IRELAND

Publisher: Aileen Lau
Project Editor: Emma Tan
Assisting Editor: Aileen Lau
Design/DTP: Sares Kanapathy
Brian Wyreweden
Sarina Afandie
Illustrations: Mohd Yasin
Maps: E T Hong

Published in the United States by
PRENTICE HALL GENERAL REFERENCE
15 Columbus Circle
New York, New York, 10023

ISBN 0-671-88277-5

Titles in the series:
Alaska - American Southwest - Australia - Bali - California - Canada - Caribbean - China - England - Florida - France - Germany - Greece - Hawaii - India - Indonesia - Italy - Ireland - Japan - Kenya - Malaysia - Mexico - Nepal - New England - New York - Pacific Northwest USA - Singapore - Spain - Thailand - Turkey - Vietnam

USA MAINLAND SPECIAL SALES
Bulk purchases (10+copies) of the Travel Bugs series are available at special discounts for corporate use. The publishers can produce custom publications for corporate clients to be used as premiums or for sales promotion. Copies can be produced with custom cover imprints. For more information write to Special Sales, Prentice Hall Travel, Paramount Communications Building, 15th floor, 15 Columbus Circle, New York, NY 10023.

Printed in Singapore

A DISCLAMER
Readers are advised that prices fluctuate in the course of time and travel information changes under the impact of the varied and volatile factors that affect the travel industry. Neither the author nor the publisher can be held responsible for the experiences of readers while traveling. Readers are invited to write to the publisher with ideas, comments, and suggestions for future editions. The publisher and the author expressly disclaim any responsibility for any liability, loss or risk, personal or otherwise which is incurred as a consequence, directly or indirectly, in the use of this book.

SAFETY ADVISORY
Whenever you're traveling in an unfamiliar city or country, stay alert. Be aware of your immediate surroundings. Wear a moneybelt and keep a close eye on your possessions. Be particularly careful with cameras, purses, and wallets, all favorite targets of thieves and pickpockets.

IRELAND

Text by Wendy Moore

With contributions from
Morten Strange

Project Editor
Emma Tan

Prentice Hall Travel

New York London Toronto Sydney Tokyo Singapore

CONTENTS

INTRODUCTION

HISTORY, GOVERNMENT & ECONOMY

PHYSICAL PROFILE

CONTENTS

C O N T E N T S

C O N T E N T S

Music comes from the Irish soul. Any festivity is the time to bring out

the pipes but there is no better day than the St Patrick's Day parade.

Amidst the green in the mountains, moors and valleys, are shouts

of color from the gorgeous Irish flora.

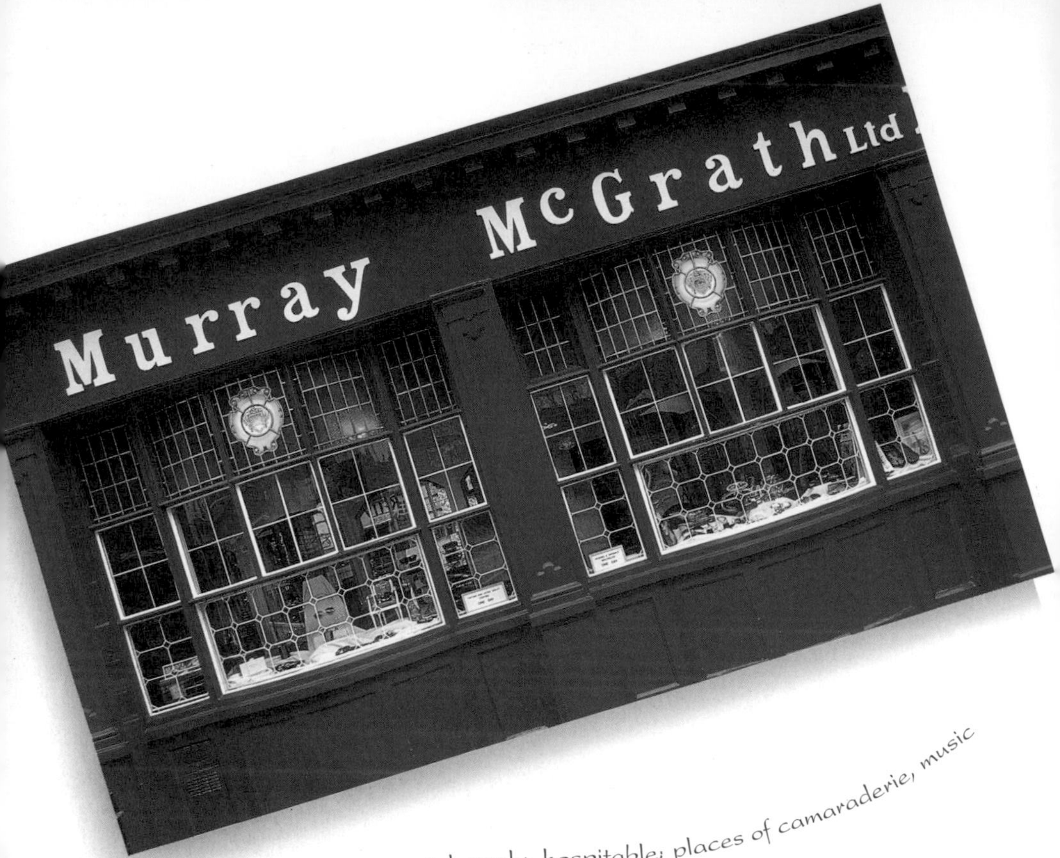

Irish pubs are quaint, homely, hospitable; places of camaraderie, music

and fun they are in the true spirit of the Irish.

I ♥
IRELAND

Introduction

Saturated in myths and legends like the soft rains that color her fields, that unique shamrock green Ireland is a land where the past is inextricably woven with the present. Mythological events, which occurred centuries before the birth of Christ, contribute to the mystical call of this land. In Amergin's incantation to Ireland when taking on the soul and spirit of the land, he compares himself to "the wind that blows over the sea", "the wave of the ocean", "a salmon in the water", and "a lake in the plain"—imagery that still beautifully depict Ireland. The Gaelic warrior then asks these immortal questions, "Who is it that creates in the head of man the fire of thought? Who is it that enlightens the assembly upon the mountain? Who tells the ages of the moon? (and) Who shows the place where the sun goes to rest, if

Welcome to Ireland.

Lush green verdure explains why green is truly Ireland's color.

not I?" Two and a half thousand years later, the answers to these questions are just as elusive. And the origins of those ancient Irish who raised them have still not been sufficiently explained. As the Celtic expert, Gerald Conan Kennedy, says, these "garrulous, aggressive, argumentative, but imaginative people...were, in fact, exceedingly strange". A description that does not fall

too far short in describing the Irish today.

Perhaps, this romantic attachment to the past flourished because during the centuries Ireland chaffed under the English yoke, everything Irish was forced underground, their religion, their language, even their music, was ruled taboo, and as history has proven this type of cultural genocide often provokes the strongest reaction.

The Irish retaliated by keeping their myths and legends intact and in so doing they have kept alive a culture which is far more traditional than the rest of Europe. When the nation finally achieved its independence from Britain only this century, fittingly, they chose the ancient name Eire for their nation, honoring the Celtic goddess who in human form was a queen of the mystical De Danaan people. Eire arrived "in a sea of smoke" to liberate Ireland from the "dark" Fomorians.

Emerald Isle

Hauntingly beautiful, the land is the nation's glory. Racehorses wade in emerald green meadows, whitewashed cottages smelling of peat fires are encircled by fences of stone, heathery hills are enshrouded with mist, and pounding surf crashes beneath awesome cliffs. When the rest of Europe lies under a pall of snow, Ireland's fields are often still green, belying its northerly latitudes. But the climate is softened by the moisture-laden winds of the Atlantic and the warm currents of the Gulf Stream. Little wonder that its conquerors lusted after the lush meadowlands of the Golden Vale where animals could graze the year round.

Ireland's history is written in stone,

Guinness Stout, undoubtedly Ireland's favorite tipple.

for scattered about the country are thousands upon thousands of rocky remnants immortalizing 5,000 years of habitation. There are megaliths from prehistoric times, circles and dolmens, monks' huts like beehives, monasteries and soaring round towers to keep the Vikings at bay, medieval castles of the Anglo-Normans, and stately Georgian manors of the Anglo-Irish landlords. There are ruins everywhere, empty and deserted; houses abandoned in rocky fields and graves and more graves, the legacy of the horrendous famines of the mid-19th-century.

From a population of eight million people in 1845, a quarter of this figure had either died of starvation or emigrated by the end of the decade. When other countries were worrying about overpopulation, Ireland was depopulating as millions flocked to greener pastures, a trend that continued unabated into the 1950s until the nation found new prosperity within the European Economic Community. Ironically, Ireland now has one of Europe's fastest-growing populations.

Literary Land

For such a small population, the nation has an enviable roll-call of famous poets, playwrights and authors, including three of this century's winners of the Nobel Prize for Literature. This literary tradition began way back in Celtic times when the *filid* (learned poets and professional storytellers)were entrusted with memorizing hundreds of stories, and then later when the early Christian monks created their beautifully illuminated manuscripts. And it was the Irish, who, after having their own language usurped by that of the conqueror, would go on to produce more famous Irish writers in their adopted English tongue, than the native English did themselves.

The Irish love of language, be it English or their native tongue which is still spoken by around 55,000 people in the Gaeltacht, west of the River Shannon, is evident wherever you are. The Irish love to talk, and as the writer Leon Uris, observed; "They speak, not as men and women talking, but as fencing masters". With tongues loosened by the

Quaint cottages and gardens dot the beautiful Irish countryside.

familiar backdrop of their local pub, and oiled by copious pints of amber-colored stout, nothing beats an Irish bar for a quick introduction to life in the land of the shamrock.

In this sanctuary from life's storms, the world's problems are solved, political careers are made and broken, relationships are dissected, business deals are concluded and gossip abounds. As Dr Samuel Johnson once said; "The Irish are a fair people, they never speak well of one another".

Then when the last round is drunk, and the pub empties, it takes on the same melancholic mood that can strike you in any of the other empty spots in Ireland. It is as if the talking somehow silences the ghosts of the past.

Mythical Beauty

The myths that make Ireland what it is, also draw the thousands who make the journey, or even as many may call it, a pilgrimage, to her shores every year. Drawn by the postcard-visions of dream-like landscapes, the castles, the ruins, the people, the pubs, the music, and the arts, most travelers arrive with enormous expectations, and surprisingly enough, they are not disappointed. True, most of the thatched-roof cottages are these days built for tourists not for locals, and kitsch bungalows and industrial estates are now just as much part of the landscape as whitewashed homes and stone fences, but somehow they too

Fast Facts

Official Name: Eire (Irish), and Ireland (English).
Form of Government: unitary multi-party republic with two legislative houses, the *Seanad* (Senate) 60 members; and the *Dail* (House of Representatives)166 members.
Chief of State: President
Head of Government: *Taoiseach* (Prime Minister).
Major Political Parties: *Fianna Fail, Fine Gael,* and the Labor Party.
Capital City: Dublin.
Official Languages: Irish and English.
Monetary Unit: I Irish pound (IR£) = 100 new pence.
Population: 3,494,000 (1991) .
Urban/Rural Percentages: urban 57.1%, rural 42.9%.
Age Breakdown: under 15, 28.9%; 15-29, 24.7%; 30-44, 18.8%, 45-59, 12.8%; 60-74, 10.7%; 75 and over, 4.1% (1986).
Ethnic Composition: more than 94% of Irish nationality (1981).
Religious Affiliation: Roman Catholic 93.1%; Church of Ireland (Anglican) 2.8%; Presbyterian 0.4%; others 3.7% (1981) .
Provinces: (4) Connacht, Leinster, Munster, Ulster.
Counties: (26) (Connacht) Galway, Leitrim, Mayo, Roscommon, Sligo; (Leinster) Carlow, Dublin, Kildare, Kilkenny, Laoighis, Longford, Louth, Meath, Offaly, Westmeath, Wexford, Wicklow; (Munster) Clare, Cork, Kerry, Limerick, Tipperary, Waterford; (Ulster) Cavan, Donegal, Monaghan.
Total Land Aarea: 68,895 sq km (26,600 sq miles).
Inland Water Area: 1,390 sq km (537 sq miles)
Major Cities & Population: Dublin 502,749; Cork 133,271; Limerick 56,279; Galway 47,104; Waterford 39,529.
Economy: Manufacturing, agriculture, tourism.
Highest Point: Carrauntoohil in the Macgillycuddy's Reeks at 1,038 m (3,405 ft).
Longest River: River Shannon (longest in the British Isles), 259 km (161 miles).
Most southerly point: Mizen Head, County Cork.
Most Westerly Point: Slea Head, County Kerry.
Most Northerly Point: Malin Head, County Donegal.
Climate: Western Maritime.
Coldest Months: January and February 4-7°C (39-40°F).
Hottest Months: July and August 14-16°C (57-61°F), sometimes reaching 25°C.
Sunniest Months: May and June, 5 $^{1}/_{2}$ - 6 $^{1}/_{2}$ hours of sun per day.

fit into the scheme of things, and have yet to become dominant as in other lands.

Dublin's highest building, the 1960s-style **Liberty Hall**, scarcely a skyscraper by any stretch of the imagination, still provokes scathing comments as to how it "stands out like a sore thumb" on the low-rise silhouette of this Georgian city. Journeying through the country, the traveler is struck by how much tradition is still preserved. In village after village, town after town, the old-style shopfronts and signs survive and the sense of keeping alive the tradition is still very strong. As the local tourguide at **Kilkenny Castle** enthused, "We are so lucky to have been given this castle to look after".

For the thousands of visitors of Irish descent who make their way to Ireland's shores every year, the homecoming is particularly poignant. Even for those whose roots are tenuous at most, there is a curious feeling that overcomes one, like a déja vu, everything somehow feels

The majestic architecture of Dublin's Custom House speaks of Ireland's glorious past.

A shy but warm welcome from Irish children.

so familiar. World leaders whose forefathers left Ireland's shores generations ago have been known to have been moved to tears on visiting their ancestral farms and villages.

What to Do

The accepted vision of a tourist in Ireland conjures up images of hordes of Irish-American video-totting retirees. However, although this group are undoubtedly well represented, especially during the high-season summer months, the young independent travelers with their backpacks, are just as prolific. For just as the older tourists come to kiss the **Blarney Stone** and ride around Killarney's lakes in "jaunting cars", the young traveler arrives for Dublin's acclaimed rock-music scene, the traditional music pubs of **Doolin** and **Galway**, and a chance to cycle the **Ring of Kerry**, or walk the **Wicklow Way**.

Opera buffs across Europe flock to **Wexford's** Opera House for the annual festivities. The racing season at **The Curragh** draws horselovers and gamblers the world over. Arts and music festivals are held in practically every major town across the republic. In Dublin the annual **Bloomsday Festival** in memory of James Joyce, is a favorite. Also, for travelers who are looking for a mate, there is even the annual Matchmaking Festival at the spa town of **Lisdoonvarna**, in The Burren.

Quality Time

Most visitors to Ireland are not disappointed. It may sound like a cliché, but there is indeed something for everyone. True, the weather may often upset well-laid plans, but no one traveling to Ireland would be surprised at this, for the rain is just as famous as their favorite drink, Guinness. It can rain at anytime, and often for days on end, but this is a land which is well prepared for entertaining folk when the weather turns foul. There is nothing quite like a wet Sunday morning in Dublin when you can pop into **Bewley's Café** for a hot coffee and listen to the jazz band in front of a roaring fire.

In fact the mood is just not the same when the sun is shining. Most of Ireland's most memorable moments come from times such as this, like the feeling you get from this vignette of J M Synge's; "I am in Aranmore, sitting over a turf fire, listening to a murmur of Gaelic that is rising from a little public-house under my room".

For anyone who has already visited Ireland, it is quotes like this that make you long for more. And indeed, most travelers to Europe's western-most nation, do end up returning for although Ireland is a small land it is not possible to do it all at once. Like a fine wine, it must be sipped slowly to appreciate its quality and you must be prepared to travel off the beaten track for great insights into traditional Irish life; "real" Ireland as the tourist guides call it.

Through the Tourist's Eyes

There are so many renowned literary quotes and poems that describe the landscape, the people, their thoughts and dreams, but I found that none of these came close to describing the feeling that travelers often have of the tantalizing beauty of Ireland, restricted as they are by their purse strings. Then, while bouncing along in an express bus from Galway back to Dublin at the end of my last visit, I chanced upon this poem by Denis O'Driscoll in *The Irish Times*, and it was all there in black and white, just what I had been thinking. His poem is entitled, *Road Not Taken.*

How tantalising they are,
those roads you glimpse
from car or train,
bisected by a crest
or grass perhaps,
keeping their
destinations quiet.

You remember a brimming
sea on the horizon
or an arch of trees
in reveries of light;
then a bend that cut
your vision off
abruptly.

Some day you must return
to find out how they end.

It is a perfect Irish type of day, the kind that the locals call "soft". There is light, but no direct sunshine, so that the absence of shadows makes the colors of the landscape stand out in sharp relief. On this kind of day, when the skies close in and the mist swirls about the emerald fields, a peculiar type of feeling overcomes those who wander about the countryside. The antiquity of Ireland seems to come alive on such days for the rocks which are found everywhere as dolmens, graves, towers, and castles, and which are the real custodians of Ireland's history, seem to take on a power of their own. One feels that if only the stones could talk, what stories they would tell.

The magnificent illuminated Book of Kells which throws light on monasticism and scholarship in the 6th century.

The Celts & the heroic age

The **Rock of Cashel** in the province of Tipperary is one of Ireland's most pregnant images of these times gone by. The ancient citadel of Cashel, taken from the Irish word *caiseal* (circular stone fort), looms on a rocky

The Rock of Cashel, an important ancient fortress founded by Conall Corc in the 4th century.

prominence, 61 m (200 ft) above the surrounding plains. The fort boasts an ancient stone tower, and a medieval complex containing a cathedral, chapel and castle within its great walls. But Cashel's history is older than any of these structures and is intertwined with the mystical tales of Ireland's first rulers.

Eoghanacht, the descendant of Eoghan, son of the legendary Oilioll Olum, was the first prominent ruler of Cashel during the 4th or 5th century AD. He ruled over the tribes of southern Ireland, while the Ui Neill claimed supremacy over the northern reaches. Four or five generations on, Conall Corc, who history credits as founding the Cashel dynasty, was more than likely the king whose foot was accidentally spiked by St Patrick's sword on the missionary's historic visit to Cashel. So the story goes, the old Pagan ruler bore his pain in agonizing silence, believing it to be all part of the Christian baptismal rites.

The Neolithic Age

Irish pre-history, according to scholars, began somewhat after the rest of Europe when the Larnian peoples began arriving on Ireland's shores around 6,000 BC. But owing to the paucity of evidence for this date, historians are now somewhat confused as to whether these Mesolithic hunters and fishermen were of a different era than the later Neolithic peoples who date from around 3,000 BC. There is no doubting the evidence, though, for this latter period as Ireland's countryside contains hundreds of megalithic tombs.

Across the northern half of the land are long barrow tombs, also known as court tombs, which derived from the same designs that occur in England and in northwest France. The most spectacular are the long-barrow type, including those at **Newgrange** which are among the best examples of megalithic tombs in all Europe.

Bronze Age Treasures

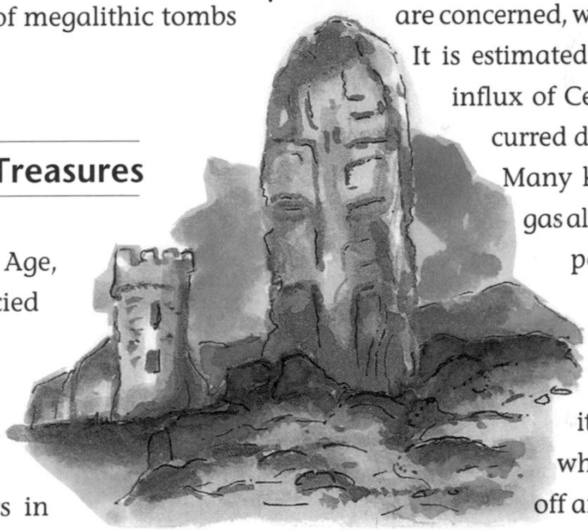

During the Bronze Age, tomb-builders fancied the limestone country of Clare's Burren, building their tombs near the copper deposits in Kerry, Cork, and Tipperary. It was during this age that Ireland's metal workers came into prominence, particularly around 800 BC when a wealth of gold and bronze works were produced, including the magnificent Clare gold hoard which was discovered in 1854 by railway workers at Mooghaun North in County Clare.

Unfortunately much of the original hoard was melted down or sold to dealers, but the remainder, including some spectacular embossed gold collars, can be seen in the extensive Bronze Age section of the National Museum, Dublin. Another fascinating display at the museum uses a cross-section of a bog to show how later medieval treasures were buried and exactly preserved in the peaty soil, looking as good as the day they were worn.

Iron Age Immigrants

The next major era, as far as scholars are concerned, was the Iron Age. It is estimated that the main influx of Celtic peoples occurred during this time. Many known Irish sagas also date from this period. Mythology and history tread a thin line, and it is difficult to tell when one leaves off and the other begins, particularly this far back in the mists of time. Earlier people were often considered god-like to later cultures, but perhaps those mythical ancestors were just as real in their own time.

Ireland's first settlers, according to the sagas, were led by Ceasair, "a daughter of Noah", who arrived in Ireland after escaping the biblical Great Flood, together with three men and 50 women. The females were then divided up among the male trio and they all dispersed to populate the land.

Browne's Hill dolmen, one of Ireland's many prehistoric monuments.

Fomorians & Nemedians

Other early peoples included the piratical Fomorians. Originally from Scandinavia these people were based at Tory Island off the Donegal coast from where they frequently engaged in battles with the Partholonians and Nemedians. Partholon, the leader of the former group, was a Canaanite from the eastern Mediterranean, who is credited by the sagas with introducing agriculture to Ireland. Nemed, after whom the Nemedians were obviously named, came from Scythia, and he and four women were the only survivors of the original fleet of 30 ships which had set sail from the Atlantic.

Although the Nemedians rapidly expanded their population, in time they fell prey to plague and then to the warring Fomorians who gained the upper hand and forced them to pay a tax at *Samhain*, a fertility and sacrificial festival at the end of summer (*Samhain* is early Irish for "end of summer"). It is from these people that the Halloween custom of "Trick or Treat" originated.

Another famous Nemedian was Macha of the Red Tresses, the charismatic 76th Irish monarch, and remnants of her fortress known as *Eamhain Macha*, or Navan Fort, still stand on the western outskirts of Armagh City in Northern Ireland. Yet another renowned Nemedian was Britain, whose name has been forever immortalized by Ireland's dominant neighbor. Strangely, though, after producing such famous Celtic personalities, the Nemedians were so few in number at the end of their era, that they were forced to flee to Greece...so the story goes.

Firbolg & the Tuatha De Danaan

The next immigrants to arrive on Ireland's shores were the Firbolg who brought the art of ploughing to Ireland. However, they were in turn defeated by the mystical Tuatha De Danaan and the surviving Firbolg moved off the mainland and settled on the Aran and Rathlin Islands off the West Coast. Of all the peoples celebrated in the Irish myths, this group that caused the Firbolg's downfall, the De Danaan, inspired the most fabulous of tales. They arrived in a sea of cloud, bringing with them the art of magic and sacred objects from the four mystical cities of Falias, Gorias, Finias and Murias.

Translated as the "People of the Goddess Danu", the Tuatha De Danaan are the most mysterious of all Ireland's early peoples and they still exert an amazingly powerful influence over Irish culture. Scholars differ as to their origins,they could have been Greeks, Finns, or Assyrians, according to varying academic opinions. They first arrived in Donegal led by Nuada Argetlamh, "Nuada of the Silver Hand", who legend has it acquired his metallic hand from a Druid, after losing it in battle.

Nuada was one of many leaders who over the millennium became godlike and together with the gods the De Danaan brought with them, the great Irish pantheon of deities came about. So the sagas go, when these people were defeated by the Milesians, the ancestors of the Gaels, at Tara, they moved underground and became the fairy folk. However, as Gerald Conan Kennedy writes in his *Irish Mythology*; "they have survived such ignominy to exert a strange and still unexplained psychic influence over Ireland." Among the Tuatha De Danaan's enormous contribution to Irish culture is the Irish-language name of Eire, which is derived from the Goddess of De Danaan,who was the wife of Mac Greine, the "Son of the Sun".

Druidic Influence

But, mystical as the De Danaan may have been, the Druids were even more so, particularly in their time, for they were the religious and learned class that the De Danaan had reputedly learnt their magic from. As Julius Caesar wrote about the Druids, they never fought wars as they "were exempted from taxes and military services" and they often spent 20 years or more acquiring their sacred knowledge.

The Druids' late arrival in Ireland has led many historians to believe that they had been ousted from Gaul by the

Dublin Castle

Dublin Castle's sumptuous State-Apartments are frequently visited by tourists.

In the historic heart of Dublin, sprawling across the high ground of Cork Hill, is **Dublin Castle**, the stronghold of mammon throughout eight centuries of Irish history. This fortress, which looks nothing like the popular version of a castle since far-sweeping renovations changed its appearance in the 18th century, is still used for important state functions as well as being one of the city's favorite tourist destinations.

Historic Foundations

Building officially started on the castle in 1204 when England's King John ordered that a treasury be built to house the considerable finances of the Irish. Thus from the outset of its construction Dublin Castle served as a constant reminder to the Irish, of British overlordship. However, the history of the actual fortress sited here goes back even further. Excavations have proved that a Viking stronghold was already here when the Norsemen took over Dublin in the 9th century. Even this was not the first edifice, as a rath, a defensive earthwork, existed here even before that, indicating that the area had been occupied perhaps for centuries before the Vikings arrived.

Strongbow, the Anglo-Norman conqueror, erected a motte in 1170, upon which King John's **Record Tower** (the treasury keep) was later built. This tower which was known under various names including the Black Tower, the Gunners' Tower and the Wardrobe Tower, still survives, albeit, much renovated. Of the original castle, only the Record Tower remains, along with the **Bermingham Tower** (a 14th century addition). Two other towers and much of the castle including the drawbridge and portcullis were dismantled in the 18th century when the castle underwent massive renovations.

Rebels & Reconstruction

Initially built as a fortress and military installation, the castle has certainly seen its fair share of "troubles". It was attacked by cannon-fire in 1534

Romans and had fled to Ireland for safety.

They mainly worked as wandering magicians but many were held in high esteem by the Gaelic kings and they often married into the ruling class. Their numbers may have been small but their influence was quite remarkable. The Druids never committed their knowledge to writing and the oral tales which were passed down by the *filid* (storytellers), were a direct result of this druidic

when Silken Thomas led a rebellion against the British. Three decades later, another insurrection against Queen Elizabeth I led by Shane O'Neill, had the monarch's representative, Sir Henry Sidney, extremely worried. When the rebel leader was finally killed, Sidney had his head brought back to Dublin Castle and displayed on a pike to advertise what was likely to happen to others should they go against the crown.

In 1684 the castle was so badly damaged by fire that an almost total reconstruction changed the face of the old fortress which then took on much of its present dimensions. The stone walls were rebuilt with bricks, the castle yards were extended, and offices and reception rooms were constructed. The magnificent **Bedford Tower** which surmounts the sumptuous **Master of Ceremonies Apartments**, were both designed by Thomas Ivory in the mid-18th century.

The **Great Courtyard**, containing most of the post-medieval buildings, was built during this Georgian era and is easily recognizable today from the well-known watercolor rendering by James Malton in 1792. In this romantic view, red-coated soldiers parley, fashionable women in high-waisted dresses walk their children, and spaniels romp about the spacious courtyard surrounded by elegant facades of Georgian-style apartments.

The State Apartments

Today, the setting is still the same but backpackers, package-tourists, and curious Irish are now the people in the square. The castle is open practically every day and a tour of the magnificent **State Apartments** features on the agenda of most visitors to Dublin. Most Georgian buildings have much more lavish interiors than exteriors and Dublin Castle is no exception to the rule. From a mushroom-pink and white foyer, hung with medieval tapestries, the tour guide takes her flock up the stairs, all the while keeping up a constant narration of the who, where, what, why and hows of history that occurred within these walls.

Visitors can witness the room where James Connolly spent his last night before being executed for his part in the 1916 Easter Rising; the room where King George IV slept in 1911; and where Margaret Thatcher slept during the last meeting of the European Community Presidents' in 1990. "No photographs, please", the visitors are requested in a room where the guide says the oil-painting on the wall may well be a Van Dyke.

The ladies' waiting and entertaining room is elegantly decorated in the Parisian style, the turquoise blue and pink colorings echoing the shades of a Chinese punch-bowl which is the centerpiece for the room. A courting couch is flanked with chaperone chairs at either end. Visitors marvel, snap photographs and ogle the over-decorated rooms where the aristocracy once ruled from. Then, in the tower room with its Gothic windows, the tour guide points out seven portraits of Irish rebels, all executed by this same administration. Their serious, often youthful faces strike a discordant note within these lavish rooms which epitomize the enormous gulf that existed between the lifestyle of the rulers and that of the common people.

Looking at the martyrs' portraits, a sensitive visitor can not help but be reminded of how long the Irish people suffered while England ruled with such an iron fist from these very rooms.

practice.

These magicians, whose ancestors historians say were originally *brahmins* from India, also bought a law system to Ireland which bears a striking resemblance to Indian Hindu laws. Other similarities between the two peoples can be found in the Irish *derbfine*, a four-generational family grouping similar to the Indian *sapinda*. The hunger strike, which was put to great use by Mahatma Gandih, and more recently by the IRA prisoners in English jails, also had its roots in druidic practice, where a man who was owed money would sit outside the debtor's house depriving himself of food until the bill was paid.

The First Division

Tuatha, meaning a petty kingdom, was the fief of an elected king, and although some of these realms combined into groups it was not until the 10th century that Ireland was ruled by a single king. Around the start of the Christian era, the country was divided into groups of *tuatha* known as the *Cuig Cuigi* or Five Fifths.

The *Cuig Cuigi* were given names: Ulster, Meath, Leinster, Munster and Connaught. The rulers were all cattle kings for Ireland then had no urban centers. But there were plenty of rural industries as Irish laws in existence from just before the Vikings arrived around the turn of the 9th century, record details of land management, animal husbandry, dairying, spinning, weaving, milling, meat-curing and malting.

Exploits of these "cattle kings" abound in the semi-legendary *Tana* which are tales of cattle raids, heroic deeds and magical events. *The Tain*, the most heroic epic in Irish literature is the amazing tale of the Ulster court and its idealized heroes the Red Branch Knights.

Among these heroes was Cuchulainn, who was often referred to as the "Irish Achilles".

A Cultural Identity

Interestingly, while the Romans made their 400 year mark on English history they never made it across the Irish Sea. This seems incredible as from Malin Head in County Donegal, Ireland's northernmost point, the coast of England is only 21 km (13 miles) distant and is visible on a clear day. However, thanks to this freak of history, Irish culture and early nationalism thrived undisturbed.

For although the tribal *tuatha* kingdoms constantly warred and shifted alliances, the Irish shared a common language, a set of laws (the Brehon Law), and traditions of music, poetry and history. As Robert Kee remarks in *A History of Ireland*, "at a time when no country was a nation in a modern centralized sense, but when British society had been at least to some extent shaped by the Romans, Ireland had its own individual cultural unity which you could certainly call a sort of nationhood".

Christianity & the Monasteries

This pagan rural society, later immortalized by Celtic revivalists as a type of mystical utopia, was, however, irrevocably changed by the coming of Christianity. But such was the strength of Gaelic society that they managed to successfully merge their culture with the new

Christianity began in Ireland with austerity, monks living in beehive-shaped huts such as these in County Kerry.

religion and flourished even more than before. St Patrick never claimed to have converted all of Ireland, but the patron saint certainly made his mark on the west and northern parts of the country, although some historians believe that his mission was preceded by the papal mission of Palladius to the south in AD 431.

Monasteries certainly existed before the national apostle began his mission, but by the 6th and 7th-centuries the new religion was totally established and in their enthusiasm, Irishmen were devoting themselves to austere lives as hermits and monks. After the saints came the scholars, and monasteries throughout Ireland became celebrated centers of learning, famed throughout Europe. During this Gaelic "Golden Age" monks toiled away producing intricately decorated illuminated manuscripts like the *Book of Kells* (see box story p.168). But even in these scholastic tomes were evidence of the unstoppable Irish wit which is as old as Ireland itself. Written as a margin note a medieval monk penned this marvellous and insightful ditty:

> Me and Panger Ban my cat
> What a nice task we are at
> Hunting mice is his delight
> Hunting words I sit all night.

The Great Transition

Monks lived incredibly austere lives in

beehive-shaped stone huts on the Dingle Peninsula, or on the sides of the cliffs of **Skellig Michael**, a rocky isle off the storm-lashed southern Kerry coast. Others, though, lived out their lives in less harsh surroundings at the great monasteries of **Clonmacnoise** and **Glendalough**. These monasteries protected by powerful kings gradually emerged as centers of trading, refuge and industrial bases; eventually they became the first walled towns.

Christianity merged into the old paganism and festivals from the old religion were renamed as saints' days. There was no brutal transition from one epoch to the other, although some Irish sagas mourned the more carefree "good ole days". But, as in many other cultures, the "Golden Age" of spirituality and learning was soon to be threatened, for on an auspicious day at the end of the 8th century the first Viking ships landed on the Irish coast and the spell was broken. The first of a long line of foreign invaders had arrived and Ireland would never be quite the same again.

The Long Travail

History in itself is rarely a series of positive happenings, seen graphically today in the negative news that pervades the media the world over, but Ireland's past and even its present is so punctuated by its travails that it seems to have suffered far more by its history than probably any other nation. It is easy to romanticize the past before the coming of the invaders to Ireland, but as it happened so very long ago – the Vikings first invaded in AD 795 and the English only pulled out this century (in fact they still control Northern Ireland) making a total of 12 centuries of occupation – the Celtic "Golden Age" is more like a mythological era fueling the spirit of the Irish, rather than a series of dates and events.

The Men from the North

An anonymous 9th-century poet voiced the feelings of his day when the Vikings sailed from Norway to raid the coastal settlements and plunder the monasteries;

> Since tonight the wind is high,
> The sea's white mane a fury,
> I need not fear the hordes of hell
> Coursing the Irish Channel.

Often known as the Danes in Irish history, the Norsemen, who were best known as pirates were also traders and they brought with them the concept of towns and changed the face of the countryside forever.

Dublin, Cork, Limerick, Wicklow, Wexford and Arklow were all founded by the Vikings. They controlled the material culture of the land, but real power still lay with traditional Irish rulers such as the High King Brian Boru of Cashel, who first ran the Vikings out of Limerick and then effectively broke their

The marriage of Strongbow to Aoife epitomized the selling-off of Ireland to the Anglo-Normans.

stranglehold by defeating them and their Scandinavian allies at the Battle of Clontarf in 1014.

Inaugurating Hostilities

By the end of the 12th century, however, the foreign Norsemen had more or less assimilated themselves into the Irish way of life. One problem had been solved, but another, the intertwining of English and Irish destinies, was just beginning.

The villain who started the whole affair was by all accounts Diarmait MacMurrough whose fief had been seized by Tiernan O'Rourke (some historians say the feud began over the former's wife who had earlier ran off with O'Rourke). MacMurrough, determined for revenge, sought an audience with French-speaking King Henry II of England and enlisted the powerful Norman barons of Wales, including Strongbow, to help him regain his lands. As an added incentive, when Strongbow conquered Waterford, MacMurrough threw in his daughter Aoife's hand in marriage, a symbolic move in the selling-off of Ireland that would be remembered for countless generations.

The English monarch himself came to Ireland in the following year, not that he considered the country to be much of a prize, but he was anxious that his barons were getting a little too big for their boots, and by seeking and obtain-

The Royal Hill of Tara

On 15 August 1843, Daniel O'Connell, the honey-voiced "Great Liberator", and the first Irishman to make popular opinion felt in British politics, addressed a multitude of protestors who had gathered for the greatest of his "Monster Meetings" at the **Royal Hill of Tara**, in County Meath. Newspaper reports put the crowd at three-quarters of a million strong, but O'Connell, who was given to exaggeration, estimated his followers at one-and-a-half million. Even allowing for the discrepancy in the figures it was an amazing turn-out, perhaps made even more successful by his choice of venue. Such was the strength of O'Connell's voice that it could be heard clearly, in those days when microphones were still unheard of. "You'd hear it a mile off as if it were coming through honey", a farmer remarked.

"We are at Tara of the Kings", O'Connell told the masses, "the spot from which emanated the social power, the legal authority, the right to dominion over the furthest extremes of the land". Historians say that he rather stretched the truth, but there is no denying that this hill is at the root of Irish culture and religion.

Primeval Roots

Situated about halfway down the eastern flank of Ireland in the rich Valley of the Boyne in County Meath, the Hill of Tara stands much higher in history and in the hearts of the Irish than it does in reality. Thomas Keneally in his book *Now and In Time To Be*, succinctly describes it as "that hill smaller than most decent sized hills anywhere else, but taller than Everest in legend".

People have lived there for the last 4,000 years, as evidenced by carbon-dated bones which archaeologists unearthed from the bottom of a ring mound. These great circular forts, known as *raths*, are not spectacular from the ground, in fact, except for some mystical carved granite pillars, there is little tangible evidence that Tara was for so long the seat of the Gael's High Kings .

Viewed from the air, however, the hill takes on a completely different character. From above, the contour lines of the ring forts look like the circular outlines of a woman's breasts upon the hillock. Seen from this angle, this ancient site evokes the power of the primeval earth mother, which is the basis of all early pagan religions. There is an organic feeling to it in stark contrast to the angular symbolism of Christianity, with its crosses and rectangular churches, which came to replace the old faiths. Significantly, it was here in the 5th century at Tara, that St Patrick lit his Pascal fire one Easter, effectively ending the traditional Gaelic pagan rites which had been at the root of ancient Irish culture since time began.

A Social Center

Tara comes from the Irish word *Teamhair* (pronounced Tawer) which means "a residence on an elevated spot, commanding an extensive view". According to the Irish sagas, the mystical Tuatha De Danaan were Tara's first inhabitants.

ing the Irish kings' submission to his overlordship he could limit their powers. The Vikings may have started the concept of walled towns but the Normans were the most prolific builders and their formidable castles like Limerick's **Bunratty** and **Dublin Castle**, which was the seat of mammon for eight centuries, still litter the countryside today.

The Flight of the Earls

During the 13th century, parliament was set up and English law was introduced to replace the ancient Brehon

The youth which archaeologists uncovered at Tara was buried here around 2,000 BC and probably belonged to the De Danaan people. He wore a necklace which had beads made of Irish copper, amber from the Baltic regions, and jet from Yorkshire, showing that even in those days Ireland had a high level of civilization and was a well-structured society. The aristocracy were the warriors, below them were the craftsmen who included doctors, lawyers, historians, and poets as well as metalworkers. Next came the peasants and then the slaves. Family clans made up a *tuath*, and groups of these constituted the five *tuatha* (kingdoms) of ancient Ireland.

Tara had a special significance, this was the place where the ancient kings and their warrior nobility assembled every three years for a gathering known as a *feis*. Laws were passed, disputes were agreed upon and after the serious business was done there was great merrymaking with songs, dances, and monumental feasting. In the ancient *Book of Leinster*, a 12th-century manuscript which records the early Tara court, the protocol of the enormous banqueting area which ran along the entire hillside, is described in great detail.

A Center of Authority

The reason why the Royal Hill of Tara is so special in the hearts and minds of the Irish, is probably because it is from here that so much of their culture is derived. Even in those early Celtic times, the Tara men were known as "the men of Erin"; and tales of the *Fianna*, the warriors who protected the Tara nobility, form the basis of much of Irish mythology. The Milesians, from northwest Spain, finally ousted the mythical Tuatha De Danaan from Tara and their descendants held sway at the royal seat until the arrival of the Anglo-Normans. Of the Five Fifths (the original Irish kingdoms), Ulster was at first dominant, but by the late 4th century, the kingdom of Meath had taken control headed by Niall, one of the Nine Hostages who founded the O'Neill clan. In the 6th century his descendants ruling from Tara claimed overlordship of Ulster, Connaught and Meath and later over all Ireland.

Pagan Eclipse

So what made the Royal Hill of Tara fall into decline after such a long and illustrious history? Probably more than anything it was the rise of Christianity that laid the death knell for the famed pagan center. Even the great leader who resided at Tara, Cormac Mac Airt, also known as "Cormac the Christian", told his followers not to bury him at the Brugh Na Boinne, the traditional burying ground for kings, as "they were burial places for idolaters". It does not seem to matter that there is so little concrete evidence of the past left here, discounting the incongruous 19th-century statue of St Patrick, for it is the aura that surrounds the Royal Hill of Tara, conjuring up the Celtic "Golden Age", that is far stronger than any mere earthly construction and which makes this a very special place.

Law. The Gaelic kings were not however, mute throughout all these upheavals and together with Edward Bruce, brother of Scottish king Robert I, they consolidated their hold on the north and tried to win back Norman lands. Inevitably, though, they were defeated and the English re-asserted their grip by creating the new earldoms of Kildare for the Leinster Fitzgeralds; Desmond for the Munster Fitzgeralds; and Ormonde for the Butlers of Tipperary. Together, these three medieval lordships formed the basis of the English administration until the Reformation. By a quirk of history, though, the Anglo-Normans were so entrenched in the Irish way of life that in time they became "more Irish than the Irish themselves". This bothered the conquerors so much that at the Kilkenny parliament in 1366 the lords drew up a statute ordering the English to speak their own language, wear their own dress, and to shun Irish customs.

The Anglo-Irish had also been weakened by plagues which swept Ireland in the mid-14th century and by the end of the century Gaelic law and custom had made a comeback and prevailed in the lands "beyond the Pale". This expression is still used today to describe a person's behavior which is unacceptable to the norm, but in those days the Pale was the region under English control which consisted mainly of Dublin and also the areas under the Anglo-Irish earls' command such as Kildare, Kilkenny, Wexford, Waterford and Tipperary.

Finally when "Silken" Thomas, (the nickname for Lord Thomas Fitzgerald of Kildare who had a fancy for silk clothing) rebelled against the English, the Tudors who had turned their backs on the Pope in Rome decided they had had enough. They were worried that a Catholic domain on their doorstep was too much of a threat. Unlike the Normans before them the Tudors, under Elizabeth I, were intent on subjugating the Gaels and were committed to war against the papacy and Spain. Throughout the Elizabethan wars, with each clash the number of Irish rebels grew; Red Hugh O'Donnell of Tyrconnel swept the English from Connaugh; Hugh O'Neill of Tyrone battered the enemy at Yellow Ford, and then joined by 4,000 Spanish troops they fought the British and lost at Kinsale. After their defeat, in 1607, rather than serve under the enemy, around 100 Irish leaders and a 1,000 of their followers went into exile on the Continent.

History records this event as the "Flight of the Earls" and it was the culmination of the power of the Tudors over Ireland. The old order was now shattered, the rebels dispersed, and Ireland was ripe again for a change-over. James I, the first of the Stuarts, was widening his dominion. He had already expanded into North America and now he looked closer to home.

In Ulster, where the English had already confiscated the land left by the fleeing earls, huge plantations were established by settling Protestant Scots and Englishmen, the most systematic attempt yet by the English at a complete take-over. Ironically, the land which was formerly the fief of Hugh O'Neill, the Earl of Tyrone and the arch-traitor of the English, was the very soil that nurtured the beginnings of Northern Ireland, the source of Ireland's religious "troubles" which still persist today.

Cromwell & the Gaelic Rebellion

Although the Gaelic Catholics still

The Battle of Boyne saw the defeat of the Catholic cause and the call to arms.

owned a large proportion of the land, they resented the newcomers settling what was historically their soil, and the Protestants knew well it. They fortified their farms which often resembled beleaguered garrisons and they were aware that thousands of Irish loyal to the departed earls still harbored a grudge against the conquerors and their representatives, the Ulster settlers. In 1641, disenchantment finally turned to fury when the Gaelic Catholics rebelled. Thousands of colonists were killed or forced to flee, and the tales of atrocities perpetrated against the Protestants, acknowledged by all historians to be grossly exaggerated, still form a vivid part of the subconscious memories of the Northern Orangemen to this day.

Loyal to his roots as Hugh O'Neill's nephew, Owen Roe O'Neill and his army of Irish and Anglo-Norman Catholics won an overwhelming victory at the Blackwater River. The euphoria of success was short-lived, however, for meanwhile England was in chaos. King Charles I, who was known to be sympathetic to the Catholic cause, was beheaded by Oliver Cromwell and his Puritans. Then the greatest villian in Irish history turned his attention to Ireland. Intent on revenge, Cromwell and his army blitzed through the land with an iron-boot, carrying out massacres at Drogheda and Wexford and burning many monasteries. The lands which the Gaelic rebellion had won, were confiscated and given to Cromwell's soldiers.

As a result, at the end of Cromwell's bloody reign of terror, Catholic landownership had shrunk to 22 per cent, down from 59 per cent at the time of the Rebellion, paving the way for future land grabs. By the first decade of the 18th century the total acreage of Irish Catholics was whittled down to an incredible 7per cent of the land total.

The War of the Two Kings

A glimmer of hope emerged for the Irish on the defeat of Cromwell's government and the re-instatement of Charles II to the English throne. Charles was however aware that he owed his position to the Protestants, thus, for fear of upsetting them, the situation in Ulster remained unaltered. As the satirist, Jonathan Swift, said at the time, the Cromwellians "gained by their rebellion what the Catholics lost by their loyalty".

Finally when Catholic James II succeeded Charles, he made some changes in Ireland by promoting other Catholics to prominent positions and re-examining the land titles. However, these moves did not go unnoticed and when James made the fatal mistake of getting his largely Irish Catholic army to put down an uprising in England's south, the Protestants recalled William of Orange from Europe to be their new monarch.

James was forced to flee to France and in 1689 he landed in Ireland with his army of French, English and Scottish soldiers. The Irish, led by the Earl of Tyrconnell whom James had made commander of the Irish army, met up with the English king's troops, and as James was counting on Irish-Catholic support to regain his lost throne he was obliged to revoke the Cromwellian land settlement at a parliamentary meeting in Dublin. But the Protestants in the North remained firm, and when a royal garrison was locked out of Londonderry, James led the siege upon this city. This turned out to be another mistake as the incredible courage of the survivors who held out against starvation fueled. Finally, William arrived with his superior army and the two English monarchs fought it out by the River Boyne. Known in Irish as the *Cogadh an Da Ri*, "The War of the Two Kings", the Battle of the Boyne was a decisive victory for the Orange over the Green – Protestant over Catholic.

Although the Irish fought gallantly at Limerick under Patrick Scarsfield, the writing was on the wall and they were forced to surrender by signing the Treaty of Limerick which became a symbol for betrayal, broken before the ink was dry on the paper. Scarsfield and his loyal troops, like other rebels before them fled to Europe, becoming the first of the famed Wild Geese, exiled Irishmen who were forced to take up arms abroad.

The Protestant Irish

The worst of Ireland's troubles, however, were yet to come. The 18th century is remembered for the draconian Penal Laws which stripped the Irish of not only their land, but of the right to speak their own language, practice their religion, be educated, hold political office, or even to own a horse worth more than IR£10. Hundreds of priests were deported to Europe, but secret masses were still held in fields and caves.

To an outsider visiting Dublin in the early 18th century, Ireland was to all extents a Protestant nation. Elegant new buildings dominated the capital which was transformed into one of Europe's most magnificent cities. But under this veneer revolt by the underprivileged masses was fermenting and strangely enough this was also being helped along by the Protestant upper-class who now considered themselves as having a distinct identity from the English. Jonathan Swift, the Protestant Dean of Dublin's St Patrick's Cathedral, was even urging the Irish to burn everything that was English-made, except English coal.

Encouraged by the American rebellion against the British in the 1770s, the "Patriot" party led by Henry Gratton and his "Volunteers" (a voluntary army recruited from Ireland's leading families) finally won a Declaration of Independence from the British in 1782 and London conceded autonomy to the parliament in Dublin. But although this seemed like a victory, it scarcely affected the common man, as the rich Protestants had mainly wanted control of parliament to strengthen their own position and were reluctant to grant any concessions to Catholics.

Quashing People Power

Meanwhile the French Revolution had occurred and downtrodden peoples the world over were realizing that government by "the will of the people" was possible. Wolf Tone, a Protestant from Dublin, caught the mood and together with the United Irishmen (a secret society who had got together with the idea of one nation for both the Orange and the Green), he organized an invasion fleet of 35 French vessels crammed with thousands of revolutionary troops to come to free Ireland. It is one of the ironies of history that bad luck once again haunted the Gaels. There was little opposition, but the weather in Bantry Bay turned foul, and the sailing ships could not land but were instead forced back to France. Wolf Tone rightly remarked that "England had not had such an escape since the days of the Spanish Armada".

The government retaliated; members of the United Irish Society were hunted down and flogged and tortured, thousands were arrested, and stockpiled arms were confiscated. Finally at Wexford in 1798 fed up with the atrocities, the people openly rebelled against the militia and began a series of successful attacks. However, the government mobilized and eventually defeated the rebels at Vinegar Hill, ultimately giving the Irish cause yet more martyrs to add to their already voluminous list.

Another débâcle occurred five years later when Robert Emmet decided to seize Dublin Castle as the impetus for a general uprising. His proclamation for an Irish Republic was printed, but the government got wind of his plans and the rebellion turned out to be little more than a street riot. Emmet's famous speech from the dock before his execution is celebrated in Irish history: "Let no man write my epitaph...When my country takes her place among the nations of the earth, then and not till then let my epitaph be written". There was still to be a long wait, however, until Emmet's wish came true in 1916 when Patrick Pearse said of Emmet's death, "It is the memory of a sacrifice Christ-like in its perfection". Indeed some Irishmen consider that as long as Northern Ireland remains under British control, Emmet's epitaph should remain unwritten.

Wolf Tone's noble aims of uniting the Catholics and Protestants as Irishmen irrespective of religion, were dashed after the Rebellion which once again saw atrocities on both sides and further widened the gulf between them. In 1800 the Act of Union dissolved the Irish Parliament uniting Ireland and England and move the power base to London, where de facto, it had always been. Tone who had landed with another French party in Donegal was taken prisoner anddied in captivity after an attempted suicide.

O'Connell & Nationalism

Naturally, the Protestants favored the Union, but the Catholics wanted it to be repealed, and they found their voice in Daniel O'Connell, a radical lawyer from Derrynane in Kerry, whose house still stands there today. Balzac wrote that

English propaganda satire on the "united Irish" training.

O'Connell "incarnated a whole people", indeed, the Kerryman, later known as "The Liberator", liberated the Irish and made them a potent force in politics. He campaigned relentlessly for Catholic emancipation, organizing "Monster Meetings" at such cultural icons as the Royal Hill of Tara in County Meath (see box story p.22) which drew upwards of three-quarters of a million Irish.

O'Connell won his cause giving Catholics the right to sit in Parliament and hold high offices. He then set his sights on the repeal of the Union and the

Daniel O'Connell rallied the Catholic Irish against union with England.

restoration of the Irish Parliament. But Westminster banned his "Monster Meeting" planned at Clontarf outside of Dublin and O'Connell was forced down by government threats. Undeniably one of Ireland's greatest nationalists, O'Connell died in 1847 before his dream of repeal came true. But his passing was overshadowed by an event of even greater calamity. The Great Potato Famine of 1845-49 was one of Ireland's most catastrophic events, suddenly politics was forced to take a back seat as families struggled to feed themselves.

The Great Blight

There is no doubt at all that a famine of this magnitude would rank with the worst Ethiopian and Somalian disasters, had it happened today. In Irish history the magnitude of an event in which at least 10 per cent of the population starved to death or died of disease, and which precipitated emigration on an enormous scale, has often been compared demographically to the slaughter of the Jews in Nazi Germany.

Travelers had long commented on how poor the Irish country folk were and their incredible dependence on a sole crop, potatoes, and when the blight struck the country's crops in 1845 rendering them unfit for consumption, it was nothing less than catastrophic. Potatoes that were edible were eaten leaving little for planting in the following year.

From an acreage of 128,400 hectares (321,000 acres) in 1846 the amount of land planted out with potatoes declined to 16,000 hectares (40,000 acres) the next year. Political economists were against giving out food as this would undermine prices; a completely unrealistic argument as the poor did not have money to buy food no matter how cheap it was. Incredibly, food was still being exported from Ireland as other crops had had bumper harvests, and food was still being imported in vast amounts to feed everyone except those that needed it.

Rural people in the west, northwest, and southwest were dying in droves, and people living close to urban centers such as Cork, were desperately attacking the flour mills. As a newspaper report of the time stated, the starving poor "staring through hollow eyes as if they had just risen from their shrouds...could no longer endure the extremity of their distress".

Mean Measures

Charles Trevelyan, as the Head of the Treasury and the chief official in charge of relief, did little but propose band-aid measures. Public works were inaugurated giving some relief to a small percentage of the disadvantaged, but Trevelyan soon closed them down in anticipation of a bumper potato harvest that year. It was a premature move, designed to save money for the Treasury and not to save lives for the harvest was again blighted and useless. Food riots occurred and then the deaths from starvation began.

A reporter from *The Times* sent to verify reports of Irish exaggerations was horrified to find that in Skibbereen town 169 people had died in only three weeks. Diseases like the deadly "Road Fever" struck down the starving by the thousands, but Trevelyan still insisted that "If the Irish once find out there are any circumstances in which they can get free government grants we shall have a system of mendicancy such as the world never knew."

However, as the pressure mounted the government was forced to act. Public works began on a massive scale, but many of the workers, already in poor health, died on the job. Soup kitchens were set up, and workhouses were given loans for food relief which were repayable by land rates. But the ratepayers could not pay for it all when two million people were starving and sometimes even landlords were forced into bankruptcy and send to the workhouse.

Trevelyan considered the job was done and in one amazing statement he commented that "too much has been done for the people". Workhouses were still reporting thousands of deaths every week, but Westminster was so far removed from the issue that they failed to realize the enormity of the problem. Trevelyan was even knighted for his role.

Emigration

As Robert Kee, in his *Ireland-A History*, writes "Dying was one way out of the nightmare". But there had for some time been another; emigration. From 1847 the land began to empty and for the next four years perhaps one million people fled the terror and migrated to the new horizons offered by the United States, Canada, and Australia. Conditions on the sailing ships were often just as frightful as those at home and it was not unusual for at least a quarter of the passengers to die *en route*.

However, those who survived and prospered in the new lands, set the pattern for the following decades when

The arrest and execution of Fenians, granted them a place in Irish myth.

emigration became more or less a way of life for the Irish. Almost one million people died from the Great Famine and one-and-a-half million emigrated during that time, changing the face of rural Ireland as never before. And not only demographic changes were at work as the dispossessed Irish, including the 75 per cent of immigrants who settled in the United States, were never to forgive England for this calamity, thus laying the groundwork for an inescapable conclusion, to break with the British government at all costs.

Following the Fenians

With their nightmarish experiences still fresh in their minds, exiled Irish in America were quick to contribute towards the newly-formed Fenian movement, a secret revolutionary group who took their name from the legendary *Fianna* warriors of Celtic times. Their aim was to injure English interests in order to secure political freedom for Ireland. These inflammatory ideals were published in the newspaper *The Irish People* but their blatancy did not go unnoticed by the government who interned the editorial staff for treasonable writing. Meanwhile the funds flocked in from the United States and the Fenians prepared for a nationwide uprising.

Planned for 11 February, 1867, the revolutionary outbreak had to be called off after an informer leaked their plans. The postponement was sent to all the Irish units save one at remote Cahirsiveen on the Iveragh Peninsula of County Kerry. When the Kerrymen rose in rebellion little did they know that they were alone. Heavily outnumbered they were forced to retreat, hiding in caves until they escaped by luggers to America.

The very next month the Fenians again made their move, but this time the uprising was easily put down by the government and the leaders were arrested. Despite their failure the Fenians were now entrenched in the Irish myth and when three of the secret society members were executed at Manchester, for the shooting of a policeman during the process of rescuing Fenian prisoners, the "Manchester Martyrs", as they became known, joined the roll-call of heroes for the cause.

Parnell & Home-Rule

By now English and Irish public opinion was so divided that Prime Minister Gladstone finally realizing the need for reforms dis-established the Church of Ireland (the Anglican Church) and in 1870 introduced the Land Act of 1870 to alleviate the problems of tenant farmers. Also, in this same year, Isaac Butt founded the Home-Rule League which aimed to bring about a union of landlords, tenants, and local government, to be ruled by Dublin, but which was to remain committed to the Empire.

In the 1874 elections, 59 Home-Rule members were returned, drastically reducing the seats of anti-Home-Rule Liberals. Butt, however, was too gentlemanly and he lacked political power, unlike Charles Steward Parnell (see box story p.42) a Protestant MP from County Meath, who was elected leader of the League over Butt. For the next decade Parnell dominated the political world, bringing widespread changes between landlords and tenants by persistently blocking parliamentary business.

In 1881 Parnell forced Gladstone to introduce the Land Act which granted fixed tenure and fair rents for tenants, but although these long-needed reforms were a considerable improvement, they were still far short of the Fenian ideal of ultimate nationalism. Parnell's speeches became more inflammatory, his meeting by torchlight in Dublin drew the largest crowds since O'Connell's Monster Meetings, and the mood was of ever-increasing militancy. Gladstone responded by jailing him in Kilmainham. This, however, was a perfect move for Parnell as it took him away from the "No Rent" extremists who were pressing for more reforms, and it laid the groundwork for his ultimate purpose, Home-Rule for all Ireland. When Parnell was released from prison in May 1882 after coming to an agreement with Gladstone, the stage was set for further concessions.

Violence again intervened; when the chief secretary for Ireland, Lord Cavendish and his under-secretary Burke were murdered in Dublin's **Phoenix Park**, by Fenian members of a new secret society known as the "Invincibles", in the ensuing mêlée the question of Home-Rule was again shelved. Parnell then used his balance of power to persuade Gladstone to introduce some measure of Home-Rule, but the Conservatives and dissenting Liberals defeated it in the House of Commons and for the next two decades Irish Nationalist ambitions were seriously thwarted.

The main reason for this setback was the completely unexpected fall of Parnell who was involved in a sensational divorce trial. Gladstone moralized that he would not press for Home-Rule while the Irish Party was led by the discredited Parnell, and as a direct result his own party turned on him and deposed him. When the church turned on the "adulterous" Parnell, the formerly "Uncrowned King of Ireland" fought a losing battle for his political life. As one historian put it, the issue of Home-Rule fell "into second place before the all-important question of whether, in a country where the influence of the Catholic Church was so powerful, an adulterer could be allowed to lead the nation's party." Parnell died a broken man at the age of 41.

The Beginning of Two Nations

The Parnell question split Irish society and left a gaping divide in political life. A fresh interest in Irish culture filled the vacuum and groups like the Gaelic League revived the Irish language and the Gaelic Athletic Association was founded to promote Irish sports; in reality the latter was a Fenian recruiting organization.

In an attempt to combine both cultural and political consciousness, Arthur Griffith started the *Sinn Fein* movement which promoted political self-help. Meanwhile the Conservatives introduced massive land reforms enabling the Irish tenant farmer to at last own the land he farmed. This was part of the Conservative ploy to "kill Home-Rule by kindness" and it certainly worked for on the rural scene political considerations took a back seat against the sweeping changes taking place on the land.

In the cities, though, it was a different story. Dublin had the worst slums in Europe and the appalling wages of workers proved the incentive for mass discontent. In 1913 the Irish Transport Union went on strike and although they gained nothing monetary they at least had the satisfaction of knowing that the bosses had failed to break the back of the Union. The irony was that many of these bosses were active Nationalists, and the Union began to mount a counter-movement against Home-Rule.

Meanwhile, the push for Home-Rule in Parliament began again. John Redmond, the leader of the Irish Nationalist Party, made deals with the new Liberal government to push the bill through in 1910. It stalled. He tried again in 1911 and the following year, but he underestimated the strength of the Ulster opposition.

Huge demonstrations were held in Belfast and hundreds of thousands of Ulstermen signed a petition, many in their own blood, against Home-Rule. The Ulstermen proposed that in the event of Home-Rule becoming a reality (which looked likely), Ulster's nine counties should be excluded. Parliament started to waver and consider Ulster's expulsion, and the alarmed Redmond stated that he and his party could never assent to Ireland's mutilation, that "Ireland is a unit...the two nation theory is to us an abomination and a blasphemy."

Many Irishmen in the south, fearful that Home-Rule might again be shelved, joined the Irish Volunteers as a counter-force to the Ulster Volunteer

POBLACHT NA H EIREANN.

THE PROVISIONAL GOVERNMENT OF THE IRISH REPUBLIC TO THE PEOPLE OF IRELAND.

IRISHMEN AND IRISHWOMEN: In the name of God and of the dead generations from which she receives her old tradition of nationhood, Ireland, through us, summons her children to her flag and strikes for her freedom.

Having organised and trained her manhood through her secret revolutionary organisation, the Irish Republican Brotherhood, and through her open military organisations, the Irish Volunteers and the Irish Citizen Army, having patiently perfected her discipline, having resolutely waited for the right moment to reveal itself, she now seizes that moment, and, supported by her exiled children in America and by gallant allies in Europe, but relying in the first on her own strength, she strikes in full confidence of victory.

We declare the right of the people of Ireland to the ownership of Ireland, and to the unfettered control of Irish destinies, to be sovereign and indefeasible. The long usurpation of that right by a foreign people and government has not extinguished the right, nor can it ever be extinguished except by the destruction of the Irish people. In every generation the Irish people have asserted their right to national freedom and sovereignty; six times during the past three hundred years they have asserted it in arms. Standing on that fundamental right and again asserting it in arms in the face of the world, we hereby proclaim the Irish Republic as a Sovereign Independent State, and we pledge our lives and the lives of our comrades-in-arms to the cause of its freedom, of its welfare, and of its exaltation among the nations.

The Irish Republic is entitled to, and hereby claims, the allegiance of every Irishman and Irishwoman. The Republic guarantees religious and civil liberty, equal rights and equal opportunities to all its citizens, and declares its resolve to pursue the happiness and prosperity of the whole nation and of all its parts, cherishing all the children of the nation equally, and oblivious of the differences carefully fostered by an alien government, which have divided a minority from the majority in the past.

Until our arms have brought the opportune moment for the establishment of a permanent National Government, representative of the whole people of Ireland and elected by the suffrages of all her men and women, the Provisional Government, hereby constituted, will administer the civil and military affairs of the Republic in trust for the people.

We place the cause of the Irish Republic under the protection of the Most High God, Whose blessing we invoke upon our arms, and we pray that no one who serves that cause will dishonour it by cowardice, inhumanity, or rapine. In this supreme hour the Irish nation must, by its valour and discipline and by the readiness of its children to sacrifice themselves for the common good, prove itself worthyof the august destiny to which it is called.

Signed on Behalf of the Provisional Government,
THOMAS J. CLARKE.
SEAN Mac DIARMADA. THOMAS MacDONAGH.
P. H. PEARSE. EAMONN CEANNT.
JAMES CONNOLLY. JOSEPH PLUNKETT.

The Proclamation of the Irish Republic.

Force which was by now armed to the teeth and had already formed an "Ulster Provisional Government" in anticipation of victory. When the First World War broke out Ireland was on the verge of a civil war. Home-Rule was delayed until the end of the war, everyone thought it would be over in a year, and Redmond pledged the Volunteers to help with the war effort.

The Rebels' Republic

Edmond's pro-English attitude, however, inflamed many Irish Volunteers who broke away to join the extremist Irish Republican Brotherhood who were actively planning a revolutionary outbreak. The ardent nationalist Sir Roger Casement, journeyed to Germany to solicit help and arms, but when he was arrested on his return and the ship carrying the arms was scuttled, plans for the projected uprising went awry. Confusion mounted and when Patrick Pearse and James Connolly led the uprising on Easter Monday, 1916, only 2,000 fighting men turned out. They took the **General Post Office** and other parts of Dublin, much to the amazement of a generally apathetic public, and then Patrick Pearse proclaimed an Irish Republic from the post office steps. At first the British were caught napping, but not for long. When they realized the seriousness of the situation they closed in, and although street fighting continued for a week, the rebels were forced to surrender. The total body count at the climax was 300 civilians, 130 British soldiers, and 60 rebels.

At the time of the Easter Rising many people found the rebels an embarrassment. The Rising had not been popular, but as the smoke cleared from the ruins, and as the number of executions rose, public opinion made an abrupt about-face. The rebels now became heroes in the awful Irish tradition. This last bloody episode on the part of the English proved to be the final straw and as the rebel Tom Clarke told his wife before his execution, "freedom was coming and Ireland would never lie down again". But he added prophetically: "Between this moment and freedom, Ireland will go through hell."

SAORSTAT
EIREANN

Government

Poems, stories and ballads by the dozen were written about the Easter Rising of 1916, about the men and youths sacrificed, of the executions and the destruction of the city, but of all the words penned none were as poignant and precise as Yeats' immortal lines: "All changed, changed utterly: A terrible beauty is born".

As the tales of executions seeped out of Dublin Castle "like a trickle of blood from under a door", the formerly apathetic public were outraged. The Irish Party were seen as an impotent force at Westminster since they made more concessions for Home-Rule, and a revived *Sinn Fein* attracted members as never before, mainly because the media had mistakenly dubbed the Rising the "*Sinn Fein* Rebellion". Meanwhile, the British Prime Minister, Lloyd-George who was keen to appease the Americans in order to woo them into World War I, had first to make some reconciliatory moves toward Ireland, as the United States had been extremely criti-

Symbols of justice, the Four Courts, Dublin.

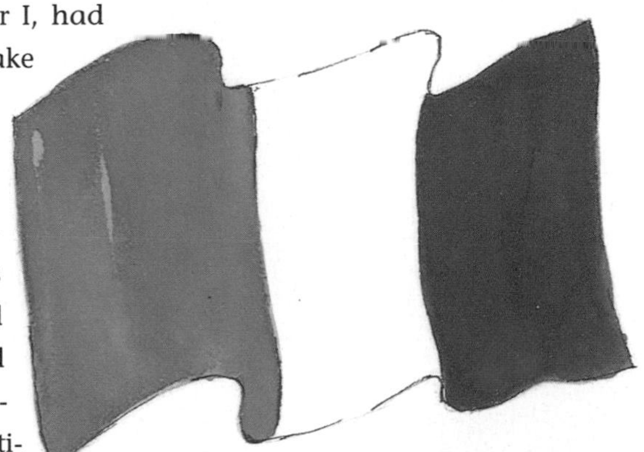

Dublin General Post Office, headquarters of the 1916 Easter Rising.

cal of England's role in executing the rebels of the Easter Rising.

United in Brotherhood

During Christmas 1917, Lloyd-George made his move and released the rebels who had been held without trial. One of the rebels was the militant republican Michael Collins, who had already organized guerrilla warfare lessons for his fellow internees under the guise of the Irish Republican Brotherhood (IRB). Once released they lost no time in reorganizing their movement and working on the now sympathetic public. The Brotherhood's electoral candidates trounced the Irish Party in the crucial 1917 by-elections; some candidates even won their seats while still in British jails.

Later the same year, the remaining prisoners from the Easter Rising were released, including the only senior rebel to be spared execution; Eamon De Valera escaped death because he held American citizenship. When De Valera contested and won a Clare seat by a huge majority, he took control of *Sinn Fein*.

Public sympathy swung even more to *Sinn Fein's* side when the prominent rebel Thomas Ashe died after being force-fed while on a hunger strike. He had been arrested that summer when the administration cracked down on the party by banning meetings and arresting well-known members. His funeral was attended by around 40,000 mourners and Michael Collins' oration at Ashe's

The executed leaders of the 1916 uprising became martyrs for their cause.

graveside publicly acknowledged the militant approach that the IRB stood for. "The volley which we have just heard is the only speech which it is proper to make above the grave of a dead Fenian."

Proclaiming the Republic

National resentment came to the boil in 1918 when the British government announced that they intended to extend conscription to Ireland. *Sinn Fein* made no bones about their opposition to such a move by declaring that "If England decides on this atrocity" they would spare no man that volunteered, and "all these having assisted the enemy must be shot or otherwise destroyed with the least possible delay". Luckily, Irish conscription did not become a reality for the war ended, the Armistice was signed, and not long afterwards the first General Election for eight years was held. It was a landslide for *Sinn Fein* who won 73 seats while the Irish Party were annihilated, their seats reduced to merely 7.

When the *Dail Eireann*, the newly-formed Irish parliament, met on 21 January 1919, they proclaimed a Republic, just as the heroes of the Easter Rising had done three years earlier on the steps of Dublin's General Post Office. At the center of their demands was the "evacuation of our country by the English garrison" and from that time on the *Dail* referred to the administration of Dublin Castle (the English headquarters) as "an enemy occupation".

However, declaring itself to be independent did not necessarily mean that Ireland was free. De Valera journeyed to the United States to rally support for the new republic, but although the Irish Americans gave generously to his cause, official recognition was still elusive.

The First Shots

While the *Dail* were discussing how to settle the deadlock amicably, two young Volunteers suddenly took matters into their own hands. With no orders from above Dan Breen and Sean Treacy shot dead two police constables and the guerrilla war against the British began. Of the shootings Breen apparently said that "If we were to have waited for orders...nothing would ever have happened".

Some of the *Dail* members would have preferred a bloodless independence, but not Michael Collins, the charismatic Minister of Finance, who led a double life as the revolutionary leader of the IRB, and later the newly-formed Irish Republican Army (IRA) or "the Army" as it became known. Collins had already announced to his fellow *Dail* members that he was all for fighting and creating disorder in the country since he felt that "Ireland is likely to get more out of a general state of disorder than from a continuance of the situation as it now stands."

The emblem of the United Irish.

"Bloody Sunday"

Throughout 1919 the guerillas waged war against the Royal Irish Constabulary (RIC), they infiltrated government intelligence, and sent in "the Squad" to eliminate informers and the police whose sympathies lay elsewhere. Then the British began to get tough. The first signs of the new approach came in March 1920 when the Lord Mayor of Cork was shot and killed by plain-clothed RIC, some of whom spoke with a British accent.

The RIC had been composed only of Irishmen, but reinforcements began to

Agitator for freedom: Charles Stewart Parnell

Monument to Parnell, O'Connell Street, Dublin.

Haughty, charismatic, aggressive, nationalistic, scandalous, passionate, all these and more, describe Charles Stewart Parnell, the mastermind who more than any other man changed Irish political life.

His rise to fame was meteoric and like a shooting-star his fall was just as dramatic. Almost overnight he went from being a hero, "Ireland's uncrowned king", to an adulterer shunned by the church and ostracized by his own party.

Ireland's Great Hope

During his decade of power in the late 19th century, Parnell transformed politics, his Home-Rule party pressurized the British parliament unrelentingly and pushed Irish questions to the forefront of parliamentary life. Parnell's Land League for tenants' rights and his nationalist push for the Home League, became the paramount questions of the day. When he fell from grace, all because of a woman, and died a broken man not long afterwards, Ireland was stunned, families were split over him, and politics stagnated.

Historians ever since have contemplated what would have happened had he lived, and most agree that the course of British-Irish relations would definitely have been different with Parnell at the helm. As the writer Robert Kee remarked, "It is possible to see now that any hopes for Home-Rule as a final settlement of Ireland's national aspirations were buried with him."

Passion of the Irish

Parnell was born into the unlikely situation of an upper-class Protestant land-owning family, in County Wicklow. The family did however have a nationalist background; his great-grandfather had been a Volunteer in the18th-century independence movement, and on his American mother's side Parnell's Admiral-grandfather had gained fame for fighting the British in the War of Independence. Parnell's early childhood years were spent at idyllic Avondale, the magnificent family estate, after which he was sent to an English boarding school at the impressionable age of six. Perhaps this early separation from

be gleaned from England. These new recruits, many of whom had recently returned from the European trenches, were known as the Black and Tans (later the "Tans") due to the color of their uniforms. A new potent fighting force made up of former officers, known as the Auxiliaries, was also created and

Ireland conditioned him to be aggressive, for while at Cambridge he was caught and fined for brawling, a prelude to his fiery political career. Before he entered the House of Commons, Irish politicians had been known for their gentlemanly behavior, but Parnell changed all that and British politics were never the same again.

Parnell was such a force for change that the British were always trying to break him. He was thrown into prison for militant talk about cutting Ireland's English links and framed by incriminating letters over the Phoenix Park murders – he was however later exonerated when the letters were proved to be forgeries. For all these controversies however Parnell's popularity shot up, the aura of martyr being added to his already considerable legend.

A Man's Undoing

Katherine O'Shea, better known as Kitty, the woman responsible for Parnell's undoing, and the love of his life, politics aside, was already married to an Irish parliamentarian when Parnell had an affair with her in London in 1880. Two years later, when he was imprisoned in Kilmainham, he found out she was expecting a child by him, and on his release from jail he visited her and the newborn on his way to Paris. Although Kitty kept up the pretence of marriage with her husband for nine years, her love affair with Parnell was still passionate. Eventually they began living together, often in rented houses under fictitious names. Her husband William O'Shea waited to sue for divorce, for fear of scandalizing an aunt of Kitty's who had pledged an inheritance to her niece. So, O'Shea, who according to friends was always short of money, bided his time, and in 1889, when the aunt passed away he sued for divorce.

The Moral Victory

Parnell's closest circle who knew about his relationship with Kitty, thought that like all the other attempted slurs against their leader, this one would also turn out to be a storm in a teacup. The divorce case was undefended, and when O'Shea and his witnesses revealed the couples' intimacies and intrigues, the media and the music halls had a field day.

Meanwhile, the public speculated as to the outcome. Parnell was re-elected as chairman of the Irish Party, but when O'Shea won the divorce case, mainly through unsubstantiated stories, England's Prime Minister Gladstone, bowing to public pressure, announced that if Parnell remained as party leader he could not continue to pressurize for Home-Rule. Finally when the church began to take a moralizing stance, Parnell's political career was shattered. At a series of by-elections in 1891 Parnell tried to pick up the pieces, but his party and indeed the Irish people at large, were divided over the issue.

After the divorce Parnell married Kitty, but the priests had branded him an adulterer. Morality seemed now to matter more to the Catholic population than Home-Rule. Parnell died in his early 40s, but the effects of his reign were to echo for decades to come.

Today, time has erased ill-feeling, and these days Charles Stewart Parnell is remembered as probably Ireland's best-loved and at the same time misunderstood patriot. On his statue in Dublin's **O'Connell Street**, a quotation from one of his most famous speeches sums up his extraordinary vision: "No man has a right to fix the boundary to the march of a nation. No man has a right to say to his country: thus far shalt thou go and no further."

together they brought terror to the Irish populace. Curfews were imposed, midnight searches for arms and rebels were mounted, houses were burnt down in reprisal for police killings, and even dairies were put to the torch to deprive sympathizers of their jobs.

But the IRA hit back in their own

uncompromising style. An entire column of 18 Auxiliaries was ambushed and gunned down near Macroom. However, when Collins' hand-picked "Squad" shot dead 14 undercover intelligence agents in their Dublin beds, some of whom had infiltrated *Sinn Fein*, the Tans responded by running amok at a Gaelic football match between Dublin and Tipperary at Croke Park and indiscriminately shooting at the crowd. Among the people killed on what was later dubbed "Bloody Sunday" was one of the Tippperary players.

As if all this was not enough, the following month a company of Auxiliaries stormed into a Cork pub, and began a frenzy of looting and torching which resulted in the burning down of most of the city's town center. The IRA hit back in May 1921 and put to the torch one of Dublin's most architecturally-renowned buildings, the **Custom House**, where the administration had been directing their operations from.

But their biggest operation turned into disaster when the IRA were surrounded by the Tans and around 120 of the rebels were forced to surrender. England's confident Prime Minister Lloyd-George proclaimed "We have murder by the throat", but as the historian Desmond McGuire pointed out, "there was little evidence to support his claim".

For the guerrilla style of warfare, which years later would prove to be the downfall of the Americans in Vietnam, was still successfully eroding the better-equipped British forces.

Eamon De Valera declared Irish independence in 1937.

Partition & Division

Then, in the middle of all the troubles when both sides appeared to be deadlocked, unbelievably a truce was signed. The fighting stopped as quick as it had started and work began on reaching some kind of political agreement. It was clear that the republic would not become a reality, so in order to end the "threat of immediate and terrible war", the negotiators settled for the Anglo-Irish Treaty which partitioned Ireland into 26 states known as the Irish Free State (with a status similar to Canada), placing the states of Northern Ireland under a separate government.

The jubilant English saw the treaty

as the solution to a centuries-old problem, but as Irish politicians were still required to make an oath of allegiance to the crown, and as the North was still under British rule, it did not require too much foresight to see that Ireland's troubles were far from over. As the IRA's Michael Collins remarked after being more or less forced to sign the treaty, "early this morning I have signed my death warrant."

Deaths & Defiance

In trying to salvage the ideals of the Irish Republic, De Valera proposed to the *Dail* that although the king should be recognized as the head of the Commonwealth, the oath of allegiance was a betrayal of all they had fought for. The *Dail* responded by voting 64 to 57 for the Treaty. A tearful De Valera resigned, and although the bulk of the Irish were relieved that the fighting had ceased and that Ireland was now to a certain extent free, the IRA, like the members of the *Dail*, were divided.

The feelings of the Anti-Treaty section of the IRA were expressed in the popular song:

> Take it down from the mast, Irish traitors,
> The flag we Republicans claim,
> It can never belong to Free Staters,
> You've brought on it nothing but shame.

In Northern Ireland riots broke out, communal violence flared, and Catholics fled for their lives to the south. Paramilitary forces, like the Black and Tans before them, were ruthless in enforcing the law, particularly after Field Marshall Sir Henry Wilson, was shot dead by the IRA in his London home. Split into the new Free State Army under Collins, and the Irregulars or Republican Army, the IRA was divided among itself and yet again things got bloody.

Civil War

When the republicans took over the **Four Courts**, Collins was forced into a no-win situation by the British, to attack his former comrades-at-arms or see the re-entry of English forces into Free Ireland. With the shelling of the Four Courts, the Irish Civil War began in earnest. Battles were fought on O'Connell Street, which had already seen its fair share of troubles during the 1916 Easter Rising, and Cork, which had been held by Republicans was retaken by Free State Troops. Collins, himself a Cork native and never at ease with the Treaty, was forced to lead the march on Cork. Less than a month later he was shot dead, something which he had never anticipated happening in his own country.

Arthur Griffiths, the founder of *Sinn Fein*, and the president of the Executive Council, had also died suddenly just weeks before Collins, and with the old guard out of the way the Free State

The Dail, Dublin, seat of the Irish Parliament.

Government moved in to restore law and order. The Republicans were hunted down and shot, others fled to the United States, or were interned in camps, but to a man they still denied recognition of the new government. The IRA were down but not out.

The Non-Violent Struggle

Although the pro-treaty party, now revamped as the *Cumann nan Gaedheal* won, the great tragedy of the Civil War was that the population who had formerly been united against British rule were now in two bitterly opposed camps. De Valera's anti-treaty party, the old *Sinn Fein*, surfaced once again and splitting from the militant section of the IRA, they decided to keep up a non-violent struggle for an Irish Republic. Although they were voted into parliament, winning 44 seats in the 1923 elections, they refused to sit in the *Dail* since in order to do so they would have had to submit to the dreaded oath to the king. Their revival in popularity, though, had the government worried and as a knee-jerk reaction they jailed De Valera.

In the meantime, the Free State government revived the question of the Boundary Commission which was in the terms of the Treaty, to settle once and for all the status of Northern Ireland. Many people believed that the Free State would gain more territory from the commission, particularly in

Tyrone and Fermanagh where the bulk of the population were keen to join with the south.

Some people even harbored thoughts that Ireland might actually become one nation, but no one dreamed of the compromising outcome when Northern Ireland actually gained territory in Donegal, which had formerly been under the Free State.

Independence

In 1926 De Valera revamped the *Sinn Fein* party into the new *Fianna Fail*, and their candidates won almost half the seats in the 1927 election, but they still refused to take the oath and as a result were not allowed admission to the *Dail*. But all this changed when after the MP Kevin O'Higgins was killed by the IRA, the government introduced the Electoral Amendment Bill which meant that members could not be elected unless they took their seats. De Valera, later nicknamed "the constitutional Houdini", turned the oath into an empty formula by not swearing on the Bible, and by sheer guile guided his flock into the *Dail*. Inevitably, in 1932 *Fianna Fail* (Warriors of Ireland) won a majority, the following year they captured even more seats and were to hold power for the next 16 years.

Fianna Fail lost no time in implementing their republican objectives. A new constitution with the name Eire (for Ireland) was introduced in 1937, the removal of the royal oath was effected, Land Annuities, a type of mortgage payment which farmers had been paying the British, were halted, and military rights to Ireland's ports were annulled.

During the Second World War, De Valera, now known as the *Taoiseach* (head of government under the new constitution) maintained the nation's new independence by declaring neutrality, which annoyed Churchill no end. In contrast Northern Ireland, which participated fully in the war, was seen as loyal and patriotic, something the British public would remember for decades.

Emigration

Although Ireland was now its own master, the government was narrow-minded in its social programs. Farmers suffered from trade restrictions with England, writers suffered from literary censorship, and emigration to greener pastures continued. The Irish felt stifled by De Valera's

Secret Dealings: the Story of the IRA

Incognito under balaclavas, shouldering sub-machine guns, planting bombs in the London tube, and terrorizing the British occupation army and informers in Northern Ireland, the IRA are well-known to television news watchers the world over. On the face of it most viewers would assume that these self-styled revolutionaries are a product of these violent modern times, but unbeknown to many people, the story of the Irish Republican Army is not a recent one, but a tale of a secret society that began over 130 years ago.

United in Brotherhood

Even as far back as the 18th century, clandestine organizations had grown in popularity in opposition to the harsh Penal Laws that British rule had imposed. Groups like the Caravats, Rockites, Threshers, Shanavests, and the Whitefeet, collectively termed the Whiteboys by the administration, were active in the rural areas, while the Ribbonmen were drawing recruits from the artisans and laborers of Dublin. These societies offered protection to the poor from avaricious landlords and middlemen, and although they were effective, their aims were seldom political.

It was James Stephens, one of the leaders of the 1848 Uprising, who decided that it was time to instigate a revolutionary secret society, along professional modern lines, in order to liberate Ireland with a nationalist insurrection. The Irish Republican Brotherhood, the fore-runner of the IRA, was founded in 1858 when Stephens and his conspirators swore to "renounce all allegiance to the Queen of England, and to take arms and fight at a moment's warning to make Ireland an Independent Democratic Republic", adding that they would also "yield implicit obedience" to their superiors in the secret society. Support, especially in monetary terms, was enthusiastically given to the society by Irish Americans whose memories of the Great Famine were all too clear, and Stephens and his colleagues had no problems in forming the twin Fenian Brotherhood in the United States, which acted as a front for the Brotherhood in Ireland.

Blood Sacrifice

By 1865, Ireland's IRB supporters numbered 85,000 and it was generally acknowledged that insurrection was near at hand, when Stephens was betrayed and arrested. However, his prison term only lasted two weeks as two Fenian warders helped him to escape. When the Fenian Rising came to a head in 1867 it was a disaster, but the insurgents' place as martyrs was established in the history books. For the next 40 years the IRB played a back-seat role until it was resurrected by Tom Clarke, a Dublin tobacconist who had served 15 years in English jails, Patrick Pearse, the poet/schoolmaster who believed in a "blood sacrifice for Ireland", and James Connolly, the trade-unionist who already commanded a workers' Irish Citizen Army. When they were all executed by the British for their part in the abortive Easter Uprising of 1916, Pearse's "blood sacrifice" became a reality.

Guerrilla Warfare

When *Sinn Fein* winners of the 1918 election were denied their Irish Republic, the Volunteers, a radical breakaway of the IRB who were soon to be known as the IRA, began a terror campaign under the leadership of Michael Collins, the fearless Sinn Feiner who led a double-life as the *Dail's* Minister of Finance. As Britain continued to deny the Irish their right to independence the guerrilla war between the English forces of the "Black and Tans" and the IRA, intensified. Police and informers were shot and ambushed and when the Crown fought back the IRA advertised that they would shoot two of the enemy for

outmoded self-sufficiency and in 1948 *Fianna Fail* lost the election to a coalition made up of *Fine Gael* (Tribe of Ireland), the Labor Party, and the radical republican *Clann na Poblachta*. The new government declared Ireland a republic the

every one of theirs.

When Kevin Barry, a teenage member of the IRA was executed, the first of 24 similar executions to follow, virtually the whole of Dublin turned out in protest. Reprisals and counter-reprisals followed, as did successes and failures for both sides, but the IRA suffered its most crushing defeat when 120 of its members were arrested in an abortive attempt to burn down the **Custom House**, seat of the British government's administration.

Divided by Violence

The IRA's unity through suffering, did not last for long. When the Anglo-Irish Treaty was signed after two years of insurrection, the organization split into anti-treaty "Irregular" forces who felt betrayed by the result, and the pro-treaty Free State Army who wanted an end to the violence.

The situation worsened and as civil war erupted between the two sides, the new government got tough; emergency powers were introduced, the Irregulars were told to "dump arms", dozens were executed and thousands were interned in jail. Order was finally restored, but as an old anti-treaty guerilla said years later in 1980, "When all the shooting was finished, and all the dead were buried, and the politicians took over, what had you got left? A lost cause!"

For decades afterwards the IRA had an image problem, and as one historian wrote, its "principal enemy was always to be its own irrelevance". Their fortunes rose again in 1932 when the pro-republican party, *Fianna Fail*, won the elections and IRA prisoners were released and offered commissions in the army. But it was the die-hard elements that were the IRA's undoing once again, and after a series of civilian killings the government once again declared that they were illegal. Embittered the IRA split into various groups, including one under Sean Russell who was determined to take the problem of partition to England's door and who instigated the still-popular tactic of leaving bombs in public places. Their public image did not improve when Russell collaborated with Nazi Germany during the Second World War and it suffered again when he died while returning to Ireland on a German submarine.

A Force of Terror

If the IRA came to be seen as ineffectual and a spent force in the south, to the Protestants in the north they were still a permanent source of terror. The IRA's goal of removing British rule and making Ireland one nation, remains a forceful weapon in Ulster to this day. After decades of maintaining a low profile, in 1969 when sectarian violence prompted the British to send forces into Northern Ireland the IRA newly-formed into the militant Provisionals or "Provos", and their Marxist-leaning officials, once again burst onto center stage. Once again the IRA became the champions of the oppressed Catholics in the North in the quest for a united Republic.

The campaign of terror escalated, British soldiers were murdered, and the IRA were back again with a vengeance. When the stone-throwing, masked supporters of the IRA exploded across the world's television screens, the myth was once again reality.

More than two decades later, despite political wranglings and peace movements, the IRA are still a force to be reckoned with. Although many Irish deplore the IRA's use of force, some still see them as following a worthy historical tradition in joining the old quest for an Ireland free of borders:

> This Ireland of mine has for long been half free,
> Six counties lie under John Bull's monarchy...

following year, the new title theoretically embracing the entire island, but in practice Northern Island was still very much a reality. Ireland stagnated in the 1950s as mass discontent and economic problems prompted the young to leave

Propaganda for Sinn Fein, the controversial republican party.

in droves. Emigration during 1956 reached 90,000. Mournfully describing his homeland during this decade, the playwright Sean O'Casey once said: "What do we send out to the world now but woeful things, young lads and lassies, porther, greyhounds, sweep tickets...We've spread ourselves over the wide world, and left our own sweet land thin."

A new age dawned, though, in the 1960s when new economic strategies were implemented which coincided with an international boom. The quality of life dramatically improved, unemployment dropped, foreign investment poured in, and the youth of the nation no longer flew away like geese in autumn.

Minority Rights

But while the Republic of Ireland was enjoying better education and a much improved lifestyle, the Catholics in the north were still disadvantaged. Tuberculosis was rampant, unemployment soared, and their right to vote was severely restricted by gerrymandering.In Londonderry, a ward containing the majority Catholic population was only given eight seats while the smaller wards of Protestants were given 12, thus preventing the Catholics from ever attaining a majority.

The Protestants were contented, with the Catholics impotent they felt safe. Their paranoia came to the fore in 1965 when Northern Ireland's Prime Minister Terence O'Neill met his Irish counterpart, the first time such a meeting had occurred in the last four decades. When O'Neill made a few conciliatory moves towards the North's Catholics, the Protestants fueled by the fiery speeches of the rabble-rousing Reverend Ian Paisley, were outraged.

Meanwhile, a new generation of Northern Catholics, inspired by Martin Luther King's black movement in the United States, began to protest their status as second-class citizens with civil rights marches. Protestant mobs attacked the marchers and the police offered no protection. Riots broke out in 1969 when Catholics armed with stones and petrol bombs were set upon not only by a Protestant mob, but also by the machine-gunning Royal Ulster Constabulary (RUC). The British Army were called in to protect the Catholics, the IRA re-surfacing as the "Provos" (Provisional IRA) became active once again, and the "Troubles" which have plagued Northern Ireland ever since, became a way of life.

Hope for the Future

In 1972, the British government suspended Stormont (the Northern Ireland Parliament) and imposed direct rule. Over 20 years later British soldiers still patrol the streets of the North, the IRA are still actively planting bombs and carrying out their campaign of terror as are their Protestant counterparts. In 1993, after yet another spate of atrocities, thousands of Irish people took to the streets to demand an end to the killings and a much awaited peace.

Emotions on the issue of Ulster run high on all sides. The British government which has always prided itself on not talking to terrorists, was in November 1993 accused of betraying the Unionists (those in favor of union with England) after Gerry Adams, the leader of *Sinn Fein* spoke of the British government's face-to-face talks with his party. The British government in turn admitted to such unauthorized talks taking place and to a secret channel of communication for dialogue with the IRA. The Irish Prime Minister and John Hume the leader of the Social Democratic Labor Party (SDLP) have in turn openly held talks with Gerry Adams in the hope of negotiating peace.

The general public remains divided as to whether governments should negociate para-military organizations. Hopes of getting all sides round the negotiating table are still dim, the Reverend Ian Paisley of the Ulster Unionists was suspended from Westminster after the talks between the Government and Sinn Fein talks were revealed, for calling the British government liars.

Meanwhile,every night on Dublin television the dream of a united Ireland quietly comes true, the Ulster counties are still included in the nightly weather reports and no mention is ever made that they are not part of Eire.

FIRST CLASS FRUIT & VEGETABLES
POTATO MARKET
053-41131
FREE TOWN DELIVERY SERVICE FROM MON TO SAT
BASKETS OF PEACHES £1.19
RHUBARB 3 FOR £1

Economy

The ancient soil and all that it stands for has long been the anchor-stone of Irish life. Throughout history, a person who had land could survive by living off the fruits of it. Centuries of antagonism against the British were mainly fueled by the fact that the Irish were merely tenants in their own country, farming the land but not receiving the profits of the soil which is still some of Europe's best agricultural country. The mild, benign climate, where winters are seldom harsh and where stock can graze outside all year round, was very attractive to foreigners. When the Normans first came to Ireland in the 12th century they were as impressed as any modern-day tourist by the lush green landscape, recording that "The country enjoys the freshness and mildness of spring almost all the year round. The grass is green in the fields in winter,

Potatoes, the traditional staple of the Irish economy.

just the same as summer".

Images of Irish country life are often one of the main reasons that so many people flock to this island on the edge of Europe. These images are often outdated but persist in one's imagination: the Kerry lass at Valencia shouldering baskets of seaweed; the crofters cutting turf in a peat bog; the Connemara fishermen catching salmon from wooden boats; the farmer digging up a potato field; the Aran Islander knitting sweaters from home-reared wool; and the hard-working wife churning butter in a thatched-roof cottage. These images have been repeatedly enforced by literature; Padraic Colum's *An Old Woman of the Roads* is poignant apropos how the Irish themselves felt about their land;

> Oh, to have a little house!
> To own the hearth and stool and
> all!
> The heaped-up sods upon the fire,
> The pile of turf against the wall!

Mechanization & Manufacturing

The biggest question for many potential visitors to the "shamrock isle" is to what extent is this romantic vision of Ireland's countryside still a reality. Well, luckily, the emerald green fields encircled with stone walls where lambs gambol in the spring sunshine, are still very much in evidence. But, although the setting is still much the same, the labor is different. Machines have taken much of the drudgery out of farm labor, tiled roofs have replaced thatch, engines have overtaken oars, but the biggest change is that although agriculture is still the mainstay of the economy, manufacturing now accounts for around 40 per cent of GNP, and tourism is now the country's latest and most aggressive foreign exchange earner.

Learning From the Past

Ireland's economic woes have long been at the heart of the country's troubles. The Great Famine of the mid-19th century, when the potato crops were hit by blight, were the cause of incredible suffering and mass emigration. The move, somewhat ironically, to greener pastures continued throughout the 20th century, despite the fact that with independence in 1922, Ireland had taken charge of its own affairs.

Emigration came to a head in the 1950s when people were the nation's number one export, a situation seen by an ex-civil servant of those times as "the valley of despondence". Ireland since attaining its freedom had looked inwards too much, self-sufficiency schemes and the banning of foreign investment and imports had seen the economy stagnate. With the 1960s, changes took place which saw enormous improvements in Ireland's economic situation. Outmoded protectionist policies were abandoned,

Peat, a useful energy-giving fuel is abundant in Ireland.

foreign investment encouraged, new industries were introduced, and together with a timely international boom, the nation began on an upward spiral which really took off after Ireland joined the European Economic Community (EEC) in 1973.

Prospects with the EEC

With the opening up of the tariff-free Common Market to Irish manufacturers and farmers, the nation entered a new era of prosperity. The number of factories multiplied, jobs were on the increase, Irish youth ceased migrating and the economic future looked rosy.

Although the state still controlled rail, air, and road transport, television and radio, electricity, and industries like peat and sugar, the way was now open for private enterprise to be a viable alternative.

Farmers were jubilant when Ireland joined the EEC as they were guaranteed prices. Shortly after the nation attained membership, farm income doubled and the price of cattle tripled. Beef-cattle rearers in the midlands, dairy cattlemen of the south, sheep graziers in the rugged west, and cereal and sugar-beet farmers of the east were at last making a decent wage.

The government's new industrial-development policy and EEC membership, provided much needed impetus for the manufacturing sector. Tourists

Farming, a prosperous livelihood for the Irish.

may bemoan the eye-jarring factory which contrasts with the traditional rural landscape, but for many towns computer-chip, pharmaceutical, and electrical-goods factories have proved to be lifesavers. Unemployment, which was as high as 30 per cent, has been drastically reduced.

One success story was Bailey's Irish Cream Liqueur, which began business the year Ireland joined the EEC. The innovative idea of making the liqueur using the well-known Irish products of cream and whiskey came about as one way of getting rid of surplus cream instead of adding to the mountain of European butter. The liqueur with its now famous creamy taste took off and five years later was utilizing 10 per cent of the nation's cream supplied by around 4,000 dairy farms.

Natural Resources

Fuel has never been a problem for Ireland even though its mineral resources are few and far between, as peat or "turf", as it is known, which is cut from bogs, covers around one-fifth of the nation's land surface.

In the far southwest, on the famed "**Ring of Kerry**", the state electricity board has set up a peat-burning power station, the largest in Eire. Some of the crofters still cut the wet peat by hand, which is a back-breaking job. The turf is then stacked and dried before it is burnt.

The dairy industry, big business in such a lush and fertile land.

At another of the seven peat-fueled power stations in **Ferbane**, County Offaly, where 80,000 hectares (200,000 acres) of bog has been developed, the peat is cut solely by machines, loaded onto railway wagons, and then transported to the station's huge hoppers.

Agricultural Diversification

Ever since the devastating famines of the 19th-century when millions of Irish starved because of the failure of the potato crop, Ireland has diversified its farming away from the mono-culture that in a way contributed to the terrible suffering of the rural folk. The Irish had been dependent on the *praities*, (potatoes), for centuries. An 18th-century writer commented that "As for their food it is notorious they seldom taste bread or meat; their diet in summer is potatoes and sour milk". Historians have, however, pointed out that in fact even in the 18th century, Ireland produced more than just potatoes and that a variety of crops were grown for export. The real issue was that the average rural person was so poverty stricken by the appalling land laws that they had no cash to buy other food, nor the ground to grow it on.

Modern day travelers to Ireland will be astonished at the apparent scarcity of potato plants, although large crops are still grown in the **Donegal** region and north of Dublin. Farmers these days

Tossing hay; fodder for Ireland's horse and cattle-breeding success.

grow a variety of produce including carrots, turnips, cabbages, and so much sugar beet that the country is self-sufficient in sugar.

In **Moore Street**, Dublin's renowned fruit and vegetable center, Irish produce is swamped by an incredible variety of foodstuffs from other member countries of the EEC; Moroccan and Spanish oranges and even potatoes from Cyprus! Irish taste-buds have correspondingly become more fastidious and eager to try a greater variety of produce. The rich peat lands are now stimulated into pro-

Ireland's horses are one of its finest exports.

ducing vegetable crops with much higher returns than that of the traditional potato.

A newcomer to the export scene could well be the "life-long shamrock" which was recently developed by University College, Dublin. Strict regulations in the United States meant that shamrocks could not be imported because of the danger of soil sticking to their roots – imported soil is illegal. Hence, the botanists have come up with a shamrock which is grown in a nutrified gel, getting around the hurdle of contaminated soil. The growers claim that 40 million Irish Americans can now buy genuine Irish shamrocks, which, "with roots intact will still be growing on your lapel".

Horse Power

Apart from whiskey, shamrocks and Guinness, Ireland is world famous for another export, fine horses. The bloodstock industry is centered around the government-run **Irish National Stud** in Tully, County Kildare, just down the road from the renowned Curragh Racecourse, home of the Irish Derby. Abundant pastures rich in calcium from the limestone subsoil are said to account for the strong-boned horses that have been bred here for centuries.

Although Ireland has always been a horsey nation, Gaelic knights first raced their steeds at the Curragh 16 centuries ago, the industry was given a

Guinnesss: Liquid Apartheid

There's alot of might behind the name of Guinness.

"Pint o' stout, please", calls the ruddy-faced stockbroker to the Dublin barman. It is knock-off time, and office workers, laborers, and professionals alike are now mobbing the city's pubs for "the crack", an expression that sums up the entire Irish drinking ritual; the camaraderie, the yarns, and most of all the famous drink which is the integral part of "the crack", Guinness stout.

The barman slowly pulls on the pump lever releasing the umber-colored liquid. Glasses fill, topped with a lacey frill of beige froth and the excess foam is scraped off with a knife. The mugs are raised, the stout pours down grateful throats, and the froth coats moustaches, but always remains like a crust on the stout. "Liquid apartheid", Dubliners call it, so Thomas Keneally says in his book *Now and in Time to Be*, when he describes it as "that exquisite demarcation between the solid froth and the anthracite nectar".

Taste of Ireland

As much part of the Irish myth as shamrocks and fairies, Guinness is also one of the "emerald isle's" greatest success stories. It all started in 1759, when, at the age of 34, Arthur Guinness, took over a small brewery at **St James Gate** on the southern bank of Dublin's Liffey River. Later, wits would describe the appearance of the muddy river waters as resembling the famous drink and some even maintained, falsely, that the water for the stout was taken from the river. Arthur signed a 9,000 year lease on the brewery paying IR£45 a year for the original $1^1/_2$ hectare (4-acre) site, and began producing both light and dark beers.

The brewery was successful almost from the beginning, but the drink that secured its fortunes, was the dark, bitter-tasting stout flavored with roasted barley, which became known as "porter", apparently because it was the favorite refreshment of London's Covent Garden porters. But, not only did this dark brew quickly establish itself in England's markets, but it also captured the taste-buds of Irishmen and women, taking over as Ireland's national drink.

After 30 years as Master of the Corporation of Brewers, Arthur Guinness made a momentous decision in 1799, four decades after the brewery was established, deciding that in view of the stout's popularity, the company would henceforth concentrate on producing only this brew.

The Guinness empire

In 1803, when his father died, Arthur II took over the Guinness helm, and while wearing two hats, that of a successful banker, he even became the Governor of the Bank of Ireland in 1820, and of a well-known brewer, he carried on the family tradition of enlarging the brewery until it was Ireland's largest. When Benjamin Lee, Lord Mayor of Dublin, and the third-generation of Guinness' brewers, took over from his father in 1855, he expanded the business overseas and during his tenure Guinness became

No pub in Ireland can be without it.

the world's largest brewery.

Situated on its original site, expanded from 4 to 26 hectares (65 acres), Guinness is now a highly-sophisticated brewery utilizing the most modern equipment available. Using nine million liters (2 million gallons) of water every day, more beer is exported from here than from any other brewery. Today, 140 countries import Guinness Stout and 9 million glasses of "the crack" are downed worldwide each day.

Caring for the Irish

The Guinness clan may have made their fortunes out of the common man, particularly the Irish, but they were also philanthropic with their vast wealth, benevolently contributing throughout the generations to many of Dublin's civic projects. The Guinness family were responsible for major city renovations especially in the Liberties area south of Dublin Castle which was formerly a notorious slum area.

Visual evidence of the family's philanthropy still stands today, including the beautiful, Palladian-style **Iveagh Trust Scheme** which houses the Liberties Vocational School on Bull Alley, the art-nouveau **Iveagh Baths** nearby, and the massive restoration of **St Patrick's Cathedral**, including the landscaping of **St Patrick's Park** which cost Benjamin Lee a cool IR£150,000 back in 1864.

Benjamin Lee's son, Lord Ardilaun, continued in the family tradition of contributing to civic projects and was responsible for buying the lease of **St Stephen's Green**, which had formerly been held in private hands, turning it into a public park. A statue of the philanthropist stands in the western part of the park, opposite the Royal College of Surgeons, thoughtfully placed so that he gazes from his stone pediment in the direction of the business that made it all possible, the brewery by the river.

A Tipsy Turn

From being the cream of society for centuries, the Guinness clan suffered a blow in 1986 when it was made public that during a takeover of Distillers Company, the world's largest Scotch whiskey distillers, Guinness had apparently used illegal and clandestine stock transactions. The resulting corporate scandal over the affair rocked Irish business to its very roots, but made no difference to the amount of Guinness that was drunk. The "dark wine of the Liffey", the nation's favorite, still remains Ireland's best-known export.

Make a pilgrimage to the Guinness Brewery in Dublin on Thomas Street. Here an audio-visual display will tell you more about the history of the Guinness monopoly and you can whet your appetite with a sample of the brew.

Ireland's woollen mills are a boon for tourism.

huge boost when a government tax exempted stallions' services in 1969. Bloodstock profits soared and the industry has proved itself a major player in the agricultural economy ever since.

Tourist Trade

Tourism is a relatively new participant in the economic field, but it has already made a huge impact, and is now the biggest contributor to the nation's net invisible earnings.

Apart from giving jobs to the construction industry for building new hotels and developing resorts, tourism has also given a much needed boost to arts and crafts. Waterford Crystal, which produces high-quality crystal wares is renowned far from Ireland's shores and is a "must-buy" for many travelers. One of Waterford's major employers, the crystal factory provides jobs for 3,000 workers.

Other crafts that have benefited from tourism include the weaving industry. Famed for its Donegal tweeds and fine weaves, the industry produces authentic coats and flowing capes, fastened of course, with a hand-tooled "Tara" brooch made by Irish silversmiths.

Tribute must also be given to the legions of women who knit the famous Aran sweaters with their characteristic cable designs, one of Ireland's best-known exports.

Recession Lessons

For much of the last half of the 1980s and up till the present day, Ireland, like many other developed nations, has been suffering from a prolonged recession. After the euphoric days of the late 1970s when the growth index soared, wages improved, and the economy staged an incredible revival, the downturn was especially felt by the farmers, whose incomes had been affected by rises in production costs. In 1991, the Program for Economic and Social Progress was selected by the government to work on improving incomes and generating jobs, but it failed on both counts. Changes in the European Community's agricultural policies also gave cause for alarm as farm incomes continued to drop, and unemployment again reached levels reminiscent of the pre-boom days.

Once again, the Irish are now doing some soul-searching to try and pick up their battered economy. In the *Irish Times*, of 16 March 1993, an article by colomnist John Waters, dealt with what he called "our national immaturity". Waters, quoted Dr Tom Collins of St Patrick's College, who refers to the problem as the "neurosis of modern Ireland" which developed in the 1960s. Before this, independent Ireland had been spurred on by Eamon De Valera's "dream speech" in which he urged the Irish to be "people who valued material wealth only as the basis of right living...satisfied with frugal comfort...a land whose countryside would be bright with cosy homesteads, whose fields and villages would be joyous with the sounds of industry, with the romping of sturdy children, the contests of athletic youth and the laughter of happy maidens, whose firesides would be forums for the wisdom of serene old age...". But when De Valera's dream failed to happen then everything that represented this old era was thrown out. It is as if, as Waters writes, the past "is associated with backwardness, poverty, stagnation, and failure. The present, on the other hand, is associated with modernity, industrialization, urbanization and prosperity." De Valera's aim of Ireland becoming a rural country was replaced by that of an urban society, and his dream of self-sufficiency was ousted. "Instead of growing their own potatoes, our farmers live off grants from the EC and sit daily down to a dinner of Cypriot spuds, while the nettles grow up to their back doors." A bitter message to chew on.

Geography

County Kildare, where emerald fields mown by sheep with black faces are bisected by hedgerows and slashed by rivers engorged by the spring rains. County Kilkenny, where the road winds across a wooded pass cloaked in pines, where the gorse is golden in the thickets. County Kerry where the only sounds are of waves dashing onto a tiny pebbly beach and the rushing wind from the mountains.In the hollows of the highlands dustings of snow remain where the sun never shines. These "sceneries" of Ireland, as the old folk are wont to call them, haunt the memory forever, and have throughout the ages exercised a powerful influence over all those who have ventured to the shores of the "emerald isle".

The spectacular beauty of the Ring of Kerry.

Much has been written, in poetry and prose, about the beauty of Ireland,

Known as the "emerald isle", Ireland is a fertile land of beauty and verdure.

balladeers have extolled it, poets romanced in it, and writers waxed lyrical of "banks with wild flowers gay", "the grey elephant pelt of hills", and where "silver waves foamed into phosphorescent mist". It is as if the landscape is part of the soul of every Irishman. WB Yeats wrote of how he always heard the lapping of the waters about the **Isle of Innisfree**, whether he was "on the roadway, or on the pavements gray, I hear it in the deep heart's core." And around the turn of the century, JM Synge, in his poem *Prelude*, wrote of how he felt when he was "far from cities, and the sights of men...".

> I knew the stars, the flowers, and the birds,
> The grey and wintry sides of many glens,
> And did but half remember human words,
> In converse with the mountains, moors, and fens.

Island Gems

Futher west than Liberia in West Africa, Ireland is the last geographical fragment of the European landmass. Like Great Britain, glimpsed on a clear day at its closest point a mere 32 km (20 miles) away, Ireland was also, way back in the dawn of geological time, part of the huge Eurasian super-continent. Eire which occupies a greater part of the

The poignant beauty of winter trees.

island which has always been known as Ireland, shares a common border with Ulster (Northern Ireland), her beleaguered sisterland in the northeast.

In crude geographical terms, Ireland is a small geographical fragment, covering only 70,285 sq km (27,137 sq miles) of the earth's surface.But with such varied landscapes and scenic wealth, the island can seem much larger, especially when traveling about by road. Distances can be deceiving, especially for visitors used to driving in nations like the United States, Canada, and Australia, where towns are often many miles from each other.

The longest distance from north to south is 475 km (295 miles), and from east to west 275 km (171 miles), but no one would ever think of driving any of these stretches in one go, that is if you really want to see the country. Time tables made up at home while consulting tourist brochures, have often been thrown out when the traveler starts to experience "the sceneries" at first-hand. And one of the reasons that most travelers to Ireland end up having to come back again is to see what they missed first time around.

Moderate Climes

Situated in the temperate zone, at around the same latitude as Germany's Hamburg, and Canada's Labrador, Ireland is vastly different from these two

Irish Rain: God's Gift or Curse?

"We just stood there getting wet with our backs against the fence. Oh, the water! Hope it won't rain all day", sings Irish rock-legend Van Morrison in his hit song *And it Stoned Me.*

Singers have sung of it, poets and writers have written about it, travelers have had their plans spoilt by it, and the incredible greeness of the Irish countryside is because of it. Rain, the gift and curse of Ireland.

Wet Statistics

According to the *Encyclopaedia Britannica*, average annual rainfall in Ireland varies from about 762 mm (30 inches) in the east to more than 1,525 mm (60 inches) in the west. Not much, compared to such saturated places as India's Assam and parts of the Hawaiian coast where the yearly readings are taken in feet instead of inches. But it is not so much the quantity of rain recorded in Ireland that is important, but how often it really rains.

Traveling eastwards scudding clouds off the Atlantic Ocean meet the Irish landmass on the western side which takes the brunt of the moisture-laden winds. This explains why annual rainfall on the west coast is double the figure for the east. On the other hand, when Europe is having snow dumped on it, Ireland, warmed by the Gulf Stream, just rains. As a cryptic Kerry saying goes, "If you look across the water and you can see Valencia Island then it is going to rain, but if you can't see the island then it is already raining."

Meadows Green

This prodigious watering is extremely beneficial to the growing of grass which, as early travelers noticed back in the 12th century, was plentiful even in the middle of winter. These pastures feed the sheep, goats, and cattle which are the backbone of Ireland's agricultural economy, so in this respect, rain is one of the nation's biggest blessings.But not for the proprietress of a Galway "Bed and Breakfast". "I'm sick of it", she remarked looking out her picture windows across the wet slate roofs to leaden-hued Galway Bay where the sky was the same shade as the water. The bogs were getting boggier, the lambs looked forlorn, but the grass looked positively luminous.

The Food of Melancholia

Rain is part of the Irish culture and impregnates its literature; there are a multitude of tales about how the maudlin, melancholic nature of the Irish is perhaps nurtured by its wet weather. JM Synge in his turn-of-the-century book *Wicklow and West Kerry*, talks of Wicklow villages where "at every season heavy rains fall for often a week at a time, till the thatch drips with water stained to a dull chestnut, and the floor in the cottages seems to be going back to the condition of the

chilly climes, moderated as it is by the warm waters of the Gulf Stream. As the 3,218 km (2,000 mile) coastline is never any further away than 113 km (70 miles) from any part of the island, the temperature stays much the same throughout the entire land, although the southwest is known to be particularly mild. In winter, temperatures range between 4°-7°C (39°-45°F), with January and February being the coldest months. In summer the mercury hovers between 14°-16°C (57°-61°F), though August and September days can often be much hotter. Along the west coast, the spectacular coastline is pounded by Atlantic breakers, while the east coast is more gently contoured by the Irish Sea. One might be surprised to learn that Ireland has some beautiful beaches.

bogs near it." This is culminated by a massive storm when the villagers "crouch all night over a few sods of turf, and the dogs howl in the lanes". The next morning the sun shines with a "supernatural radiance" and the population look like they "have recovered from a fever", but then in the evening it rains again. He writes that this "peculiar climate" acts like a depressant on the locals who seem to be inflicted with a more-than-average dose of melancholia.

Luminous Lushness

But as much as the rain gives rise to melancholy thoughts it also contributes to days when the pure Irish character of the land seems at its most essential. A "soft" day is how the Irish describe those special days when fine, misty rains give a gloss to the landscape, creating a depth and luminosity like "the brilliance of wet sea pebbles". Such was the day Frank O'Connor experienced in his *Irish Miles* when on the Dingle Peninsula he encountered "a spattering rain that chased us frequently to the uneasy shelter of a bush". However, as frequently happens, the wind soon rent the clouds and the land was gloriously illuminated as "little colored rags of light fluttered through". Sunbeams like Hollywood spotlights, search out the patchwork fields with their borders of stone fences, and Ireland glows again washed anew by the capricious rains that are both its bounty and its curse.

Lush Lowlands

Geologically, the heart of the country is formed by a rolling limestone plain which varies from 61-122m (200-400 ft) above sea level, although low hills up to 305m (1,000 ft) high, give the countryside an undulating look. This grassy plain, known in Tipperary as the **Golden Vale**, for the lushness of its pastures, is riddled with rivers, lakes, and bogsides. In some places like County Meath it is said that the meadow grass grows so fast that you can "throw down your stick of an evening..." and "in the morning you will not be able to find it".

The spectacular waterfall at Powerscourt in the Wicklow Mountains.

In the rich pasturelands of the Midlands, especially in the famed "Bluegrass" region of County Kildare, world-class racehorses graze on bone-enriching grasses nutrified by the underlying limestone soil. This was the heartland of Ireland that her conquerors always lusted after. The climate made certain that animals could graze all year round, a fact not missed by a 12th-century Norman commentator who noted that "the island is richer in pas-

A moment in timelessness, Ireland's beauty seems infinite.

ture than in crops, and in grass rather than in grain", adding that "the meadows are not cut for fodder, and stalls are never built for the beasts".

Peat, once the only fuel of Ireland, and still the most popular, being used to fire power stations, comes from the peat bogs which cover around one-fifth of the nation's landspace.

The Irish Highlands

Encircling the lush lowlands are coastal highlands and mountain ranges. Although they are only mountains in Irish terms, elsewhere they would be thought of as mere hills, they often appear higher than they actually are because they rear up suddenly from the lowlands. Ireland appears to be a hilly country, however, in fact only 15 per cent of the total land area is over 213m (700 ft) above sea level.

Carrantuohill, Ireland's highest peak at 1,041 m (3,414 ft), forms part of the **Macgillicuddy's Reeks** located in the **Killarney National Park** in Kerry. Snow-capped in winter and lightly dusted with snow in spring and autumn, the mountain descends towards Killarney in a jagged profile which gives rise to part of its Irish name, *carran*, which means a reaping hook. Other main ranges are the picturesque **Wicklow Mountains**, dominated by 926 m (3,039 ft) high, Lugnaquilla; the **Knockmealdown** and **Comeragh ranges** near

Waterford; the **Twelve Pins** of Connemara, and the **Brandon Range** of the Dingle Peninsula which contains Ireland's fourth-highest peak.

Geologically, these ranges are quite complex as the southern mountains are of red sandstone, drained by limestone river valleys, whereas in Wicklow and the western hills of Galway, Mayo, and Donegal the region is predominantly granite.

In the distant past two major glacial upheavals shaped the Irish countryside, creating its diverse landscapes and the large peat bogs which are characteristic of land shaped by glaciers. The best farming soils, like that in the "Golden Vale", originated from the drift which during the Ice Age was frozen at the base of the glaciers and then melted when the temperatures became warmer. Granite and shale regions are by their nature unproductive, but in some of the valleys, the glacial drift which originated from limestone regions has helped to make fertile pockets in some of Ireland's most forbidding regions.

Creating a natural border between Kerry and Clare counties, the **River Shannon**, the longest waterway in Ireland, empties into the Atlantic. From its source in the plateau country of Sligo, it slowly meanders 259 km (161 miles) through the central lowlands, creating the lakelands of **Lough Ree** and **Lough Derg**.

The Shannon meets the tidal mark near Limerick, and from there it opens into a wide bay and eventually meets the ocean at the Mouth of the Shannon. Ireland's other major rivers include the Slaney, Boyne and Liffey in the east; the Blackwater, Bandon, and Lee in the south, the Barrow, Nore, and Suir in the southeast; and the Corib and the Moy in the west.

The Rugged West

Beautiful, stark and containing some of the nation's best loved scenery is the rugged west and southwest, encompassing the counties of Kerry, Clare, Galway, Mayo, Sligo, and Donegal. Scoured by the rolling breakers of the Atlantic, the coastline is broken by deep bays formed where the mountains meet the sea. The deepest of these, **Bantry Bay**, in the southwest, is 32 km (20 miles) long and up to 8 km (5 miles) wide, and is one of Europe's best deep-sea anchorages, a

The famed majestic Cliffs of Moher, County Clare.

fact not missed by the writer Thackeray who remarked that "Were such a bay lying upon English shore, it would be the world's wonder".

Looking at a map, the entire coast from Cork to Kerry resembles the tassles of a shawl, so indented is the land, making for some of Ireland's most spectacular scenery. Offshore lie the rocky outcrops of the **Skellig Islands**, once the home of penitential monks, and now a teeming refuge for migratory birds, and the **Blasket Islands** which, until 1953 when the last of its natives moved to the mainland, was Europe's most westerly inhabited spot.

The Clare coast north of the Shannon is world-famed for its remarkable ramparts known as the **Cliffs of Moher** which rear up 213 m (700 ft) vertically from the foam-lashed coast. Other spectacular cliffs include those at **Slieve League** in Donegal, and the 244 m (800-ft) high **Minaun Cliffs of Achill** in Mayo, which are of quartzite weathered over the eons into unique shapes like the so-called **"Cathedral Rocks"** at the northern end.

Off the coast of Galway, like beacons at the mouth of Galway Bay, the limestone **Aran Islands** of Inishmore, Inishmaan, and Inisheer, also contain some of the country's most magnificent cliff scenery. "Like a blessed barrier reef protecting holy Ireland", is how one writer described these bleak outcrops that seem to defy their isolation. Early occupants cleared the fields of rocks by building stone walls around each tiny plot, then painstakingly built the soil up with seaweed and sand. But if the Aran Islands seem desolate, then **The Burren**, a unique limestone region of Clare, seems almost lunar-like.

Sprawling across 259 sq km (100 sq miles), bordered in the north by Galway Bay and to the west by the pounding Atlantic, this completely treeless and what looks like at first glance a barren landscape, is a geographical marvel. In this austere limestone environment wild flowers stud the stony crevices watered by the rainwater that trickles off the rock and down into subterranean passages. (See box story "Burren: Land of Limestone", p.278).

Beach praise

Some of Europe's prettiest beaches stud Ireland's coast, particularly in the west where pale crescents of sand alternate with rugged cliffs and bays that are showered by the spray of the Atlantic. Beaches have long been a popular place of leisure for the Irish, as an old Gaelic saying testifies; "Praise the beach when you come to it".

Many of the sunniest beaches are found along the popular **Ring of Kerry** which encircles the Iveragh Peninsula, Kells Bay, Ballinskelligs and Waterville; and on Dingle Peninsula is the renowned sand strand of **Inch**.

In Donegal, where the land juts into the sea "like a thousand tongues" the sands are golden and the beaches

Seascape at Valencia Island.

plentiful. One of Ireland's finest strands is at **Rossnowlagh** where the beach fronts the Atlantic on Donegal Bay, and where the wave formations are good enough to surf on. The eastern beaches have an entirely different character to the west, and although there is no denying that the Irish Sea can get rough, the eastern resorts are gentler and tamer than their counterparts to the west. Popular beaches include **Arklow** in Wicklow, and **Tranmore**, meaning "big beach" in Gaelic, in Waterford.

Untamed Culture

History probably played the major part in the settlement of Ireland, but geography also helped to shape Ireland's population patterns. Even today, the lush meadow lands east of the River Shannon and the coastal regions around Dublin, are the most populated, while the remoter west with its stony infertile soils is still the poorer cousin. But the scenario is not as bleak as the landscape in much of the west, for as tourism keeps expanding it is bringing more and more visitors to the untamed southwest and west coasts.

Known as the Gaeltacht, these regions are where the traditional Gaelic language and traditions are still well preserved, thanks ironically to their geographical isolation which once their curse, may well turn out to be their saviour.

Flora & Fauna

"Spring is in the air – daffodils and young lambs" exclaims the Dublin disc-jockey on a particularly pleasant morning in late March. He is not alone in his observations, for anyone strolling through the city gardens where beds of golden daffodils are blooming, or driving past fields where lambs are frisking, feels very much the same way. These two events are seen as joyful portents heralding the arrival of spring. Travelers who are most interested in Ireland's flora and fauna would be well advised to plan their trip during spring or early summer, when the nation's verdant countryside and glorious gardens are at their very best.

Living elegance, flowers in the Ring of Kerry.

From Near & Afar

Typically Irish scenery such as the fuchsia hedges of Kerry, window boxes full of flowers, rhododendron gardens, and idyllic pictures of livestock grazing on green fields, are ironically not native to Ireland at all. In fact many of the existent flower, tree and ani-

Irish horses are famed for their agility and grace.

mal species were introduced thousands of years ago during the last Ice Age, when Ireland was joined by an ice-cap to Great Britain and the European mainland.

There are indeed some native species that only occur in the republic, but the vast majority, including many floral species, migrated across this land connection from northern Europe. Some plants even originated from the Mediterranean, reaching Ireland along a drowned coastal corridor, while others journeyed from as far as North America, via Greenland and Iceland.

Irish and English plant and animal species are very similar, although as Ireland split from Great Britain before the latter broke away from Europe, some creatures which are common in England, such as weasels and moles, never made it to Ireland.

The most famous animal which is notably absent from the republic, but which is plentiful in both Great Britain and Europe, is the snake, which as legend has it was vanquished from Ireland by St Patrick while he was preaching on **Croagh Patrick**, the rocky pilgrimage mount in Mayo.

Mythological Roots

Fossils discovered from the Pleistocene Era which ended around 10,000 years ago, show that a giant elk, about the size of a moose with antlers spanning 4 m (13 ft) once roamed throughout Ireland, and that these creatures, known as *Megaloceros*, could actually have survived up until 500 BC. The early Celtic hunters would have been around at that time and probably contributed to the animal's extinction.

Like all pagan peoples, the mythology of the Gaels was bound up with all living things and each different tribe was associated with a particular animal, or even a plant. The Firbolg, who arrived around 800 BC revered the pig, the mystical De Danaan held the horse as sacred, and the Milesians cherished the hawthorn or thorn bush which later became known as the "fairy tree".

Legendary figures, like Fionn the great warrior of Tara, even had animal links in his family tree. It was said that his hounds were his sister's children, and that his son was the offspring of a faun, a half-man, half-beast with goats' horns, legs and a tail. Other famous tales from that era include that of the Children of Lir who turned into swans for 900 years, and the Salmon of Knowledge, which when eaten gave the diner second sight.

Irish Dogs

Familiar to bus travelers across Ireland, is the Irish wolfhound which is not often seen in the flesh, but is painted as a logo on the side of every Bus Eireann. Tallest of all dogs, this ancient breed first mentioned by Gaelic writers back in the 2nd century, is renowned for its hunting ability and its speed.

Masters of the manor, the Irish Wolfhound, the tallest of dogs.

Another dog breed developed in Ireland is the Irish terrier, one of the oldest of all terriers which is famed for its dare-devil nature. These sturdy little dogs, standing about 46 cm (18 inches) tall, became well known during World War I when they served as messengers and sentinel dogs.

The Irish are almost as sentimental about their dogs as the English and they are loved as pets and companions alike. Most popular in the Irish countryside are the irrepressible, black-and-white sheepdogs. A working dog, their beady, forever-watchful eyes are a useful aid to many a farmer but they are often also the family's pet.

A congregation of swans in Galway.

Birds & Bird-watching

In the old days Ireland teemed with wildlife but as deforestation became rampant and more land was cleared for agriculture most large game became extinct, although native red deer still survive. **Killarney National Park**, in Kerry, has the country's last remaining herd numbering around 450, and for visitors wanting to take a look at the republic's original forest and wildlife this 10,000-hectare (4,000-acre) park is Ireland's best untamed corner. Extensive natural woodland still exists here including oak-woods and yews, and plants like St Patrick's cabbage and butterwort. Birds easily sighted here include stonechats, peregrines, ravens, robins, chaffinches, herons and kingfishers. The famed lakes are well stocked with salmon, brown trout and char.

While in Kerry, avid bird-watchers should also take a trip to the **Skellig Islands**, a group of rocky crags 13 km (9 miles) offshore, which are home to large breeding colonies of storm petrels, puffins, razorbills, guillemots, fulmars, kittiwakes and Manx shearwaters. Little Skellig, characterized by its white cape of guano, is among the world's largest gannetries, boasting around 22,000 pairs of birds. The gannets jealously guard their own niche on this popular nesting ground, as Des Lavelle writes of a gannet returning from a fishing trip in his book *Skellig, Island Outpost of Europe*:

Ireland just would not be Ireland without its cuddly sheep.

"Both birds stand face to face, wings half open, bowing to each other and knocking their bills together with much contented grunting. No doubt it could be a very graceful affair if they had enough space, but in the crowded conditions of the Small Skellig, any protruding wing-tip or tail which encroaches by an inch on a neighbor's territory is liable to provoke a sharp stab of retaliation which upsets the whole ceremony."

Bird-watching is so popular in the republic that every year in early spring the Irish Wildbird Conservancy stages an Ornithology phone-in, in which the public is invited to take part, to report on where and when migrating birds arrive back in Ireland, from their wintering grounds. Also, if birders want to check on what birds have arrived all they have to do is make a phone call to the society.

Another spring phenomenon, which is easy for even the most hopeless of bird-watchers to evidence, is watching the rooks rebuild their nests. Before the trees have their new leaves, when they are still in their wintery skeletons, these rather sinister-looking black birds, which seem to fancy flying around gloomy castle ruins together with ravens and magpies, are busy gathering nesting materials. Apparently the male birds are the ones that build the nests, and ravens can often be seen flying along with branches up to $2^1/_2$ cm (1 inch) thick and $1^1/_2$ m (5 ft) long, which they hold on the nest with their claws and then pull into place with their bills.

Irish cattle on the Dingle Peninsula.

Male magpies really know how to pamper their females, they are sometimes seen lining their mates' nests with horsehair.

Forest & Aquatic Fauna

There are 253 state forests in Eire, and of them **Lough Key Forest Park**, covering around 350 hectares (865 acres) of County Roscommon in the mid-north, not only has some marvellous giant cedars and conifers but it is also a good viewing park for stoats, deer, hedgehogs, badgers, otters and red squirrels. This lake country is also good for bird-watching with grey herons, curlews, kingfishers and cormorants, numbering among the most easily spotted bird species.

However, it is for river cruising and fishing that most visitors make the trip to Lough Key, Lough Ree, and the River Shannon that nourishes both these lakes and much of Ireland's midlands. Known to the Irish as coarse fish, bream, pike, and roach have an open season all year round, but fishing for salmon, the passion of most serious anglers, is regulated and fishermen must buy a permit first. Rivers are open according to the season and they vary from one region to another. Donegal's Bundrowse River, Kerry's Blackwater, and Mayo's Errif and Moy rivers all offer excellent salmon fishing at different times of the year. **Sneem**, a picture-postcard town on the

Every spring Dublin's St Stephen's Green is covered with daffodils.

Ring of Kerry, also has excellent salmon fishing. Sea fishing is also popular and anglers can try their luck with shark and tuna that can be the stuff of great fishermen's yarns to entertain the folks back home with. **Blacksod Bay** off Achill Island in Mayo is a favorite venue, as is most of the wild west coast. Boats also operate out of the resort port of **Kinsale** in Cork, and further north in the same county at Youghal.

Seals can often be seen lolloping around the rocks and cavorting off the steep cliffsides of **Howth Head** just north of Dublin; they are easily viewed from the cliff walk. Further afield, seals can be spotted at the Skellig and Blasket Islands, and at **Achill Island** in Mayo, there are regular boat-trips to the renowned seal caves.

Floral Festival

While most wildlife viewing is dependent on luck as well as on patience, the beauty of the republic's floral bounty is, from early spring onwards, flaunted publicly throughout the land. Hillsides glowing with yellow gorse light up the rock-strewn countryside long before the mountain grasses turn green. Later, the Kerry hedgerows are a splash of red and purple, festooned with delicate fuchsias. Window-boxes in Georgian townhouses are a rainbow-palette of primroses and pansies, and city gardens, like Dublin's **St Stephen's Green**, are heady

A pretty Bunratty hedgerow.

Fuchsias are resplendent in many an Irish garden.

with banks of pastel-hued hyacinths, and vivid with daffodils and tulips. As summer approaches the rhododendrons bloom in a shower of pinks and purples at **Howth Castle** where they were immortalized by Joyce, in his novel *Ulysses*. Walkways are bright with azaleas and trellises are heavy with wreaths of scented wistaria. In Cork, pink magnolias shed their petals on fine green lawns, and at **Blarney Castle** the blossom trees issue a sweet smell and provide a glorious border to many a tourist's snapshot.

Great Gardens

Ireland is famous for its "great gardens", and some travel agencies run a grand tour of the pick of the crop, many of which are within a day's touring distance of Dublin. Visually, **Powerscourt**, an 18th-century garden just south of Dublin at Enniskerry in County Wicklow, is the most impressive. This feeling is somehow reinforced by the blackened ruin of the adjoining mansion which was destroyed by fire in 1974 leaving the gardens in magnificent solitude amid the Wicklow Mountains. Powerscourt has been described as "garden as theater" for incorporated into its scallop-shell shape are statues of Greek warriors and minotaurs, a Japanese garden, a grotto made of petrified moss, and acres of manicured lawns and trees. Daniel Robertson, the 18th-century landscaper responsible for this grandi-

Birding in Ireland– by Morten Strange

No wonder the national color of Ireland is green, because that is exactly what this country is. It is a landscape of rolling hills which seldom rise more than 1,000 m (3,280 ft) above sea level. Most land is utilized as green fields for grazing and pasture, and in the lowlands there are extensive peat bogs. Forests are few and far between; tree cover is mostly coniferous plantations cultivated quite recently on the higher slopes. Since there is therefore little leaf fall in the autumn and the winters are short and mild with little snowcover, Ireland indeed appears green all year round.

In the farmlands and the village gardens, some common European birds are plentiful such as **Skylark, Song Thrush, Blackbird, Robin, Magpie, Linnet and Chaffinch**. They can be seen all over the Palaearctic region. You may however find it odd that several other common European birds appear to be missing. Many passerine birds such as the Nuthatch, Redstart, Reed Warbler, Lesser Whitethroat, Wood Warbler, Pied Flycatcher, Tree Pipit, Yellow Wagtail, Woodchat Shrike and Hawfinch, are absent from Ireland. The main reason is because the forest habitat is poorly developed and also because many birds never seem to settle on islands which generally have fewer resident species than large land masses. Outside the diverse passerine order other bird families such as owls, woodpeckers and birds of prey, are also poorly represented in Ireland by just one or a few species while where are several or a dozen in mainland Europe.

The main reason to go birdwatching in Ireland, is to look for wetland birds, especially seabirds along the coastlines, and also for migrants and rare vagrants not found further east in Europe. You will also be able to see a good number of European resident birds.

Freshwater Wetlands

There are countless rivers and lakes cutting through the Irish countryside, draining and collecting the precipitation which is generous in most places. **Lough Erne** is such a freshwater wetland site in the northern part of the republic.

Puffin Island in County Kerry, has large colonies of puffins.

Kittiwakes gather in their thousands every summer.

It is a tangled maze of water and islands intermingled to form a rich birding location. There are several species of ducks breeding here including **Mallard, Teal, Tufted Duck, Red-breasted Merganser** and a few pairs of the northerly species Common Scoter which is found nowhere else in Ireland. Other resident waterbirds include **Mute Swan, Grey Heron, Moorhen** and several **grebes, gulls** and **terns**. On the small heavily vegetated islands many landbirds occur. During migration season and winter the lakelets are visited by other species of ducks and flocks of **Whooper Swan**. Part of Lough Erne is now a nature reserve.

In the southwest corner of Ireland just south of the village of Ballyheighe near Kerry Head lies **Akeagh Lough**. Compared to other Irish lakes this one is tiny; in fact it almost dries up during late summer. It is however an important breeding location for some wetland birds including the Gadwall duck, which is somewhat rare elsewhere in Europe. Most significantly the small lake is just behind the seashore and many migrants end up here when they rest during migration. This is about as close to America as you can get in Europe and therefore it is no coincidence that Akeagh Lough has become something of a "twitchers" heaven; a "twitcher" being birdwatching slang for a person obsessed with spotting new birds and preferably rare species new to the area. Many shorebirds of North American affinities which rightly should not occur in Europe at all, have turned up here as rare vagrants, these include **Least Sandpiper, Baird's Sandpiper, Western Sandpiper, Kildeer, Pectoral Sandpiper** and also several **American ducks**. Some of these sandpipers are notoriously difficult to recognize and identify positively in the field - if you do go to Akeagh Lough or another Irish shorebird location be sure to bring a high quality telescope and a camera, you might produce a "first for Europe" sighting.

The Magnificent Seacoast

Of all the locations in Ireland, the coastline is perhaps the most pleasurable and interesting. The southern and western coast is a rugged landscape of tall cliffs dropping off steeply down into the sea below. In between are long stretches of coves with the most beautiful sandy beaches; if only the weather had been a little more agreeable the popular charter vacation spots around the Mediterranean may have palled in comparison. As it is you have these miles of enchanting beaches exclusively to yourself - you only have to share them with the birds!

The most exposed points along the coast are, for a few short summer months, breeding grounds for some spectacular congregations of pelagic sea birds. These birds live almost their entire lives on the rough Atlantic seas, often venturing far offshore with apparently no affiliation to land. They satisfy their need for water by drinking sea-water and excreting the excess salt in concentrated droplets through a tube above the bill, therefore the label "tube-nosed" birds; the **Fulmar, petrels** and **shearwaters** belong to this category. But even pelagic birds cannot lay their eggs on the sea; reluctantly they have to venture ashore during the breeding season. They select the most remote islands and capes facing the sea, preferably steep cliffs where they are safe from predators and where

Shags populate the Irish coast, living in colonies.

they can fly straight in to perch. When the young have hatched and matured all they have to do is jump out from the ledge to become airborne and glide out to their beloved sea environment below.

A bird cliff colony in May or June is one of Europe's great birding spectacles when thousands, sometimes tens of thousands of **Kittiwakes, Razorbills, Guillemots, Shags** and **Fulmars** congregate on various sections of the 200-300 m (656-924 ft) high, vertical cliff faces. In Ireland these and other sea birds can be viewed close to Dublin at **Howth Head**. Other important spots include **Bray Head, Helvick Head**, the **Cliffs of Moher**, the **Mayo coastline, Horn Head, Fair Head** and **Islandmagee**. Near these bird cliffs look out for other coastal residents like **Black Guillemot, Eider Duck, Oystercatcher, Common and Arctic Tern, Great and Lesser Black-backed Gull**. They breed on the lower, grassy slopes or the shingle beaches below, near to the sea.

Bird cliff birds on the mainland are usually quite tame and easy to view from trails above the ledges or from a boat out on the sea. But this is even more so on offshore islands where the birds are sometimes very numerous, breed very densely and can be approached to within a few meters distance. Besides, some species are mainly found on the islands. There are large colonies of **Puffins** on **Puffin Island** in County Kerry and **Rathlin** in County Antrim. The **Manx Sherwater** and the **Storm Petrel** also prefer offshore islands along the west coast, but they only come ashore at night and are therefore a bit more difficult to view.

Perhaps most renowned of all Irish bird islands is the **Little Skellig Bird Sanctuary**

...Birding in Ireland – by Morten Strange

which is home to 20,000 of the dazzling Gannets, one of the largest colonies of Gannets in Europe. The **Skellig Islands** are part of the Kerry Islands group in the southwestern corner of Ireland, which is probably the best place to go in Ireland to see seabirds. Boats to visit the islands can be rented from the fishing villages on the mainland. All species of seabirds resident to Ireland and Great Britain can be found here.

Migrating Birds

Migrating coastal birds congregate on tidal mudflats and saline marshes mostly on Ireland's eastern and southeastern coast. Near Dublin the **Bull Island** is accessible by car via a causeway and is feeding and resting ground throughout the non-breeding season for migratory shorebirds, divers, ducks and geese, including large flocks of Brent Goose. Even more famous among birders are the **Wexford Slobs** near Wexford harbor, south along the coast from Dublin. This extensive area of flooded fields and marshes is home to up to 10,000 geese, mainly the **White-fronted Goose** of the subspecies *Anser albifrons flavirostris* from Greenland, which can be seen here and in a few other places in the world.

A little further south from Wexford are more good birding areas. Offshore, **Carnsore point** and the **Great Saltee island** have many seabirds and on the mainland **Lady's Island Lake, Tacumshin Lake, Gull and Bannow Bays** are all known as regular haunts for migratory water birds. Rare land birds also turn up during the migration season. This is even more the case on the exposed **Cape Clear Island** in the southwest corner of Ireland. The bird observatory on the island does provide accommodations and if you can manage to arrange a visit to this remote spot by mailboat from the mainland town of Baltimore near Cork, you are bound to see rare birds. Migrant landbirds stray onto the island and from the shores many pelagic vagrants can be spotted, including Great Shearwater, Wilson's Petrel and Black-browed Albatross. Whether these species which have never set foot on European soil can truly be regarded as European birds is of course a matter of discussion, but you can see them in Ireland!

More Information

Being part of Europe, Ireland is covered by all the excellent field guides available for identifying birds occuring on the continent. One of the newest titles is the very comprehensive *Birds of Europe* by Lars Jonsson which will help you identify all the birds that have been seen in Europe including North Africa and the Middle East more than five times this century. Specifically on the status and distribution of birds in this country *Ireland's Birds* by R F Ruttledge will be the book to get. John Gooders' *Where to Watch Birds in Britain and Europe* has a useful chapter on Ireland. At the Irish Wildbird Conservancy, work is being co-ordinated to inform about and protect Irish birds and their habitats, the society publishes *IWC News* which contains all the latest details. The address is 8 Longford Place, Monkstown, County Dublin, Tel: (01) 2804322, Fax: 2844407.

osity, was apparently pushed around in a wheelbarrow to oversee the project, as he was too crippled by gout to walk. A later edition to the garden is an intricate herbaceous border designed by the prominent landscape gardener JJ Costin.

Continue further south in Wicklow for the exquisite gardens of **Mount Usher** near the village of Ashford. The site was formerly a 8-hectare (20-acre) potato patch before being changed into one of Ireland's most famous gardens. During early summer, Mount Usher is a vision of lilies, poppies, and peonies. Dense with eucryphia and eucalyptus, with masses of magnolias and maples, the

Rhododendrons in bloom, Glengarriff.

gardens boast a riotous azalea walk and they even have a fernery located in a secluded gully accessible across a gangplank which spans a rushing stream. Another "great garden" in Wicklow is **Killruddery**, which has a beautiful conservatory, often the lunch stop for garden tours, complete with elegant statuary and fountains. "The most benignly haunted garden I have ever visited" writes Miranda Innes, the gardening expert of the English *Country Living* magazine.

Other notable gardens include **Graigueconna**, also in Wicklow, the county commonly known as "Ireland's Garden", which has a conservatory engulfed in fuchsias, geranium and passion-fruits. There are 80 different types of roses, and trees with unusual multicolored bark on display. Further north in Meath is **Butterstream**, here pyramidal box trees provide a contrast to an exuberant flower garden where a white garden is ringed with conifers and a mock-Doric temple is wreathed in flowering clematis.

In the mid-north are the magnificent rhododendron gardens of **Lough Key Forest Park** and near Galway is **Coole Park**, the former home of Lady Gregory. The house, now in ruins, is survived by a yew walk and a garden, where, scratched in a tree, are the initials of some of the hostess' famous guests, among them, WB Yeats, Sean O'Casey, and Douglas Hyde (Ireland's first president).

People

In his generalizations about the comparative friendliness of different European nations, William Makepeace Thackeray, talks of how in order to get an Englishman to "laugh cordially or to speak unreservedly...it requires a long sitting, and a bottle of wine at the least". He writes also of the idiosyncrasies of how to get the Germans, the Irish, and the French into a similar mood. But of all these nationalities, Thackeray decides that "it is clear that for a stranger the Irish ways are the pleasantest, for here he is at once made happy and at home."

A young Irish of genteel refinement.

Tourism, Ireland's fastest growing industry, is surely an indication that Thackeray was not alone in his feelings. Although many people come for the republic's scenic beauty, even more visitors arrive to experience the camaraderie, the charm, the earthy irreverent wit, and the deep faith of its inhabitants.

At Home & Abroad

The reputation of the

The great character of Dublin attracts a diversity of people.

Irish, though, certainly outweighs their numbers, for Ireland's population figures for 1991 list just under $3^1/_2$ million inhabitants – about the size of a moderately-large American city – a fact which comes as a surprise to most visitors. Since the mid-19th century, unlike most other European nations, Ireland was a demographic freak, for its population was declining instead of growing.

Today's numbers are only half that of a century-and-a-half ago when even after the massive losses caused by the Great Famine, the population in 1851 still numbered $6^1/_2$ million. But it was emigration that made the biggest difference to Ireland's population pattern, for poverty forced these economic refugees to search for greener pastures in the United States, Canada and Australia. The poignancy of this situation is brought home in an old etching entitled *The Causes of Emigration in Ireland*, dated January 1849, in which evil-visaged rent collectors thrust eviction notices on a poor Irish family while a glowing sun on the horizon entitled "America", beckons.

The final emigration tallies were incredible, and these days the number of Irish who live outside their homeland far outnumbers those who stayed behind. Americans of Irish descent are said to number around an astonishing 40 million, which obviously accounts for a large number of tourists, many returning to the "emerald isle" in search of their roots.

Aristocratic elitism at The Curragh.

Rebellious Irreverence

Of course many travelers come to Ireland with a preconceived idea of what an Irishman or woman is supposed to be like. Roy Kerridge, the author of *Always Ireland: An Englishman in Ireland*, talks of how he always imagined the Irish to be like Brendan Behan, the bawdy playwright, whose works he read "with horrified fascination". He recalls that it was not the violence of Ireland that he had always feared, but that he would, like Behan, succumb to drink. Kerridge, however, goes on to say that in 1991 he met what he considered, these days, as a real, typical Irishman. The fellow lived in a suburban estate, mowed the lawn, washed the car, and ate trendy dishes prepared by his wife in a stripped-pine kitchen. However, what Kerridge omits to say, is that under this veneer of modernity, this middle-class suburbanite was probably just as irreverent as Behan.

Irreverence is something that has long been remarked upon in the Irish character, and is a trait which still runs deep despite their independence from their colonial masters the English, whose rule some historians say contributed to this behavioral pattern. Anarchy springs from oppression, which is something the Irish, often referred to "as lawbreakers at heart", have always been reminded of through their long history.

These days the Irish have mellowed,

Gaelic: The Mother Tongue

A Gaelic class, County Waterford.

Comedians the world over have mastered the slow drawl of the Irish accent. And anyone who is aware of the different dialects of English can easily identify an Irishman from a Liverpudlian, a Scot, or a London Cockney, but what most people fail to realize is that this Irish language is but an import, and a comparatively recent one at that, and that Gaelic is the mother tongue of the republic. Enshrined as the national language in Ireland's constitution, Irish, or Gaelic (pronounced *Gaylick* as opposed to Scotland's *Gallik*) as it is sometimes referred to, may play second fiddle to English as the republic's most popular tongue, but for the more than 70,000 Irish who speak their native language, and the perhaps one million others who have an understanding of it, the original Celtic tongue is at the very roots of Irish culture.

The Inventive Celts

First introduced by the Gaels, the ancestors of the Milesians who arrived on Irish soil around the same time that Romulus and Remus were founding Rome, Irish belongs to a branch of the Celtic languages known as Goidelic, which includes Scottish and Manx. During Roman and pre-Roman days, Celtic languages were spoken over much of Western Europe as the Celts were responsible for bringing civilization to Europe, north of the Alps. Inventive and energetic, they introduced Europe to the iron industry which revolutionized agriculture and transport. They were a people of both inventive genius and cultural brilliance, capable of producing stunning artworks, like the Tara brooch, and a rich mythology which still endures today. Celtic culture was well-preserved in Ireland, owing to the failure of the Romans to travel across the Irish sea. Today, the only remaining areas that speak Celtic languages apart from Ireland, are the Scottish Highlands, Wales, some parts of Cornwall in England, and France's Brittany.

Digging for Roots

Surviving the Viking and then the Norman raids, Irish endured as the principal language of Ireland until well into the mid-19th century. But for centuries there had really been two linguistic Irelands: Gaelic was the tongue of the countryside while English was popular in the Anglo-Norman towns. The survival of the language parallels Irish history, for with Cromwell's scorched-earth policy and the planting of Protestant settlers in Ulster, the Gaelic-speaking population were forced out of the rich pasture-

although old habits still survive. On Dublin's **Westmoreland Street**, the traffic lights show red, but that does not deter the pedestrians who merrily jaywalk against the lights, scuttling like rabbits between the vehicles, while three

lands of the midlands and the east, to the rugged country of the southwest and the west. Although Irish speakers still numbered around four million (more than Ireland's total population today), mass starvation during the 1830s, and the wholesale emigration of the rural people in the next decade, saw the number of native speakers on the decline.

The Gaelic death knell came when English was declared as the language of instruction at all national schools, and the speaking of Irish was penalized by beatings with a tally stick. It was considered regressive to use Gaelic, and even the "Great Liberator", Daniel O'Connor, a Kerryman and a fluent speaker of his mother tongue, thought that it was "an encumbrance to the Irish people in the modern world". Thomas Davis, who wrote for the radical newspaper *The Nation*, did not agree, proclaiming that "a people without a language is only half a nation". Half a century later, Davis's call was taken up by the scholar and linguist, Douglas Hyde, who saw the need "for de-anglicizing Ireland" and founded the Gaelic League. He realized that the key to Ireland's survival was the revival of its language, a view shared by many nationalists of the time and one which developed into a powerful literary movement led by WB Yeats and Lady Gregory. This movement was responsible for the formation of the first Irish national theater. When Ireland achieved independence the restoration of the Irish language was given top priority, being introduced into schools and government departments. However, although the sincerity was there, it was all too late for English had become the language of choice for most of the Irish, although they still had a romantic attachment to their old mother tongue and all that it represented.

Surviving the Gaeltacht

The Gaeltacht, the name used for the officially Irish-speaking regions of Ireland, was always different from the rest of the country. In this region, which comprises much of the southwest, the west coast, and the far northwest, Gaelic has always been the most popular language.

Today it is not only common to hear Irish being spoken, but these rugged lands east of the English "Pale" are the areas where Irish culture is at its purest and least homogenized.

Road signs provide an easy first step for learning Irish, as often both the English and Gaelic names are given, but the former are not always included in the Gaeltacht. *Baile*, pronounced "bally" and spelt variously as "balli", "bally", "valli", and "bal" means "town", which accounts for the hundreds of Irish place names starting with these prefixes, like Ballyconnell, Ballina, and Baile-atha-cliath, the "town of the hurdle ford", also known as Dublin. *Cashel*, home of St Patrick's Rock, means "castle"; *inis*, the prefix of all the Aran Island's names is Irish for "island"; and "lough" or "loch", which is usually thought of as being Scottish for "lake", actually had its roots in Gaelic which was brought to Scotland by the Irish.

Winning Friends

English is well understood all over Ireland, but a smattering of Irish phrases, even badly pronounced as beginners are apt to, is always a sure way to win friends and influence people, especially in the Gaeltacht. Start the day with the greeting *"dia duit"* ("good-day"), pronounced "jee-a-ditch". Raise your glass if someone shouts *"slainte"* ("cheers"), pronounced "slawn-che" in a pub, and remember to watch out for the *gardai* (police) when you are attempting to drive after too much *craic* (alcoholic, tipples that accompany good company). In this case, a winning smile and a *"go raibh maith agat"* ("thank you") should work wonders.

policemen patiently wait for the green light. Further south, in a Cork public park a woman walking an overweight Corgi dog helps herself to a large bunch of daffodils, completely oblivious to the sign at the gate which prohibits flower

Juniors on an outing.

picking. Again, nearby, at the old waterworks on the Lee River, a fisherman calmly climbs the fence and sets up his rods beside the "No Trespassing" notice.

A Most Tolerant People

Like the *gardai* (police), though, who watched the jaywalkers but let them be, the Irish are also well known for their tolerance towards others. No cause is rejected, no matter how strange or radical it may appear. The Dublin youth wearing a green apron painted with "Please Help the Starving in Bosnia" has no problems soliciting donations on St Patrick's Day. At the **Winding Stair**, a second-hand bookshop cum alternative food center, silver-haired pensioners in brogues and tweeds browse the shelves and sip their herbal teas beside youths in leather jackets emblazoned with Harley Davidson symbols. On the counter there is a free newspaper published by the gay and lesbian movements.

Opposite the restaurant, on the other side of the Liffey River, in full view of the passing parade, a photographic gallery is running an exhibition of photos of naked men, their painted penises framed with twirling Celtic designs. Somehow, it seems ironic to see such things in such a strictly Roman Catholic country, but perhaps as these works are considered as "art" they are therefore unattached to reality.This attitude is

Gypsies prefer to go where the spirit takes them.

indicative of the elusiveness of the Irish mind which James Joyce often railed against. His fictional hero, or alter-ego, proclaimed: "I go to encounter for the millionth time the reality of experience and to forge in the smithy of my soul the uncreated conscience of my race".

Humble Humor

Like Joyce, the Irish are always best at picking faults with each other rather than with outsiders. At the pub, drink in hand, the regulars banter freely. As Samuel Johnson observed in the 18th century, "the Irish are a fair people, they never speak well of one another". And another Irishman, much adored and maligned, the audacious Oscar Wilde, made a claim that few people would deny: "We are the greatest talkers since the Greeks". At the pub, at the corner-store, and on radio talk-shows across the country, the gossip flows unabated like Guinness from the tap.

In true Irish style no one is afraid of speaking out. A woman phones the radio station to complain about a street hawker who was fined IR£25 for selling shamrocks without a licence on O'Connell Street. She compares that with the IR£29,000 the politicians have just spent on a trip to Australia. "They claim to be selling Ireland, but they are just wasting Ireland's money. The shamrock seller should be allowed to make an honest living", says the Limerick housewife.

At Dublin's Moore Street markets, the talk becomes a barrage of words. Hawkers shrill their wares and housewives banter with shopkeepers. On the street corner, a dapper old gent asks a woman half his age, "Are you waiting for me, love?" then he apologizes for his indiscretion by saying, "You've got to make people laugh". The joke, the "ability to turn suffering into music", is what the Irish are most adept at. But they have had to do so in order to survive a history darker than most nations have had to suffer.

Home of Hospitality

Hospitality is another of the Irish traits

The Women's Movement

Since mythological times Irish women have always held their own in both marriage and war. Even in Celtic days, if a woman happened to own more property than a man, she was the governing force in the household, and if the marriage broke down she was allowed to keep all her personal possessions. In war, the Celtic Amazons were legendary. Sixty years after the birth of Christ, Queen Boudicca burned London to the ground, and a Roman historian of the time told of Gaelic women that were a match against troops of foreigners: "Steely-eyed...she swells her neck, gnashes her teeth, flexes her huge white biceps, and rains wallops and kicks as though from the twisted cords of a catapult".

Famous Women

Other accounts tell of the beauty of Celtic women, how they painted their faces with berry juice, perfumed their bodies with aromatic herbs, and draped themselves in colorful flowing cloaks. Female Druidesses who often presided at pagan rites presenting offerings and sacrificial animals, were noticeable by their elaborate body tattoos. Even Ireland's name is based on a feminine principle as Eire was a goddess of the mystical De Danaan people in whose cosmology she was the wife of Mac Greine, the "son of the sun". Together with her two sisters Banba and Fodhla, Eire formed a trinity of goddesses.

Other notable women from those legendary days include Macha of the Red Tresses, the 76th monarch of Ireland who ruled Ulster and founded the great Navan Fort near Armagh; Queen Medb who reigned at Rathcroghan, Roscommon; and Saint Brigid, who before her conversion was a Druidic priestess and whose Christian followers kept a sacred fire going in memory of her until it was extinguished by the Normans.

Changing Mores

In the old pagan days sexual mores were even more liberated than the wildest dreams of modern-day feminists. Women rulers took their pick of the virile warriors under their command, and wives were even known to present young women to their husbands as gifts. Of course it was not all fun and games, some women were chosen as sacrificial victims, but they usually met their death at the hands of powerful female priestesses, so although some of their practices were barbaric, women were far from being oppressed.

Christianity, however, changed all this as social mores took on a new moral code which profoundly altered the role of women. Men became monks, forsaking the pleasures of the flesh for the austerities of the monastery, women fell into the role of wives and mothers, and Ireland's political and social arena began to be dominated by men. A woman's place was in the home and her main role was to bear children, a situation which remained virtually unchanged until recent times.

Marriage was frequently arranged by relatives, usually to cement a land deal, but this arrangement was not only confined to women but also to men. To be landless often meant that one would end up unmarried, and after the Great Famine figures show that 26 per cent of women were unmarried, an amazing figure given that in those days to be single was almost a social sin.

which travelers have been commenting upon for generations. You can always find homely touches in the Bed and Breakfasts and guesthouses. "I give you more soda bread this mornin' cause I knows you like it", said pretty Catherine, the proprietress of a Gardiner Street establishment. And amongst the bar paraphernalia and stickers there is always one that reads, "There are no strangers, only friends you've never met".

One traveler who was especially charmed by Ireland was Asenath Nicholson, who wrote of his 19th-cen-

Raven Beauty

But although Irish women played the role of good Catholic mothers and daughters there was always a streak of Celtic pride and vigor that seemed to separate them from other more oppressed European women. Poets have penned sonnets on women with "eyes as soft as darkness and a voice like a singing swallow", and travelers like19th-century writer Asenath Nicholson believed that a buxom Kerry matron who danced barefoot on the beach was "more graceful in her movements, more beautiful in complexion or symmetry" than "the daughter of Herodias herself". On a more current theme, was this recent notice in the "Personal" column of the *Irish Times*: "Sheila, Memories of Egypt Fade With My Tan But You Remain, Beautiful Raven You Stole My Heart, Mark".

Irishwomen, though, are hard to label. Take a glance at a cross-section of women walking along a Dublin street. There are the moneyed trendies with fashionable clothes and stylish coiffures; there are the mini-skirted, leather-jacketed girls with their perms and dyed hair; and what about the frumpy, overweight mums puffing on a cigarette and screaming at the kids; or the earnest student types dressed in black, as well as the freaks and the hippies. They may present a thousand different faces to the world, but there are some common facets of Irish womanhood.

Frank & Free

Firstly, despite the fact that divorce and abortions are still illegal in Ireland, women are forthright, outspoken and frank. Take the radio phone-in caller who had her own ideas as to why the actress Kim Bassinger had decided to "cover-up" for future films after appearing seven times in *Playboy*, and being notorious for her nude scenes. "Her boobs no longer stay vertical when she's horizontal", remarked the Dublin housewife, adding that "she must be over the hill". Or there is the anti-abortionist campaigner on O'Connell Street thrusting pamphlets showing gruesome aborted eight-week-old foetuses at unsuspecting shoppers.

This freedom for women to speak out is in fact relatively new, for prior to the 1970s women were bound to the home, churning out baby after baby. They used to joke about having their annual holiday at Dublin's Rotunda, Europe's largest maternity hospital.

With the rise of the women's movement many Irishwomen began to opt for the liberty offered by contraception, although this is far from being accepted by the papacy in Rome. Contraception has marked the beginning of what some writers have coined "a la carte Catholicism" where a woman gets to pick and choose what she wants.

The Roman Catholic Church has become more a source of guidance than of rules and thus women are making more decisions for themselves. Such liberty is a far cry from the 1920s when an Irish bishop, railing against the evils of a new dance craze, advised fathers that "if your girls do not obey you, if they are not in at the hours appointed, lay the lash upon their backs. That was the good old system, and that should be the system today." Nowadays women have more say in how they live their lives.

tury wanderings in *The Bible in Ireland.* Nicholson tells of sleeping the night in a one-room cabin with a family of six and a menagerie of pigs, ducks, geese, hens and dogs. His bed consisted of a bundle of straw with a woollen covering. "In my own native land I had slept under rich canopies, in stately mansions of the rich, in the plain, wholesome dwelling of the thrifty farmer, the log-cabin of the poor, and under tents on the hunting-ground of the Indian, but never where poverty, novelty, and kindness were so happily blended".

Coping with Difficulties

The Irish, like the Scots, are known to be penny-pinching, but it is not out of a miserly nature, but rather out of a tradition of having to make do with so little. "I don't see many millionaires in my job", said the Clonmel bus-driver. But they are also generous when they feel the need; when the actor Paul Newman approached the government for assistance in finding a summer camp for sick children, Albert Reynolds, the *Taoiseach*, responded by giving the Hollywood star a castle in Naas for the rent of only IR£1 per year.

Having had such a troubled past, the Irish are expert at turning a deaf ear to current troubles, especially the ongoing problems of Northern Ireland. When a newscaster was relating the latest atrocity, an IRA bombing in England where an infant was killed, the restaurant crowd did not even pause in their chatter. At first this attitude may seem callous, but the longer one stays in Ireland, and the more these types of broadcast are repeated, one begins to become immune to "the troubles". It is a bit like a complaining relative that you have grown to endure.

The statues of dead martyrs and heroes that adorn every village and town square all over the republic make the traveler realize that this apathy to the Northern problems is due to so much pain in the past. Not that the south does not have its own problems to worry

Starting young: life on the farm.

On the Ancestor Trail

At breakfast, the proprietress of a Galway guesthouse told the tale of an Australian couple who had only last year discovered their long-lost Irish relatives. The grand-daughter had always remembered the name of their ancestral farm and the county where it was situated, from childhood stories. When she found the farm, although it had long since passed out of family hands, the neighboring church graveyard revealed her grandfather's tomb, and enquiries at a nearby residence eventually led to the family's reunion."Others are not so lucky, though", added the proprietress, recalling families who had searched for ancestors with no result.

Every year thousands of Irish Americans, Irish Australians, and the descendants of those who emigrated throughout the English-speaking world, continental Europe, and Central and South America, return to their motherland intent on discovering their roots. The ancestry business has therefore become a lucrative adjunct to Ireland's booming tourist trade.

Useful Preparations

The key to success, in locating relatives or even just discovering an ancestral village, lies in obtaining prior knowledge of forefathers' names, dates and places of birth, death and marriage, and other relevant details. Usually the more information a traveler provides, the more successful the search will be. Offices in Dublin which provide valuable information include **The Genealogical Office** and **State Heraldic Office**; the **National Library**, in Kildare Street; **The General Registery Office**, in Joyce House, Lombard Street; the **Registery of Deeds** in Henrietta Street; and the **State Paper Office** in Dublin Castle.

For visitors who want professional help, the oldest and best-known research company is the Hibernian Research Co Ltd, PO Box 3097, Dublin 6, Ireland, who were responsible for successfully investigating the ancestry of former US President Ronald Reagan, former Canadian Prime Minister Brian Mulroney, tennis ace John McEnroe, and Patrick Duffy, star of the TV soap-opera *Dallas*.

On the Name Trail

The following is a list of some popular surnames, their meanings, and approximate family locations:

Ahearne: Originally *O Heachtighearna*, meaning "Lord of the Horse" who were descendants of the High King Brian Boru. Later known as Aheron, Ahearne, Herne, or Hearne (the most common of today's variations) the sept originated from Clare and Limerick counties.

Barry: Also Barrymore. Arriving from Wales with the Anglo Normans in 1170 they settled in Cork where their hunting lodge, **Fota Island**, still survives. The Barrymores of theater fame, first made their mark in Irish theater in the 16th century.

Blake: Originally Normans they successfully settled in Galway becoming one of the rich "14 Tribes of Galway". Many of their castles still survive in Connacht, and in County Kildare there are three Blakestowns.

Butler: One of the most successful Norman-Irish families, whose members included Anne Boleyn and WB Yeats. For centuries, the Butlers, known as the Earls of Ormonde, ruled from **Kilkenny Castle** where they still have a world reunion every three years.

Carroll: Originally *O Cearbhaill* meaning "warlike champion" from the 3rd century King of Munster, Oilioll Olum. Found in **Tipperary** and **Offaly** counties.

Connolly: Originally *O Conghaile* meaning "valorous", the family is still found in Cork, Meath and Monaghan counties.

Doherty: Originally *O Dochartaigh* meaning "obstructive", descended from the 4th century King Niall of the Nine Hostages. Still numerous in **Donegal** where they often hold clan rallies.

Donoghue: Originally *O Donnchadha*, claim descent from an 11th century King of Munster. They settled **Cork** and **Kerry** (Killarney's Ross Castle), Galway, and Kilkenny where they founded **Jerpoint Abbey**.

Egan: Originally *Mac Aodhagain* and sometimes known as Keegan. Old Gaelic name meaning "son of Aodh", the sept originated in **Galway, Roscommon** and **Leitrim** and are also found in **Tipperary** (Redwood Castle in Lorrha, Tipperary holds clan rallies), **Kilkenny** and **Offaly**.

FitzGerald: Powerful Norman family dating from the 1170 invasion who became the Earls of Kildare, Dukes of Leinster, and the Earls of Desmond (Kerry and Cork).Many of their castles still survive.

Gallagher: Originally *O Gallchobhair*, meaning "foreign help", claim royal blood through the son of Niall of the Nine Hostages. Still numerous in **Donegal**.

Guinness: Originally *MagAonghusa* meaning "son of Aonghus", the family date back to a 5th century chieftain. Originally the Lords of Iveagh in Down county they are best known as the famous brewing and philanthropic family.

Hennessy: Originally *O Haonghusa*, also known as Hensey and Henchy. Towns named **Ballyhennessy** (Hennessy's town) abound in Connacht and Munster and many families are still found in **Limerick, Tipperary** and **Cork.** Most famous for the well-known cognac.

Hogan: Originally *O Hogain*, they descended from the 10th century High King Brian Boru. The family settled **Clare** and **Limerick** counties.

Joyce: Comes from the French name "Joy". They arrived with the Norman invasion in Galway and were one of the original "14 Tribes of Galway". **Ross County** is today known as Joyce's Country, and the most famous family member is writer James Joyce.

Kavanagh: Originally *Caomhanach*, they were direct descendants of the 12th century King of Leinster, Diarmuid MacMurrough, responsible for the Norman invasion. The family is still numerous around **Wexford** and **Carlow**, and their castles still survive at **Enniscorthy** and **Ferns**.

Lynch: Originally *O Liongsigh*, this family owe their roots to a Norman, de Lynch, and to Labradh Longseach, King of Ireland in 600 BC. They settled **Clare, Sligo, Limerick, Galway** and **Donegal**. The Norman Lynches were one of the powerful "14 Tribes of Galway".

MacCarthy: Originally *MacCarthaigh* who descended from a 3rd century King of Munster. Their fine castles and buildings include Cormac's chapel at the **Rock of Cashel, Muckross Castle** beside the Lakes of Killarney, and **Blarney** where Cormac started the "Blarney Stone" legend.

Maguire: Originally *MagUidhir*, also known as MacGuire and McGuire came from the Irish word meaning "pale colored". As Barons of Enniskellen, there are still castle remains in the region, including **Enniskellen Castle**, Fermanagh.

Malone: Originally *O Maoileoin*, meaning "one who served St John". Kinsmen of the Connacht kings, they originated from Offaly, and many served as bishops and abbots at **Clonmacnoise**.

Moore: Originally *O Mordha* meaning "noble", the sept descended from Conal Cearnach a chieftain of the Knights of the Red Branch. The family territory was at **Leix**, and other Moores include the Marquess of Drogheda who built **Moore Abbey** in Kildare.

Murphy: Originally *O Morchoe* meaning "sea warrior", they originated from **Tyrone, Sligo** and **Wexford**, and later many moved to Cork. The present chieftain is "The O Morchoe" a farmer from Wexford.

O'Brien: This sept are named after the 10th century High King of Ireland, Brian Boru. This powerful family settled in **Clare, Limerick** and are numerous in **Munster**.

O'Connor: Originally *O Conchobhair*, meaning "hero". The sept date back to the 2nd century, but their name derives from a 10th century King of Connacht. They settled **Clare, Offaly, Kerry** and **Ulster**. The family seat is **Clonalis** near Roscommon.

O'Grady: Originally *O Gradaigh* meaning "illustrious" originated from Clare, and then moved to **Limerick** where they are still numerous.

O'Kelly: Originally *O Ceallaigh*, now often known as Kelly, they descended from Ceallach a 9th-century chieftain whose name meant "war" or "contention". Their territories were in **Galway** and **Roscommon**, and famous Kellys include Princess Grace of Monaco and the Australian bush-ranger Ned Kelly.

O'Kennedy: Originally *O Cinneide*, now known as Kennedy. The name originates from a kinsman of Brian Boru called "ugly head". They first settled in Clare, then later in **Tipperary** and **Kilkenny**, and are best known for the famous Kennedy political clan of the US.

...On the Ancestor Trail

O Neill: This famous family claim descent from the legendary Niall of the Nine Hostages and originated in **Ulster** where they are still very numerous.
O'Sullivan: Originally *O Suileabhain* meaning either "one" or "hawk-eyed" originated from Olioll Olum, 3rd century King of Munster. Numerous in **Tipperary, Cork** and **Kerry**. Sir Arthur O Sullivan wrote the music for the Gilbert and Sullivan operas.
Power: Came to Ireland with the Normans, their name "Le Poer" meant "poor" but they became rich estate owners in **Wicklow** and **Waterford**. Famous names include the movie star Tyrone Power.
Regan: Originally *O Reagain* also known as Reagan were one of the "Four Tribes of Tara" and one sect, which the ex-president of the US, Ronald Reagan, descends from, are derived from one of Brian Boru's brothers. Numerous in **Leix, Clare, Leinster,** and **Tipperary**.
Ryan: Originally *O Maoilriain*, also known as Mulryan from either the word for "administrator" or "water", they descend from a 2nd century King of Leinster. They settled in **Carlow, Tipperary** and **Limerick**.
Sheridan: Originally *O Sirideain* who first settled in Cavan, of obscure origins. Well known for centuries for their literary talent. Another famous member is the famous American Civil War general.
Walsh: Originally *Breathnach,* the Irish name for "Welshmen" this clan descended from the Welshmen who arrived in Ireland with the Normans. They settled **Dublin, Kilkenny, Leix, Waterford** and **Wicklow**.
Irish-Americans can go to the US National Archives to discover where and when their ancestors came to the New World. There are also a number of interesting books.

Other names

Other prominent Irish names are as follows: Barrett, Beirne, Blake, Boland, Boyle, Brady, Breen, Brennan, Browne, Buckley, Burke, Cahill, Carey, Cassidy, Clancy, Cleary, Collins, Connolly, Conroy, Conway, Cooney, Corcoran, Costello, Crowley, Cullen, Curtin, Cummins, Curran, Cusack, Daly, Delaney, Dempsey, Devine, Devlin, Dillon, Doherty, Dolan, Donoghue, Doran, Dowling, Doyle, Duggan, Duffy, Dunne, Fagan, Fahey, Fallon, Fitzpatrick, Flanagan, Flynn, Fogarty, Foley, Gaffney, Galvin, Garvey, Geraghty, Healy, Hickey, Higgins, Hogan, Jennings, Kavanagh, Kelleher, Keane, Keogh, Kirwan, Kinsella, Lacy, Lalor, Lee, Lyons, MacAuley, MacAuliffe, MacBride, MacCabe, MacCann, MacCormack, MacDermot, MacElroy, MacEvoy, MacGee, MacGrath, MacGovern, MacHugh, MacInerney, MacKenna, MacLoughlin, MacMahon, MacManus, MacNally, MacNamara, MacNulty, MacQuaid, MacQuillan, MacSweeney, Madden, Maher, Martin, Molloy, Moloney, Monahan, Mooney, Moran, Moriarty, Morrissey, Mulcahy, Mulligan, Nugent, Nolan, O'Byrne, O'Callaghan, O'Casey, O'Connel, O'Connor, O'Dea, O'Donnell, O'Donovan, O'Dowd, O'Driscoll, O'Dwyer, O'Farrell, O'Flaherty, O'Flanagan, O'Gara, O'Gorman, O'Hagan, O'Halloran, O'Hara, O'Hegarty, O'Higgins, O'Keeffe, O'Leary, O'Mahoney, O'Meara, O'Malley, O'Reilly, O'Riordan, O'Rourke, O'Shaughnessy, O'Shea, O'Toole, Phelan, Plunkett, Quinlan, Quigley, Quinn, Rafferty, Redmond, Rice, Roche, Rooney, Scanlan, Scully, Shannon, Sheehan, Sheehy, Tierney, Taaffe, Tobin, Treacy, Tully, Twomey, Wall, Ward, Woulfe.

about. Reading the news reveals a host of problems: Dublin bus drivers went on strike after a series of youth attacks and refused to operate after 2100 hours; more disenchanted youth rioted in another Dublin suburb after their stolen car rammed a taxi; again, in Limerick two teenage boys "with everything to live for" committed suicide. Unemployment is seen as the root cause of the problems. But these ills are the same for all industrialized societies, and Ireland will have to find its own solution.

A Close-Knit Nation

One problem that Ireland is remarkably free of, though, is ethnic divisions. While England once struggled with the huge influx of Pakistani and West Indian migrants, and modern Germany tries to find a solution to its "guest worker" woes, Ireland is practically a monoculture, where 95 per cent of the population is of Irish nationality, and where the same percentage is of the Roman Catholic faith. It was not always so. At the dawn of time, the Celts and other earlier peoples migrated from Europe, and then a millennium ago there were the Viking waves, and then the Normans, who contributed so much to the fabric of the Irish personality. But such invasion and colonization all occurred so long ago that today there are no racial or ethnic distinctions.

The smallness of Ireland, and its geographical isolation, made for a homogeneity that is still so apparent. Talk of someone you met in a distant county and coincidentally it turns out to be some long-lost relative. "Paddy! I haven't seen you in years", exclaimed a woman spectator at Dublin's St Patrick's Day

A wry smile to the rustic life.

procession. "He's me cousin from Donegal", she explained to her friend.

Perhaps this is why so many travelers of Irish descent keep returning to Ireland, year after year. In order to feel and experience part of what they once were, or would have liked to be. To do as George Bernard Shaw had berated his countrymen for: "Oh, the dreaming! the dreaming! the torturing, heart-scalding, never satisfying dreaming, dreaming, dreaming...!"

Religion

Proof of the importance of religion in Irish life is shown by this recent advertisement in *The Irish Times* which listed seven good reasons for buying a JVC video camcorder: "(1) First Communion, (2) Confirmation, (3) Weddings, (4) Holidays, (5) Sports Events, (6) Birthday Parties, (7) The Price, IR£499". Where else would the first two of these events be given top priority but in Ireland where over 93 per cent of the population are Roman Catholics? And imagine any other country where a quiz-show participant would be asked and correctly respond to the question of "What colors are the Vatican flag?".

Ireland, the stronghold of the Roman Catholic faith.

The Christian Mission

Christianity, which usurped the pagan Celtic rites that preceded it, officially arrived in Ireland in AD 431 when Pope Celestine sent Pelladius as bishop to the Irish Christians. This historic event, however, has been overshadowed by

Huts on the Dingle Peninsula were home to some of Ireland's first monks.

the popularity of Patrick whose divine mission to bring Christianity to Ireland was such a success that the Irish made him their patron saint. Born in Roman Britain, Patrick, so the legend goes, was captured by Irish pirates and taken into slavery in County Down.When he escaped he declared his aim of Christianizing Ireland, a task that he took to with great zeal producing astonishing results.

Celtic Christianity

The fact that the Romans never conquered Ireland was important for the Christian church there, which was thus allowed to grow on the foundations of earlier pagan religions and hence evolved in an unorthodox tradition. Old earth goddesses became Christian saints, and ancient pagan festive days were reinvented as Saints' Days.

Monastic life, introduced by Saint Finian of Clonard, was similar to old pagan practices which revered sacred bones. Stone cells, like the beehive-shaped huts of the **Dingle Peninsula** and the austere hermitages of **Skellig Michael** were built around these skeletal reliquaries, and in these simple constructions monks lived out their solitary and harsh lives.

The church did however, have to adapt to the modern age, for example the *filid* (professional story-tellers), who had previously committed all their genealogies and tales to memory, be-

Clonmacnoise, one of early Christianity's great monastic settlements.

gan to learn how to read and write in order to keep themselves relevant, and scribes who were gleaned from the peasantry of the Celtic hierarchy set to work producing the intricate, illuminated copies of sacred Christian manuscripts.

One of the strongest advocates of the isolated monastic life, and also a dominant force in combining the old religion with the new, was Columba, a high-ranking member of the powerful O Neill's, who was later canonized. He founded the famed monastery of Iona on Scotland's western isles in the 6th-century. A clever preservation of Celtic traditions together with new elements meant that despite a certain nostalgia for the old days the new religion fused remarkably well with the Gaelic culture.

Great Monasteries

Ireland soon became famous for its great monasteries, such as **Glendalough** in the Wicklow Mountains, founded by Saint Kevin, and **Clonmacnoise** the monastic city founded by St Ciaran, overlooking the Shannon River near Athlone. These centers rapidly took on the role of monastic cities housing vast numbers of monks who toiled away learning sacred tomes and writing and copying manuscripts. Monasteries employed a number of craftsmen such as stone-masons who built churches and carved the high stone crosses. Gold and silversmiths produced sacred objects set with precious gems,to be used in the religious rituals. Protected by powerful clans, these monasteries became more than centers of learning and culture as they also developed into a center for traders and merchants and in time took on the shape of Ireland's first walled towns.

Meanwhile, on the mainland, Europe slumbered through the Dark Ages while Ireland became the "Jewel in the Crown of Christianity". Scholars flocked to Irish religious centers and Irish monks went abroad to export their expertise. The wealth of the monasteries was legendary and so it was hardly surprising that when the Vikings plundered the Irish coast in the 9th century they made a beeline for the great monastic cities. Circular towers made of stone, which occur at most major religious sites dat-

The tower of the 11th century monastery at Glendalough.

ing from this era, are leftovers from this age when the monks were forced to flee into these fortified towers with their valuables. In time, though, the Vikings integrated into the Irish way of life and even built their own churches like King Sitric's magnificent **Christ Church Cathedral** in Dublin.

Harnessing the Church

In the 12th century, Adrian IV, the only English pope in history, attempted to reorganize the Irish church into the Roman mould. But his papal bull *Laudabiliter* fell on deaf ears, and his attempt to bring Ireland under the See of Canterbury was rejected by Irish bishops at the Synod of Kells. However, it was only a matter of time before the status quo changed and when the Normans invaded and successfully conquered the country later that century, England's King Henry II convinced the bishops to hand him the overlordship of the Irish church. In reality, though, this move ended up splitting the Irish church into two: the Gaelic or western group and the Norman, or eastern group, setting the stage for further upheavals.

During Elizabethan times, after the Reformation had made England a Protestant state headed by the English monarch instead of the Pope, Catholic monasteries and abbeys were ordered to be dissolved, and Protestants were settled on the old church lands. The Irish church

The crucifix witnesses from the mountain tops in County Kerry.

Croagh Patrick

A statue of St Patrick awaits the pilgrims.

Every year on the last Sunday in July, as many as 70,000 Irish Catholics, some barefoot, climb the barren, rock-strewn hill of **Croagh Patrick** in County Mayo, enacting a pilgrimage that goes back to Celtic times.

Croagh, or *Cruach*, as it is known in Irish, means a "rick or stacked-up hill", and Croagh Patrick translates as "Saint Patrick's Hill". Standing only 765 meters (2,509 ft) high, there are many hills in Ireland that are higher, but none that are as sacred as this inhospitable, scree-covered slope situated in the rugged mountain wilderness southwest of Westport.

Pilgrims who prefer their penitential climb to be as harsh as possible in atonement for their sins, even forgo their shoes for the 3 km (2 mile) ascent to arrive at the summit barefoot and bleeding. Although the pilgrimage is done in summer, the weather is seldom kind, fierce winds blow in from the Atlantic, and the hill is usually wreathed in cloud and mist. The elderly struggle up the slopes which are covered in small, loose stones, leaning on their walking sticks and fingering their rosaries all the while. At the prayer stations, young and old, rich and poor alike bend to their knees to give thanks to St Patrick, on the cold, wet rocks where he fasted, and as legend has it, vanquished all the snakes from Ireland.

Celtic Rituals

Ireland's patron saint made his epic climb back in the 5th century when he ascended the hill in order to christianize the peak, which was sacred to *Crom Dudh* (The Black Crom) a powerful ancient god to whom human sacrifices were offered. The Black Crom, was a sinister pagan deity and from Ireland's earliest days the last Sunday in July was known as "Black Crom's Sunday". Pilgrims had probably been climbing Croagh Patrick for millenia before Patrick made

was still divided, evidenced in 1641 when Irish Catholics went on a rampage against the Northern Protestants. Thus the stage was set for Cromwell to reconquer Ireland with a bloody thoroughness that is now legendary. Hence began the religious divide of Ireland which has been the source of much violence to this day.

Oppression & Republicanism

In 1697, imprisonment or banishment was the penalty for failure to comply with the Banishment Act which decreed

his historical ascent as the practice was part of the Celtic ritual associated with the pagan festival of Lugnasadh. Folklorists maintain that the early pilgrims made the climb at the end of the month known as "Hungry July", a traditionally lean time before the yearly harvest. At the summit they would await the arrival of the god Lugh, known as "The Shining One" who had successfully fought with a primitive earth god in order to ensure a successful harvest.

Vanquishing the Gods

Patrick needed to prove that Christianity was more powerful than the old pagan ways. Legend has it that he climbed to the summit and fasted for 40 days and 40 nights, during which time he battled with the ancient, evil spirits like the Black Crom and some say that he even fought with the Devil's mother. Unbelievers, realists, and sceptics would say that anyone who deprived themselves of food for such a long period of time would obviously suffer hallucinations, and that a mind in this state could easily conjure up visions of evil spirits. But, St Patrick, was merely doing what most other famous prophets had done throughout history in order to strengthen their faith and it was a practice that again proved successful to his cause. When he descended the mountain he proclaimed that the pilgrimage would still be commemorated on that same day, but that from then onwards Croagh Patrick would be sacred not for the old, pagan gods of old but for the One God of Christianity.

that "all popish archbishops, bishops, vicars general, Deans, Jesuits, monks, friars and all other regular popish clergy...shall depart out of this kingdom before the 1 May 1698". Repression, however, entrenched the fervor of faith; masses were staged in ruined churches and outdoors in the countryside where boulders were used as improvised altars. Catholicism had retreated underground, but despite the enforcement of Protestantism the numbers that changed ranks were indeed few.

In the 18th century harsh Penal Laws declared that Catholics were forbidden to hold public office, stand for Parliament, vote, practice law, join the armed forces, or buy land. And although priests were allowed to practice, no higher orders were allowed on Irish soil, therefore effectively ending the ordination of new priests, a plot whereby the authorities hoped Catholicism would be rendered impotent. However, since the majority of the population were still steadfastly Roman Catholic, these laws were difficult to implement.

The establishment of Irish nationalism was from the beginning inseparable from religion and the history of the movement parallels that of Catholicism. This is not difficult to believe for throughout centuries of oppression the church was the fulcrum of national identity. To be Irish was to be Catholic. As the freedom-fighter Pearse declared: "Like a divine religion national freedom bears the marks of unity, of sanctity, of catholicity, of apostolic succession".

The Catholic Tradition

When Ireland eventually attained independence from Britain, the Catholic religion was given a special place in the new constitution, not that it needed

A trio of priests await their mission.

official recognition for it had already infiltrated Irish life "from the *Dail* to the bedroom". In Ireland the church permeates not only the lives of the Irish people, but is an inescapable part of the landscape. Ruined abbeys and monasteries are scattered about the country, churches and cathedrals dominate the villages, towns and cities, wayside shrines are found along most roads, and on Sundays the pealing of church bells and the flocks of Irish that still "get mass", as they say, is proof that Catholicism is very much a part of the fabric of Irish life.

Modernizing the Church

With over 18,000 men and women ordained in the various Catholic orders it is a rare Irish family that does not boast of at least one nun or priest. These days, however, not every family adheres to the old practice of giving up an offspring for a religious career, such vocations are often considered by the young to be old-fashioned. Although a remarkable 82 per cent of the population still attends mass, numbers are dropping, particularly

Sunday Mass, Skibbereen.

among Ireland's youth. In view of this, the Catholic church is probably now facing its greatest challenge since the introduction of the Penal Codes. In an attempt to make religion more accessible, the church has dropped the Latin mass and is working hard to develop a more human face.

Recently, the state and the church have realigned their roles, and the new adage is "we preach, you govern". Divorce and abortion, still illegal, are now not the sole affair of the church, and it is expected that in the near future politicians will give the green light for the introduction of divorce and limited legalized abortions for special cases. Ultramontanism appears to be on the decline.

Choirboys head to church for Sunday duties.

C.Y.B.

Festivals

It would be bad timing indeed if a traveler to Ireland managed to miss out on a traditional Irish festival, so plentiful are they, but it would near impossible for a visitor to spend any time in Ireland without coming across at least one festive event, the like of which increases annually, especially during the peak tourist months in the summer. It may sound a lot like tourist propaganda to say that Ireland has a celebration to suit everyone, but even a cursory glance at a calendar of yearly events would be enough proof that this is indeed not a hollow promise.

Preparing for parade on St Patrick's Day.

Sporting buffs are more than well looked after with a superb racing agenda which includes the Irish Grand National, and the added interest of the Gaelic sports calendar, offering the spectacle of hurling and football. Music, dance and theater fans are positively pandered to with traditional music fests, opera sea-

Proud to be Irish and happy to celebrate it.

sons, folk, rock and jazz festivals. Irish dance contests and dramatic performances happen throughout the year; and then there are the pure Irish events like St Patrick's Day, and those that date back even further, like Killorglin's Puck's Fair which had its origins in a pagan fertility rite. And if that is not enough to whet the appetite of even the most jaded of travelers there is a plethora of other events and contests celebrating literature, fishing, motor-racing and oyster-eating, for starters.

Celebrations of the Ancients

The idea of festivals and feasts is not new to Ireland, starting as it did way back in the days of myth, when legend and fact were inseparable. In those days the annual calendar was halved into two major events which corresponded with the start and end of summer and then quartered into four major festivals which heralded the seasons, a system that was common not only to the Celtic world but to most early civilizations the world over.

Beltaine, translated as "the fires of Bel", known today as **May Day**, was always celebrated on the first day of May, which for the ancients was the first day of summer. On this day, bonfires were ignited by the Druids using the sun's rays and all household fires would be put out and relit with kindling taken from the sacred fires. ***Lugnasadh***, the harvest festival which was originally held for 15 days in August, is now celebrated on the last Sunday in July and is the date when pilgrims climb **Croagh Patrick** (see box story p.112). Traditionally, it was a feast staged by the pagan god Lugh in honor of his foster-mother Tailtiu and was celebrated in great style, with merrymaking and courtship rituals at Teltown (originally *Tailltenn*) in County Meath. In the Irish language, the month of August, *Lunasa* is still derived from the name of this original harvest festival.

Celebrated on the evening of the last day of October, ***Samhain***, meaning "the end of summer", is the forerunner of today's Halloween. On this eve, wandering spirits from supernatural realms visited the earth causing mischief, and

A big day for a wee lass, dressed in her finery.

in order to appease them, sacrifices and fertility rites were enacted. These days, Halloween is celebrated much as it is in America, but many Irish still eat the Barm Brack, a currant bun which contains a lucky ring. The last of the four major festivals of old was ***Imbolg***, celebrated on the first day of February. Sacred to the goddess Brigid, the festival name derived from the Irish for "sheep's milk" as this was the time of the year when the ewes would first come into milk.

In addition to these major pagan festivals there were numerous others, and these days the best known is **Puck's Fair** which is held annually from 10th-12th August in the picturesque town of **Killorglin** on the Ring of Kerry. Historians claim that the festival originates from a pagan fertility rite, but the most common reason for its existence, townsfolk have it, is that the fair commemorates the day when goats apparently saved the town from Cromwell's army and to this day a goat is still crowned as King Puck. The "traveling people", Ireland's version of gypsies, still flock here to trade horses and to join in the unabashed merrymaking. With the pubs staying open for the entire three-day festival, Puck's Fair is a real Irish experience not to be missed.

Religious & Fun Fests

Christmas and **Easter** are celebrated as

Confederation of Kilkenny Festival.

they are all over the Christian world, but there are some aspects that are special to Ireland. Hot-cross buns, are traditionally baked and eaten on Good Friday, and the Easter feast of lamb is often accompanied with colored eggs, sometimes dyed with gorse flowers which bloom around Easter. Christmas cakes are often flavored with Guinness stout, a real Irish touch.

Christianity also brought a score of Saint's Days, the most famous of which is **St Patrick's Day**, joyously celebrated with parades, "wearin' o' the green", and full pubs, on 17th March throughout Ireland, and in other Irish-expatriate centers the world over, notably New York. (See box story p.122).

Other festivities based on historical events include the newly-launched **Confederation of Kilkenny Festival**, held in mid-June, which commemorates Kilkenny's 17th-century status as Ireland's capital with jousting matches, street parades and riotous merrymaking. Another fun fest which has its origins in the popular ditty, "The Rose of Tralee", is the **Rose of Tralee International Festival**. Held, obviously in **Tralee**, in Kelly, in late August, these extremely popular celebrations are capped by a beauty parade to find Ireland's bonniest and best.

The winner of the Rose of Tralee would do well to meet her equivalent from the **Ballybunion International Bachelor Festival**, a "must see" for aspiring brides.

Pipes and tartan for a true Irish celebration.

Music & Dance

Ireland is famous for its traditional dance and music so it is hardly surprising that the festive calendar is crammed with musical events. The *Fleadh Ceoil na hEireann* (The All-Ireland festival of Irish music), the top-ranking traditional music fest, is held in the last week of August in a different city each year. Check with the Tourist Board for details. Other well-known traditional music festivals include the **Ballyshannon Folk and Traditional Music Festival** which is held in early August at Ballyshannon in Donegal; the **South Sligo Traditional Music Festival** held at **Tubbercurry** in July; and the **Dublin Irish Music Festival** held in Dublin's pubs around mid-March.

Other famous music festivals include the marvellous **Music in Great Irish Houses Festival**, where classical music concerts are staged in sumptuous mansions around **Dublin**; the ***Feile***, a three-day pop/rock/traditional music happening hosting big-name stars, held in early August at **Thurles** in Tipperary; the renowned **Guinness Jazz Festival** held in Cork in late October; the **Willy Clancy Summer School**, a mid-summer musicians' gathering specializing in uillean piping at **Milltown Malbay**, Clare, in early July; the national fiddling competition at **Sligo's Summer Festival** in July; and **Galway's** three-day **Busking Festival**, the mecca for

"Wearin' O' the Green": St Patrick's Day

Wearing the flag on St Patrick's Day.

Days before the big event on 17th March when all Ireland, and folk of Irish-descent the world over celebrate St Patrick's Day, hawkers are making the most of the occasion. Wrapped up against the cold wind howling down Dublin's O'Connell Street, women push prams which are not filled with babies as is usually the case, but with punnets of emerald-green shamrocks. "Twenty pence for a bunch", the vendors shout and wave green plastic hats and Irish flags, all necessary accessories for the grand parade.

Drawing upwards of 350,000 spectators, Dublin's parade is Ireland's largest in terms of both onlookers and participants, the latter usually numbering around 6,000. Coming as it does in mid-March, often referred to as "the grayest month", St Patrick's Day for many Irish is a time to celebrate the passing of winter and the coming of spring. It is a time to lift the spirits, when the grayness gives way to colorful costumes, and the Irish rejoice in their Irishness.

Preparing to March

St Stephen's Green in Dublin is the start of the parade and it is here that all the excitement begins, hours before the big event. Dressed in red-and-white costumes with a Viking boat as their symbol, the Dublin All Stars Marching Band are jamming. The up-beat drumming stirs the crowd to yell for encores. A black American is rap-dancing to the beat on the pavement, and the parade has not even started. Outside the Shelbourne Hotel, the Kirkebride Pipe Band, all dressed in tartans with the ubiquitous shamrocks pinned to their lapels and painted on their faces, is warming up. Girls in Victorian-period costumes climb aboard the "Arnott's 150-Years" float, and beside them the Liberties of Dublin are flinging their batons about, getting the right feel before the big event. Youngsters dressed in white and green tap-dance, a man and his two sons walk past, their hair dyed green for the occasion, and hawkers brandishing spray cans will even give you an Irish tricolour hair-color for a mere 20 pence. The rock band on the "Born-Again" Christian float strike up "When Irish Eyes Are Smiling", and at 1100 hours the parade is underway.

Every statue, lamp-post, traffic-light, and tree, is draped with onlookers along the traditional 2 km (1 $^1/_2$ mile) route which winds from St Stephen's Square, through Cuffe Street, George's Street, Dame Street, Westmoreland Street, and O'Connell Street to end up at **Parnell Square**. Even the lofty statue of Parnell, inscribed with his famous "No man has a right to

street musicians, held in either July or August.

Opera buffs flock to the seaside town of **Wexford** in October and November for the highly-acclaimed **Wexford Festival of Opera**. Lesser known operatic works are often featured at the town's unimposing Theater Royal. **Cork** is also

Carnival mood in Dublin and the coming of spring.

fix the boundary to the march of a nation" speech is covered with spectators. Some wag has even put an Irish flag in Parnell's hand, something which the great nationalist would not have minded in the least.

A Carnival Scene

Vintage cycles trundle past, and open carriages are crammed with bonny-faced grandmothers dressed in period costumes. There are floats of youth groups, and bands, and even more bands, sometimes following each other in a cacophony of sound. All along the route the streets are packed thick with Dublinites, and the best spots were bagged hours before the parade started. Late arrivals have to make do with peering over the throng to catch a glimpse of the tops of the floats, or are just hanging back and enjoying the music. Children sit on the kerbside waving their flags and streamers, and laughing at the clowns. They are all dressed in their festive best, the cute, freckle-faced girls wearing white stockings with their carrot-colored hair braided with green ribbons, unconsciously and patriotically reflecting the colors of Ireland's flag.

After the parade, the pubs are filled to brimming with not only the spectators but with plenty of the participants looking for some liquid refreshment after the hard work of blowing bagpipes on the march. Not so long ago all Ireland's pubs were closed on St Patrick's Day, and the only place in the capital with an open bar was the Royal Dublin Society's annual Dog Show. Dublin wits say that during those "dry" days there was a huge interest shown in pedigree dogs, but that with the opening up of the pubs on this festive day, the interest has been somewhat quelled.

Critics might say "what's so special about a parade." Although many events the world over have much more spectacular floats, there is something so essentially Irish about Dublin's St Patrick's Day parade, that it is hard to express it in words, and for those of Irish descent who first witness this outpouring of nationalist pride, it is an emotional experience. In the Irish calendar it could not come at a better time, for apart from paying homage to their patron saint, in an indirect way the Irish also come to pay homage to the start of spring. By doing so, they combine elements of both Christianity and the older pagan religions of the Celts, who lived according to the seasons. On this day, Ireland's cities and towns are transformed out of their gray, leafless, March-ness into a riot of color and excitement. All credit to St Patrick.

well-known for its opera season during March, and for its **Summer Revels**, comedy and burlesque performances, which are also held at the **Cork Opera House** during August.

Traditional Irish dancing was popularized during medieval times and then revitalized during the early-20th-century Gaelic revival. Dancing can still be seen at weddings, fairs and sports events, but for true lovers of dance, the event of the year is the **Irish Dancing Championships** held at Dublin's **Mansion House** in early March. Also on the agenda is the **World Irish Dancing Championships** which are staged later the same month. Ask at the Tourist Bureau for venue details as these can vary year to year. **Cobh**, the harbor town outside of Cork, also hosts a week-long **International Folk Dance Festival** in mid-July.

Arts Fests

Some of the most popular events for visitors, especially those pressed for time, are the festivals and fairs which combine music, dance and drama. Scenic **Kenmare**, over the mountains from Killarney, hosts an annual **Cibeal** during June, which attracts some of the country's best artists.

In late August, the **Sligo Arts Festival** also offers a packed agenda of dance, music (classical, rock, traditional, jazz and blues), comedy, and short-story readings. **Galway** hosts its **Arts Festival** over two weeks in July and is renowned for its musical and dramatic presentations. **Kilkenny** stages an **Arts Week** during the last week of August with poetry readings, concerts, art exhibitions, and recitals. Tickets can be purchased for individual events or for the week-long event.

Works by Ireland's renowned playwrights, both historical and contemporary, are enacted every year at the extremely popular **Dublin Theater Festival** held in late September and early October. The capital also hosts a particularly Irish event on 16th June when James Joyce buffs from all over the world gather for **Bloomsday**. On this day,

The Irish Derby at The Curragh, an important part of the festive calendar.

Joyce immortalized Dublin's streets in the publication of his mammoth novel *Ulysses*, and today, revelers dressed in Joycean garb trace the footsteps of his protagonist Leopold Bloom on his epic-walk. Events on the day include lunch at Davy Byrnes Pub, a garden party at Merrion Street, and selected readings.

Another of Ireland's brilliant literary lights, WB Yeats, is remembered every year at the **Yeats International Summer School** in **Sligo**. Although not a festival, it is actually a two-week study course on the poet, the school holds events that are open to the public including musical revues, poetry readings, lectures, and concerts. **Listowel** in County Clare holds the Listowel Writers' Week in late May/June.

The Racing Calendar

Horse racing is a passion with the Irish, and not surprisingly their bloodstock and racing events are famous the world over. The highlight of the racing calendar is the **Irish Derby**, a race for three-year-old colts, held in late June at the **Curragh** in County Kildare, the heart of horse country, where steeds have been racing since Celtic times. Other classic races held during the season at The Curragh are the **Irish Oaks** for fillies, staged in early July; the **Irish 2,000 Guineas** for three-year-old colts, and the **Irish 1,000 Guineas** for fillies, held during May.

Not as serious, and much more informal, are the well-known horse races where the partying and people-watching are as important as the racing. These include the **Galway Races** which are held at **Ballybrit** near Galway) during the last week of July; the **Killarney Races** also held during mid-summer; and the amazing **Laytown Strand Races** in County Meath, held in either July or August, where the horses thunder along the beach during low tide, reminiscent of the horse-races of old.

Steeplechasing, which originated as a cross-country race between two gentlemen from one church to another, hence the "steeple", in the mid-18th-century, celebrates its Irish roots every year at the renowned **Irish Grand National** held at **Fairyhouse** outside of Dublin on Easter Monday. Other "must-see" horsey events on the annual calendar include the National Hunt's jumping meet at **Leopardstown** (Dublin) in January; and the **Dublin Horse Show**, the top show-jumping event of the year, held every August at **Ballsbridge**.

Gaelic Sports

Ireland's unique national sports of hurling and Gaelic football, have their season from October to March, an excellent reason (among many others) to plan a trip to Ireland during the off-season. Rooted in ancient Celtic times, hurling, often referred to as one of the world's toughest and fastest ball games, has its high point in September, when the finals are staged in Dublin's **Croke Park**. The finals for *Camogie* (women's hurling) are also held during the same month.

Regional games, though, are often just as exciting, and easier to buy tickets for. Famous venues include **Cork**, where hurling is the city's favorite sport, and **Kilkenny**. At **Mountshannon**, an attractive village on Lough Derg, north-east of Limerick, the **Mountshannon Sports Weekend** in late July, is renowned not only for its watersports but also for its hurling contests.

Fun at the fair.

Gaelic football, often touted as "the game with no rules", and similar to Australian Rules, a football game that was probably invented by Irish immigrants, holds its **All-Ireland finals** in Dublin's **Croke Park** in September. Kerry is home to many of Ireland's greatest footballers and any of their regional matches are just as exciting as the finals. Try Killarney's **Fitzgerald Stadium** any Sunday during the season.

Miscellaneous Entertainment

Other well-known sporting events on the annual calendar include the **International Rugby Championships** held at **Lansdowne Road** in Dublin during January and February; the **Circuit of Ireland Car Rally** held over the Easter weekend; the **Westport Sea Angling Festival** held at **Westport**, Mayo, in late June; the **Dublin City Marathon** in October; and the **Killarney Regatta** held on Lough Leane in July.

Last, but not least, especially for gourmands and food-freaks, is the **Galway Oyster Festival** held in late September which kicks off with the first "oyster shucking" of the season. The oyster-opening contest draws an international crowd of contestants whose skills have to be seen to be believed. The classic way to eat Galway oysters is to wash them down with "black velvet", a heady mix of Guinness and champagne.

Literary Greats

When AS Byatt, the author of *Possession*, and the winner of the 1990 Aer Lingus Prize for Literature, came to the republic to accept her award she was awed by the nation's "literary passion" as she called it. "In Ireland", Byatt told a reporter, "you feel everyone goes into a pub and actually talks about poetry".

To those who are unfamiliar with Ireland, Byatt's remark may seem exaggerated, but for those in the know, she is quite correct, for Ireland celebrates literature with a fervor which probably surpasses every other country. Where else but Ireland would you find a busker who recites poems requested by passers-by from his 100 or so repertoire? And where else would you find an entire city annually celebrating the writing of a novel like Dublin does every year on "Bloomsday", the day immortalized in James Joyce's *Ulysses*. The amount of renowned writers, poets, and dramatists that this small island has produced far outweighs its size, particu-

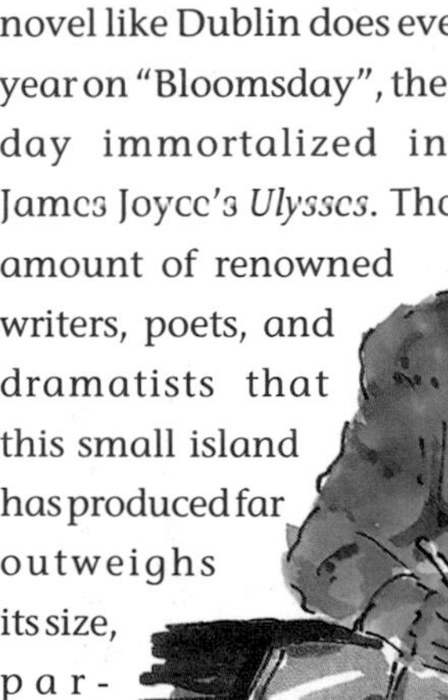

William Butler Yeats, one of Ireland's greatest poets.

Trinity College old library, Dublin, houses Ireland's greatest literary collection.

larly since Ireland boasts three winners of the Nobel Prize for Literature.

Literary Origins

Irish literary history goes back a long way, with its origins shrouded by the mists of time. Although the practice of recording information on manuscripts only arrived with the Christians in the 5th-century, the *filid*, a class of learned poets and professional storytellers, had their own oral traditions and memo-

Tomb of writer Jonathan Swift, genius of satire.

rized complex genealogies and epic tales for centuries, before they were written down. *Filid* were known to be able to memorize 250 main tales known as *Primscela* and 100 *Fo-scela* (subsidiary tales) which were later classified by scholars into four cycles: The Mythological, Ulster, Kings (or Historical), and Fenian.

Tana, meaning "cattle raids", were one of the main groupings of tales, and these epic stories embraced more than just plundering expeditions for they were also tales of magic and the supernatural. *The Cattle Raid of Cooley*, the most famous *tana* is the tale of Queen Medb's Connaught warriors fighting against the Red Branch Knights of Ulster led by Cu Chulainn, often referred to as the "Irish Achilles". Love stories were also popular. There is the *Dream of Aonghus* where Aonghus, the "love god", falls in love with a beautiful maiden who is disguised as one of a flock of 150 swans. Aonghus successfully identifies her and they live "happily ever after" at Newgrange. Another classic tale is *Deirdre of the Sorrows* the story of a chieftain's daughter who a Druid prohesized

Oscar Wilde, one of Ireland's best-known playwrights.

would bring war and destruction to Ulster.

The great cultural flowering of the monasteries during the 8th and 9th centuries saw illuminated manuscripts being produced like the *Book of Kells* (see box story p.168), *The Book of Armagh*, and *The Book of the Dun Cow* which appears on the Irish pound note. These intricately written texts are superb examples of Irish script which had its own distinctive alphabet until it was Romanized in the 1960s.

Anglo-Irish Writers

One of the greatest effects of the English colonization of Ireland, was the gradual replacement of the Irish language with that of English. By the 18th-century, Jonathan Swift, the outspoken Protestant Dean of St Patrick's Cathedral, through his satirical writings, was urging the Irish to burn anything English except coal. Best known for his *Gulliver's Travels*, Swift was a prolific writer, with a genius for scathing satire. In his pamphlet entitled *The Irish Problem Solved* he suggests that young children should be fatted for the table and sold as an alternative to other meats, adding, tongue-in-cheek, that although "this food will be somewhat dear" it would be "very proper for landlords, who, as they have already devoured most of the parents, seem to have the best entitlement to the children".

Another 18th-century writer, Oliver Goldsmith, a wordsmith of immense talent, who Thackeray described as "the most beloved of English writers", was not as many people would suppose, an Englishman, but an Irishman. Born north of Athlone in Longford County, the region is now known as "Goldsmith Country". Best known for his *Vicar of Wakefield*, and *She Stoops to Conquer*, his haunting poem *The Deserted Village*, which tells of an idyllic rural village which was destroyed by a tyrannical landlord, is believed to have been set in one of the villages near Ballymahon.

Born in Dublin in the mid-18th century, Richard Brinsley Sheridan came from a well-known theatrical family. His father, Thomas, was a well-known actor and theatrical manager, but his career was much less eventful than his son's who became not only the most successful dramatist of his time, writing such classics as *The Rivals* and *School for Scandal*, but a noted Whig politician in England. Sheridan moved to London when he was still young, and never returned to Ireland, so although he was a native Irishman which showed in his writings, particularly his satire, the subject of his plays was always life and times in Georgian England. Ireland's great Anglo-Irish writers and playwrights of the 18th-century were all masters of the English language and Protestants rather than Catholics, but in the following century a new movement appeared fueled by the growing nationalist aspirations of the Irish, which favored the Gaelic Catholic traditions and along with this historical turn-about came a host of new Irish writers.

The Gaelic Revival

Philologists discovered how to read Old Irish, and manuscripts written prior to the 18th-century were deciphered laying the groundwork for the Gaelic revival. Intellectuals and poets discovered their long-lost roots in the rich imagery of the ancient tales. The nationalistic newsletter *The Nation* published poems by Sperenza, the pseudonym of Lady Wilde, whose son Oscar was later to become one of Ireland's best-known and notorious playwrights. James Mangan composed his own poems in Gaelic and also translated Gaelic poems into English such as Mac Liag's 12th-century ode *Kincora* which laments the passing of the great Irish High Kings. J J Callanan broke new ground by utilizing Gaelic refrains in his nationalistic verses like this extract from *Gougane Barra*:

> Though loftier minstrels green Erin can number,
> I alone waked the strain of her harp from its slumber,
> And gleaned the gray legend that long had been sleeping,
> Where oblivion's dull mist o'er its beauty was creeping,
> From the love which I felt for my country's sad story,
> When to love her was shame, to revile her was glory!

Shattering events like the mid-19th-entury Great Famine, tempered the Gaelic revival but the seeds were sown, and by the turn of the century Ireland was experiencing a great blossoming of talent, now known as the Irish literary renaissance.

William Butler Yeats

Aesthete, poet, dramatist, and nationalist, William Butler Yeats, winner of the Nobel Prize for Literature in 1923, was the central figure in the new literary force. With his upper-class Protestant background Yeats should have fitted in at his boarding school in London, but

James Joyce:The Literary Legend

James Joyce, influenced the future of modern English literature.

"The demand that I make of my reader", James Joyce once said to a friend, "is that he should devote his whole life to reading my books". This call for a total lifetime immersion in one author's works, may seem to smack of egoism, and no doubt seem like a tall order, but for the average reader struggling to make sense of the tortured prose of *Finnegan's Wake,* his last novel, (if it can be called that), there is a ring of truth to his statement. For in order to really understand his mammoth works like *Finnegan's Wake* and *Ulysses*, often referred to as "masterpieces much praised but little read", the literary scholar would probably have to devote as much time as Joyce specified.

Literary Beginnings

Born in 1882, James Augustine Aloysius Joyce spent his early childhood in **Bray**, a seaside resort south of Dublin, where the family moved to when he was five-years old. He began his studies at home with a governess, then at Clongowes, a Jesuit institution in Kildare where his early, impressionable schooldays were immortalized in the first chapter of *A Portrait of the Artist as a Young Man.*

When his father, a rate-collector, retired, the family moved back to Dublin and James was admitted to **Belvedere College**, where he regularly won the annual prizes for literature. During his years at Belvedere, which feature in later chapters of *A Portrait of the Artist as a Young Man*, Stephen Dedalus, the moody, sometimes brilliant student who was Joyce's alter-ego, flirts with a career in the church, then goes through religious torment, has his first sexual experiences, develops his intellect and a rebellious nature which includes a bitter hatred of Catholicism which seems to have been nurtured during Joyce's Jesuit schooldays.

Harry Levin in his introduction to *The Essential James Joyce,* talks of Joyce's initial attraction to a religious career and then his loss of faith, by summing up Stephen's central dilemma as being "between carnal sin and priestly absolution", and that "with the self-dedication of the priest Joyce took the vows of the artist". In 1898, Joyce left Belvedere for University College where his literary career began with an article on "Ibsen's New Drama" which was published in the *Fortnightly Review*. He also began writing the poems which later appeared in *Chamber Music.*

A Life of Exile

After graduation in 1902 Joyce made the acquaintance of WB Yeats and other advocates of the Gaelic cultural renaissance, but they had problems coping with his crudity and arrogance, although they could not deny his obvious intelligence and imagination. In that same year Joyce enrolled at Dublin's **Medical School** but family poverty made it impossible to meet the fees, and when he looked without success for work as a tutor, Joyce left Ireland, like so many Irishmen had before him, joining the ranks of the "Wild Geese". From the age of 20 except for the occasional visits home, Joyce spent the rest of his life, until his death in 1941, in Europe. Ironically, though, it was not of Paris, Rome, or Trieste, that he wrote, but of Dublin. And although he often affected an attitude of dislike for his home, Joyce showed that by continually writing of his homeland, he was at heart an incurable Irishman, and like so many other exiles before and after him, he was obsessed by his Irishness. As a result his books have put Dublin so firmly on the world's literary scene that the old adage that once said "you can take Joyce out of Dublin but you can't take Dublin out of Joyce" can now be turned around to insist that "you can't take Joyce out of Dublin" , Joyce has become so much a part of the city of which he wrote.

Dublin Immortalized

While abroad, Joyce lived out the role of the impoverished artist, but this was certainly not by choice. He earned a meagre income from book reviewing, and tutoring, but it was always insufficient, particularly after 1904 when he began his life-long liason with Nora Barnacle, who he eventually married almost three decades later. They moved to where Joyce could secure work, a nomadic existence that saw them move to Paris, Zurich, Trieste, Rome, and Puli in Yugoslavia. His brother, Stanislaus, joined the household which had enlarged to a family with the addition of two children, and when Joyce suffered with rheumatic fever which affected his eyes, Stanislaus took over the role of provider.

During this time abroad Joyce was working on *Dubliners*, and his few short visits back home in 1909 when he caught up with old journalist friends and immersed himself into Dublin life, obviously inspired his forging of the everyday characters of this city that the book so faithfully depicts. When he finally finished *Dubliners*, the Irish publishers who had initially accepted the book, bowed to colonial pressure and insisted that Joyce delete the "offensive" remarks about Queen Victoria and Edward VII. When he declined, the company destroyed the manuscript, but as luck had it Joyce still had his original and it was later published in London in 1914. Although sales were trifling, the reviews were complimentary, and when Ezra Pound serialized *A Portrait of the Artist as a Young Man*, in his avant-garde magazine *The Egoist*, Joyce had definitely arrived on the world literary stage.

Monetary success was, however, still elusive and poverty was still a constant companion during the years when Joyce worked on *Ulysses*, in three different European cities. His mammoth novel which took seven years to write, chronicles a day in Dublin, and each chapter relates only one hour in the life of Leopold Bloom, who wanders about the city in a 20th-century version of Homer's *Odyssey*. The book was first serialized in the United States in 1918, but then the editors were charged with publishing obsenity, and *Ulysses* was banned from American bookshops until 1933. As one historian relates "the progress and reception of (*Ulysses*) were to be at least as much a part of 20th-century literary history as of Joyce's personal life".

Statement of an Artist

His last literary masterpiece, *Finnegan's Wake*, originally called *Work in Progress*, took up the last 17 years of Joyce's life, and although it has been described as a "novel", the resemblance is merely superficial. It is really a "literary experiment". Critics were hardpressed to make head-or tails of this "Joycean creation", where words and thoughts become more like music than literature, where spelling and grammar becomes immaterial. Some historians maintain that with his failing eyesight (Joyce suffered from glaucoma), his prose took on more of the "aural character of music and moved away from rationality". Other critics though suggest that in this final statement, Joyce ended his literary and physical life together by "inventing an artificial language of innuendo and mockery". The language of genius is certainly not easy to understand.

his thoughts were always of Ireland. He was caught between two worlds, for although he favored the aesthetics of the Gaelic Catholic literary scene, he was not of the faith, and his sensitive artistic nature rebelled at the Protestants who he saw as "thinking of nothing but getting on in this world". Eventually he settled on a more profound solution by celebrating the hidden Ireland of old, the pagan customs and beliefs that had existed before Christianity.

As a member of the Theosophical Society, Yeats believed that international peace could be achieved through mysticism. He studied the works of William Blake, dabbled in magic and astrology, and was repelled by the scientific age that surrounded him. Yeats' early poems like *The Wanderings of Oisin* reflect this sensitivity to the legends of what he considered to be a time of simplicity. When he teamed up with Lady Gregory, a Galway aristocrat who was sympathetic to the rural folk and fascinated with ancient west-coast lore, Yeats found a soul-mate, and together they formed the nucleus for the setting up of Ireland's first national theater, Dublin's famed **Abbey Theater**.

Yeats threw himself into writing plays and poems, stirred by his belief that somehow these works would lift the nation to a new moral plateau, a kind of purely Irish combination of ancient peasantry and proud aristocracy. He abhorred the middle-class and anyone whose ideal was conventional success, and because of both his views and his lordly presence, Yeats was not a popular figure. His plays lauding the old pagan times were seen as being anti-Catholic and anti-Irish, and after spending several years at the helm of the Abbey he felt that the theater was becoming too concerned with middle-class values. Consequently he gradually moved away from the theater and into writing more aesthetic dramas inspired by the avant-garde poet Ezra Pound.

In 1922, Yeats became a member of the Irish Free State Senate, and after winning the Nobel Prize for Literature, the year after, he attained celebrity status. Fame, however, pressed him to work even harder to formulate his ideas on the sacredness of art. In 1925 *A Vision* was published, but dissatisfied he worked on it until the definitive version appeared in 1937.

During the 1920s Yeats wrote some of his best poetry including *The Tower*, and *The Winding Stair*. His contribution to Ireland's literary scene was immense, and many of his poetic quotes are widely remembered. No one else summed up the feeling of the Irish after the abortive 1916 Easter Rising like Yeats' immortal lines:

> Now and in time to be,
> Wherever green is worn,
> Are changed, changed utterly:
> A terrible beauty is born.

Yeats' preoccupation with the mystical being part of Ireland's identity comes across with exquisite sensitivity in these lines from *The Stolen Child*:

Famous faces at the Dublin Writers Museum.

Come away, O human child!
To the waters and the wild
With a faery, hand in hand,
For the world's more full of weeping
than you can understand.

John Millington Synge

Poetry was Yeats' forte, his dramas were often above the understanding of the masses, unlike John Millington Synge, a powerful dramatist who was inspired by Yeats to give up his academic pursuits to delve into the lives of the people Aran Islands. Synge visited and lived periodically on the islands from 1899-1903 when he mingled with the people, observing their day-to-day life and learning their language, which formed the basis of his book *The Aran Islands*, and his plays *The Shadow of the Glen* and *Riders to the Sea*. Writing in a stylized peasant dialect, referred to by his critics as "Synge-song" (Synge is pronounced "sing"), he is best-known for his famous play *The Playboy of the Western World*. This melancholic comedy is about a rural youth who is treated as a hero in a strange village when he boasts of having murdered his father, but who fails to hold the villagers' respect after his father appears alive. When the play was staged at the Abbey Theater the audience rioted, enraged by Synge's unsentimental portrayal of the Irish, as a people who encourage boastful talk and who glamorize the lawless. Riots also broke out in New York, Boston, and Philadelphia, where the Irish Americans were just as enraged by the play. Gradually, though, Synge's later plays were accepted, but as fate always decrees he is most remembered for this controversial play, rather than for his other achievements.

Sean O'Casey

Sean O'Casey, another remarkable writer and dramatist, was born into Dublin's slums and was no stranger to hunger, disease, drunkeness, and poverty. Dublin's houses he saw as "a long, lurching row of discontented incurables" their "doors...scarred with time's spit and anger's hasty knocking". He edu-

George Bernard Shaw, yet another Irish winner of the Nobel Prize.

cated himself, worked as a laborer, dabbled in nationalist politics, and then after being disillusioned with the latter he began writing tragi-comedies about his fellow slum-dwellers. Although the Abbey Theater, first rejected his works, it later accepted and produced his plays. O'Casey, in gratitude, told Lady Gregory that "All the thought in Ireland for years past has come through the Abbey. You have no idea what an education it has been to the country".

O'Casey's most popular play was *Juno and the Paycock* set during the turbulent civil war, and his most controversial drama was *The Plough and the Stars* which saw an indignant audience riot over what they thought was the denigration of Ireland's "Easter Rising" heroes. O'Casey's humorous scenes were among the best in modern drama. Later, like James Joyce, O'Casey became disenchanted with Ireland, the Abbey had rejected his anti-war drama *the Silver Tassle*, and he moved to England, where his works became more cynical and satirical. His targets were Irish intellectuals, and the puritanism that he considered had befallen his native land.

George Bernard Shaw

Two years after Yeats won the Nobel Prize, another Irish-born playwright bagged the world's top literature prize. George Bernard Shaw was born in "genteel poverty" in Dublin in 1856, a situation which later prompted him to become totally involved in Socialism. When he was 20-years old he joined his mother in London, determined to be a writer, and set about educating himself at the British Museum reading room. His writings were systematically rejected by London publishers for at least a decade, but he was finally noticed when he edited and wrote articles for the Fabian Society, and also from his work as a witty and polemic theater critic.

From this base Shaw began work on the plays that were to be his greatest accomplishments: from *Candida*, where the heroine is forced to choose between a poet and a cleric; *Antony and Cleopatra*, where the heroine is a spoilt 16-year old girl; *Man and Superman* where Shaw expounded his evolutionary philosophy;

Major Barbara a comedy about the Salvation Army and hypocrisy; *Pygmalion* his most popular and famous work which was later adapted into the musical and cinema classic *My Fair Lady*; and the masterful *Saint Joan* for which he was awarded the Nobel Prize. Shaw kept on producing plays until well into his 90s. He was lauded as having "helped mold the political, economical and sociological thought of three generations". The *Encyclopaedia Britannica* calls him the "most significant British playwright since the 17th century", which he no doubt was, except that he was an Irishman!

Samuel Beckett

Ireland's third recipient of the Nobel Prize for Literature in the 20th century was Samuel Beckett, who, although he wrote extensively in French and English was best known for his plays in particular, *Waiting for Godot*. After graduating from Trinity in 1927, Beckett went to Paris where he met, and was inspired by, James Joyce. Like Joyce, although Beckett returned periodically to Ireland, he lived most of his life in self-exile in Europe.

After the First World War, during which he had served in the French Resistance, Beckett embarked on an intense literary period when he wrote a number of stories, novels (or rather narrative prose) and the play which was to pave his way to international recognition, *En attendant Godot* (waiting for Godot), which first opened in Paris to critical acclaim in 1953.

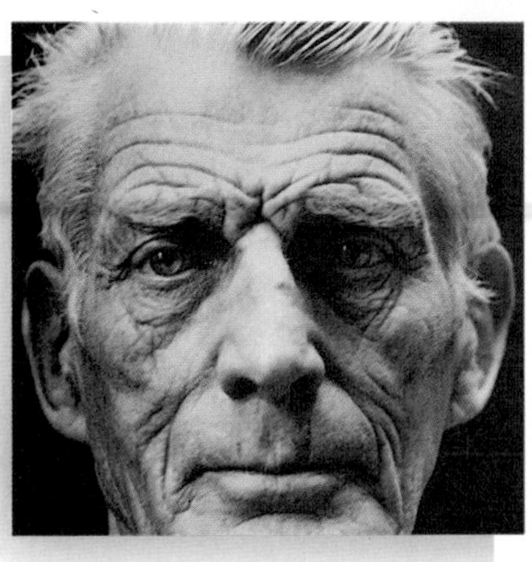

The Irish playwright Samuel Beckett.

In a life dedicated to art, Beckett avoided the press, never gave interviews, and when he was awarded the Nobel Prize in 1969, although he accepted the honor he would not travel to Stockholm as he could not have made the acceptance speech. His plays and narrative works were austerely written with a brevity of words that he also adhered to in real life.

His *Come and Go* which he called a "dramaticule" contained only 121 words and Rockabye, one of his last plays, lasts for a mere 15 minutes. Beckett always tried to get to the essence of self in his works, and explored totally new ground in human experience. Existence for him was seen as a stream of thought, probably best summed up by Beckett's favorite philosophic phrase by Descartes; "I think; therefore, I am".

Bram Stoker & Dracula

On the north side of Dublin's Liffey River, there is a rather unremarkable looking church, but if its exterior is singularly unimpressive, its interior more than makes up for it. **St Michan's** has a long history, founded by the Danes in the 11th century, for half a millennium it was the only parish church this side of the river. At the end of the 17th-century it was rebuilt and the new structure which has survived to the present day still contains some remarkable artifacts including sacred reliquaries, superb wood carvings and the organ which Handel composed *The Messiah* on. However, its most famous relics are some ancient mummified bodies which legend has it inspired Bram Stoker to write his spine-chilling novel *Dracula*.

Chilling St Michan's

In the vaults under St Michan's the bodies of these long-forgotten ancients have been perfectly preserved over the centuries by the limestone in the ground which has kept the air absolutely dry. A visitor to the church in the 1960s recalls the irreverant "keeper of the dead" raising one mummified hand and asking the horrified tourist to "shake hands" with him. These days, though, tourism is not such a casual affair, and it is definitely "hands off". But there is still a certain sinister air to not only these nameless mummies, but the whole atomosphere of Saint Michan's, it is easy to imagine that these very settings could have been the inspiration for the world's most famous horror story.

Stoker's Beginnings

Bram Stoker was born in Dublin in 1847. He was a sickly child; throughout his early childhood until he was seven-years old he could neither stand or walk. However, in his later youth he overcame his illnesses and during his undergraduate days at Dublin University he excelled at athletics and was an outstanding football player. Stoker spent the first decade of his working life as a civil servant at the administrative headquarters of Dublin Castle, and it was during this time that he sowed the seeds of his later literary achievments by writing drama critiques for the Dublin newspaper, *The Mail*. Stoker loved the theater and this work, although unpaid, gave him the opportunity to mingle with and become friends with the leading dramatists, actors, and actresses of the time.

The turning point in Stoker's dull civil-servant existence came when he met his idol, the actor Sir Henry Irving. In 1878, he became Irving's manager, managing his correspondence, writing, so the story goes, up to 50 letters a day for the actor and accompanying him on tours to America. The job lasted for 27 years until Irving's death.

The Horrendous Masterpiece

Late in life, Stoker began writing fiction. *The Snake's Pass* his first novel was published in 1890, and nine years later his masterpiece *Dracula* appeared. The novel's namesake, Count Dracula, is a vampire blessed with supernatural powers, who journeys to England where he preys on innocent victims in order to suck their blood which he needs in order to survive. *Dracula* was not written like a conventional novel but in the form of diaries and journals penned by the main characters, who embark on a series of adventures and eventually are able to overpower and annihilate the vampire Count.

A Living Nightmare

Bram Stoker was a prolific novelist in his old age, turning out *The Mystery of the Sea* in 1902, *The Jewel of Seven Stars* in 1904, and *The Lady of the Shroud* in 1909. But none of these had half the audience appeal of *Dracula*, which enjoyed immense popularity not only in its original form as a novel but had equal success on the stage and screen and spawned a number of imitations. Almost a century after its first release *Dracula* is just as popular as it was when it was first written and the character *Dracula*, is more universally known than any other character in Irish fiction.

A memento to Ulysses, Joyce's masterpiece.

James Joyce

No doubt, the most towering figure in 20th-century literature was James Joyce (see box story p.134). Because of his preoccupation with writing of his homeland, although he lived in voluntary exile most of his life, unlike Shaw there was no doubt of his origins of birth. Joyce became a legend in his own time, his works were considered classics even while he was still alive, a feat not achieved by many writers, perhaps because as one literary critic said Joyce had been so severely tested during his lifetime. His works had been rejected, suppressed, confiscated, attacked and misunderstood, the consequent end event being that he was then imitated.

Bound, as Joyce once said "to the cross of his own fiction" his masterful works written during a tortured life include *Dubliners* which accurately portrays the barmaids, loners, dreamers and workers of his native city; *A Portrait of the Artist as a Young Man* which is his autobiographical novel of a young man's developing mind; and his later monumental works *Ulysses* and *Finnegan's Wake* which explore a hitherto unknown "universe of discourse". His enormous contribution to literature is aptly summed up by the comment by the *Times Literary Supplement*; "James Joyce was and remains almost unique among novelists in that he published nothing but masterpieces".

John Millington Synge immortalized the lives of the people of the Aran Islands.

Music & The Arts

A bus rumbles down Eden Quay, with a giant-sized guitar painted across its length. Plastered on the walls of old Georgian town houses, luminous-colored posters advertise a plethora of music events ranging from Christie Hennessey, to The Chieftains, and U2. Folk-music drifts from the doorways of the city's pubs, buskers entertain the passers-by and most of the young people walking Dublin's street, so the story goes, "are either in a band, writing a novel, or dreaming of being famous".

But it is not only in the capital that music and the arts flourish, as around the countryside, especially in the Gaelic-speaking Gaeltachts, traditional Irish music is very much alive and widely appreciated. Ireland has Europe's most flourishing folk-music scene which is a major attraction for tourists both young and old, who flock to the republic every year, particularly in summer, for the music season and the *fleadhs*, loosely translated as "music feasts".

Irish arts and crafts, including

Street music, Dublin.

Plucking at the heart strings; the harp is the symbol of Ireland.

the renowned Waterford crystal, weaving, silverwork, fine arts and sculpture, are also thriving particularly with increased tourism which generates the need for Irish-produced crafts, and centers like the award-winning **Kilkenny Design** group, are producing arts and crafts of superb quality.

The Gifts of Lugh

Ireland's abundant legacy of musical and artistic traditions draws its earliest

inspirations from the pre-Christian Celtic days. Lugh, the god of arts and crafts, who gave his name to France's Lyons, Netherlands' Leiden, and England's *Lugdunum* (London), was apparently the creator of the first leprechaun, the "fairy craftsman". These "little folk" were accredited with passing on their skills to fortunate mortals, a belief which still persists in some rural areas, evidenced by the popular tale that the Sligo-based fiddler Michael Coleman, had learnt the tricks of his trade from the leprechauns.

Although most traditional Irish music dates from after the Gaelic "golden age", with its roots in the depressed peasant-class of the colonial times, there are remnants that are as old as Ireland itself. The harp, the nation's symbol, dates from the Celtic courts when harpists played accompaniment to the poetry of the *filid* (Storytellers). Bagpipes were played to rouse soldiers into battle and to enliven early sporting events. Known as uilleann pipes, Ireland's bagpipes differ from the well-known Scottish variety in that they use a bellows rather than an inflated bag.

Other musical instruments which contribute to the lilting jigs and mournful melodies that are the hallmarks of Irish traditional music, are the *bodhran*, a goatskin drum which is played with a double-ended drumstick, tin-whistles, fiddles, concertinas, flutes, and even the guitar, a later addition.

In the decorative and fine arts, early Celtic traditions are popularly utilized as motifs, particularly the famous Tara brooch which is still being reproduced. The original, elaborately filigreed and chased in silver, which is on display at the **National Museum of Ireland**, dates from the 8th century, but there were obviously earlier versions as this type of brooch was used to fasten cloaks from time immemorial. Legend has it that

Dublin's Music Trail

Follow the prolific posters to the concert of your choice.

As the graffiti splashed on Dublin's O'Connell Street exclaims, "Dublin is the rock-music capital of the world", a fact certainly not argued by the thousands of international music freaks who annually flock to Ireland's capital, just to be near the action. Most of the nation's best-known musicians all spent at least part of their rise to fame playing at pubs and gigs around the nation's capital, and as many of these venues are still operating, what better way to immerse yourself in Dublin's music history than to follow the trail where bands like U2, and singers like Sinhead O'Connor first made their mark on the music world.

Musical Hang-Out

A fitting and central place to begin a stroll of Dublin's historic music venues, is at the **Gresham Hotel**, located just north of the Tourist Information Center in O'Connell Street, where the Chieftains, Ireland's best-known traditional music band, first got together in the early 1960s. The sextet inspired a host of later bands and artists, including Van Morrison. Head south from the Gresham, following Henry and Mary Streets, to **Slatterys Pub** on Capel Street. Dublin's best-known music pub, still hosts traditional Irish music, rock, blues, and set-dancing every night of the week. A regular performer here during the last decade was the renowned singer and songwriter, Paul Brady, whose compositions have been recorded by Tina Turner and Santana.

Follow Capel Street to the river, then follow the south bank downriver to the medieval **Merchants' Arch** area where the late Phil Lynott first played with his acclaimed rock-band Thin Lizzy. In the maze of old streets behind the Merchants Arch is Crown Alley, where at the **Bad Ass Café**, young music hopefuls sip their drinks where Sinhead O'Connor worked as a waitress during her stint as a singer in Ton Ton Macoute in the mid-1980s before she rocketed to international stardom. On nearby Dame Street is the historical **Olympia**, Dublin's oldest surviving theater, where Mary Black, one of Ireland's best-loved singers and perennial winner of female-vocalist awards, has often appeared.

From Dame Street head for Trinity College and down **Grafton Street**, a vibrant pedestrian shopping area which is always home to plenty of entertaining buskers. The well-known traditional group, the Furey Brothers, whose prodigious musical talents were inherited from their

Macha of the Red Tresses, who founded Navan Fort in Ulster, which was occupied from 300 BC, marked out the perimeter of the fort with her brooch, and then forced captive prisoners to construct it.

Sculptors, artists and artisans carry on the Celtic tradition today and their

Fan's tribute, Windmill Lane, the recording studios of U2.

parents who were "traveling people", first performed in Grafton Street pubs. Duke Street which branches off Grafton is the home of **The Duke**, also known as Tobins, where Hothouse Flowers, Ireland's latest internationally-famous rock band honed their skills in front of Dublin's critical pub audiences.

Remember While you Eat

Back on Grafton Street, hop into **Bewley's**, one of three like-named establishments in the city, which are famous for their coffee, snacks, talk and entertainment. Bewley's on Grafton was where Bob Geldof's Boomtown Rats often entertained the throng and where his classic hit-single *Rat Trap* was first publicly performed. Cross Grafton Street for **Captain America's**, a hamburger joint, which was the unlikely venue for the start of Chris De Burgh's career. This smooth-voiced singer, known for his international hits like *Lady in Red*, is one of Ireland's greatest concert draws (a recent concert sold out for ten consecutive nights). De Burgh apparently tried out his earlier renditions on Captain America's customers.

In nearby Baggott Street is the **Gaiety Theater** where Christy Moore, often referred to as Ireland's Bob Dylan, and a foundation member of Moving Hearts, began his career in the early 1970s. Also on Baggott Street, past St. Stephen's Green, is **O'Donoghues Pub**, where the traditional-music group The Dubliners, who took their name from James Joyce's stories, first got together in 1962 as the Ronnie Drew Group. A block east of here, is the **Baggott Inn**, where U2, undoubtedly Ireland's most internationally-successful rock band, first wowed their audiences.

Windmill Lane

The last destination, but possibly the most loved and well-known of all the stops on the rock-music trail is **Windmill Lane**, the studio where U2 first recorded their music. It is located near the southern bank of the River Liffey in the lane of the same name. Graffiti from visitors from all over the world adorns the brick walls of the narrow passageway, singing the praises of Ireland's musicians. Windmill Lane is a fitting tribute to the nation's musical tradition, and the best place to end our homage to all those musicians who first tasted success in the pubs and clubs of Dublin.

works displayed in galleries throughout Ireland, reflect the strong presence of their Irish roots. Two major sculptures in Dublin's streets were inspired from traditional tales: *Cuchulainn* by Olive Sheppard outside the General Post Office in O'Connell Street, depicts the dying Cuchulainn with Morrigan, the

The National Gallery, Dublin, houses Irish and European masterpieces of art.

Goddess of War, as a bird on his shoulder; the *Children of Lir*, by Oisin Kelly, in the Garden of Remembrance (commemorating those who died for Irish freedom) in Parnell Square, depicts the legend of the children who were changed into swans for 900 years.

Music of the Peasantry

When the Gaelic High Kings were ultimately replaced by the aristocracy of the Anglo-Irish, Irish music, once a feature of the royal courts, moved into the

The Irish love the opportunity to sing.

countryside as the new lords were more interested in cultivating refined music tastes imported from Europe. Music traditions suffered under Cromwell's puritan hand, and as the Gaelic Catholics were forced to practice their religion underground, music was the most popular release for the oppressed peasantry. As the anonymous author of *Ballinderry* wrote; "He would whistle, and I would sing, Till we would make the whole Island ring".

Traditional folk music is not difficult to find in Ireland, and as most of it is played for an appreciative home-grown crowd and not solely staged for tourists, the rollicking jigs, and the haunting ballads, are completely authentic. Pubs, all over the country, but especially in **Dublin**, and the west-coast towns, are the best venues to hear traditional music in a real Irish atmosphere. The **Abbey Tavern** in Howth, just north of Dublin, is renowned for its musical evenings, as is Galway's ***Seaghan Ua Neachtain*** (shortened to "Nocktons") on Quay Street, Dublin's **Brazen Head** or **Slattery's**. However, the best (according to *Time* magazine) and the most popular music (judging by the crowds of international tourists) is to be found in the small town of **Doolin** on the Clare coast, where just about every pub on its mile-long main street hosts traditional music. Try **O'Connor's**, **McGann's** and **McDermott's** for starters.

Comhaltas Ceoltoiri Eireann, the national traditional music association, has

Ireland's own type of bag-pipes; the uilleann-pipes.

contributed immensely to Ireland's music scene, and its regular musical happenings, known simply as *fleadh* pronounced "flah", culminate each year with the **All-Ireland *Fleadh Ceoil***, a three-day event, (see "Festivals" chapter p.117 for more details).

Irish Jigs

Irish dance, often known as "Irish jigs", and the perfect complement to traditional music, is also very much alive and well. Before the advent of movies

Music & Guinness in a pub.

and television, jigs, reels and hornpipes were the main entertainment for much of rural Ireland for centuries. Dancing masters were respected members of the community and would often hold competitions to show off their prowess, the forerunner of Ireland's **World Irish Dancing Championships**, which are held in early March. Dances were held at weddings, fairs and festivals, at sporting events, and their popularity can be judged by this lament by a rural youth about to embark into exile from William Allingham's *the Winding Banks of Erne:*

Adieu to evening dances, where merry neighbours meet,

And the fiddle says to boys and girls "get up and shake your feet!"

Music of the 1970s & 1980s

It is not surprising that with such a bounteous heritage of musical traditions, Ireland's modern musicians have made such a mark on the international music scene. By mixing their own traditional music with American rock and blues, Irish musicians have come up with a completely new sound which has put them at the forefront of popular music since the 1970s.

Paving the way in the 1960s, the Chieftains popularized Irish traditional music led by Paddy Moloney and his uilleann pipes. Three decades and 22 albums later they are still as popular as ever. The Dubliners, another renowned "traditional" band, began their rise to fame in the 1960s with their controversial song *Seven Drunken Nights.*

In the same decade, Thin Lizzy, Ireland's first famous rock band, burst onto the scene, infusing their heavy-metal style with their Celtic roots, a combination of acid rock and folk. Phil Lynott, their lead-singer and song-writer, used the tales of Gaelic heroes to create their hit songs throughout the 1970s and early 1980s until his tragic death in 1986.

U2 & "The Rats"

Following the inspiration of Thin Lizzy, Bob Geldof, who was later nominated for a Nobel Peace Prize for his "Live Aid" concerts to help the world's starving, formed the Boomtown Rats in Dublin. As the first Irish "punk" band, "The Rats", as they were popularly known, went on to record a string of hits including the aptly-named *Rat Trap* which soared up the world's hit charts. Ironically Geldof, who these days is accorded something like saint-ship in his native land, was in his earlier days, as one rock-critic says "an arrogant, loud-mouthed malcontent" who used to wear a shirt emblazoned with the words "Geldof is God!".

U2, Ireland's most famous contribution to the rock-music scene, were legends at home before they made it internationally. After winning a national band contest in Limerick, the four Dublin schoolboys burst into prominence. Bono's impassioned lyrics, and Dave Evans' innovative guitar riffs, are now hallmarks of this incredibly successful group who are renowned as one of rock music's greatest bands. In 1985, the year U2 teamed up with Bob Geldof for the Live Aid charity concert, no less than six of their albums appeared in the British charts at the same time.

Van Morrison

Other Irish musicians were also making their mark during the 1970s and 1980s. Van Morrison, undoubtedly the best-known Irish rock singer, was born in Belfast, Northern Ireland. His music has spanned over three decades, from his classic rock n'roll hit *Gloria* which he recorded with his original rock-band Them in the 1960s, to his haunting *Moondance, Brown-Eyed Girl,* and *And It Stoned Me*. Morrison's music, a fusion of rock, jazz, and blues, has been a major inspiration to both Irish and other musicians, worldwide. His many years spent away from his birthplace are poignantly recalled in his 1993 song *Too Long in Exile*, where he compares himself to other famous exiles like James Joyce, Samuel Beckett and Oscar Wilde.

The late 1980s & 1990s

The 1980s also saw the rise of a number of other bands like Moving Hearts, who synthesized traditional music, jazz and blues; and Clannad, whose Irish-language single made it to the British top-10. This decade also saw the rise of Sinhead O'Connor, the shaven-headed Dublin lass who became the hottest property in rock in the early 1990s. Sinhead

Whatever your choice you cannot be disappointed in Dublin's music mecca.

burst onto the music scene in 1982 at the impressionable age of 14, although Sinhead O' Connor started her singing career by recording traditional songs on her father's dictaphone.

In 1987 while still working as a part-time waitress in a Dublin café she recorded her first LP and the rest is history. In 1990 her version of Prince's *Nothing Compares 2U* rocketed to the top of the US charts placing her in the world's music spotlight where some of her controversial and irreverant ideas put her under attack by the American public. In 1993 Sinhead put in an impromptu appearance at a Dublin peace rally.

Irish rock's latest phenomenon is Hothouse Flowers, whose winning combination of traditional styles, soul, blues, and rock, fused in their hit single *Don't Go*. Their irrepressibly Gaelic roots, are intertwined in their music and they have even included Gaelic hymns in their performances.

Rock-music, and rhythm and blues affecionados flock to Ireland by the thousands, especially during summer when music festivals are staged throughout the country. For intending music-freak visitors, a good introduction to Ireland's music scene would be to catch a screening of the award-winning movie *The Commitments*, a happy/sad story of a Dublin rock band who look to American soul music for inspiration. *Hot Press*, Ireland's music "bible" will fill you in on what's happening throughout the republic.

Dublin

"We loved it", said the prize-winning writer Louis Begley when asked about Dublin. "It was so friendly. We went to a pub to try to cure the flu with some hot toddies and a couple of men who looked like builders started talking about Verdi. I had the feeling that conversations here could go in all directions". As Begley along with thousands of other visitors observed, there is a depth of feeling and a neighborliness in Dublin that sets the city apart from other European capitals. Often it seems like an overgrown town, with its population of just over half a million, its sidewalk pubs and its traditional shop windows. This town-like ambiance is reinforced by the absence of skyscrapers, Dublin is marvellously low-rise. The predominance of street after street of Georgian architecture further adds to the city's human scale.

St Patrick's Cathedral, where its former Dean, Jonathan Swift, is buried.

A Truly Great City

Dublin, like its inhabitants, is a moody place with

IRELAND
Scotland
Coleraine
Limavady
Antrim
Letterkenny
Londonderry
Ballymena
Donegal
Derry
Larne
Strabane
Donegal
Tyrone
Belfast
Omagh
Ballyshannon
Northern Ireland
Armagh
Enniskillen
Down
Sligo
Fermanagh
Armagh
Ballina
Monaghan
Sligo
Newry
Monaghan
Leitrim
Mayo
Cavan
Boyle
Carrick on Shannon
Cavan
Dundalk
Westport
Castlebar
Roscommon
Louth
Castlerea
Irish Sea
Claremorris
Longford
Meath
Roscommon
Longford
Navan
Drogheda
Westmeath
Tuam
Mullingar
Galway
Athlone
Moate
Ballinasloe
Galway
Dublin
Tullamore
Kildare
Dun Laoghaire
Loughrea
Offaly
Naas
Atlantic Ocean
Gort
Birr
Laois
Clare
Portlaoise
Athy
Wicklow
Republic of Ireland
Wicklow
Ennis
Nenagh
Carlow
Limerick
Kilkenny
Carlow
Arklow
Thurles
Limerick
Tipperary
Gorey
Kilkenny
Cashel
Tipperary
Wexford
Tralee
New Ross
Dingle
Wexford
Clonmel
Waterford
Rosslare Harbor
Mallow
Fermoy
Waterford
Killarney
Cork
Kerry
Cork
Youghal
Bandon
Bantry
Celtic Sea
N
0
Kilometers
80

Dublin's pubs, where the jovial Irish spirit bubbles over.

its personality swings intimately connected with its changeable skies. Clouds always seem to race across the city and skies can be a cornflower-blue or gray and overcast, all in the space of a few minutes. "Half-mournin' skies for ever over us", wrote the Dublin playwright Sean O'Casey. But it is a magical place when the sun shines, when the pavements gleam opalescent from the early-morning rains, when a sunbeam strikes a brass door-knocker on a mellow-colored Georgian town house, when the daffodils bloom in St Stephen's Green where office girls with peaches and cream complexions chatter and hurry along the paths, their coats swirling in the wind.

Dublin is also a very musical place. Youths in Levi jackets tote guitars through the city's cobblestoned lanes while buskers serenade passers-by. On O'Connell Street a billboard proclaims, "Dublin, the rock-music capital of the world". Ireland's capital is literally a throbbing city and every evening the city's bars and clubs burst into song.

Culture does not end with music for Dublin is a well-known source of great literature. Every second street has either featured in a novel or has housed, fed or watered famous writers, poets, and playwrights. Dublin's impressive roll-call of local-born literary greats includes Jonathan Swift, Sheridan, Bram Stoker, Oscar Wilde, WB Yeats, James Joyce, JM Synge, Sean O'Casey, Brendan Behan and Samuel Beckett.

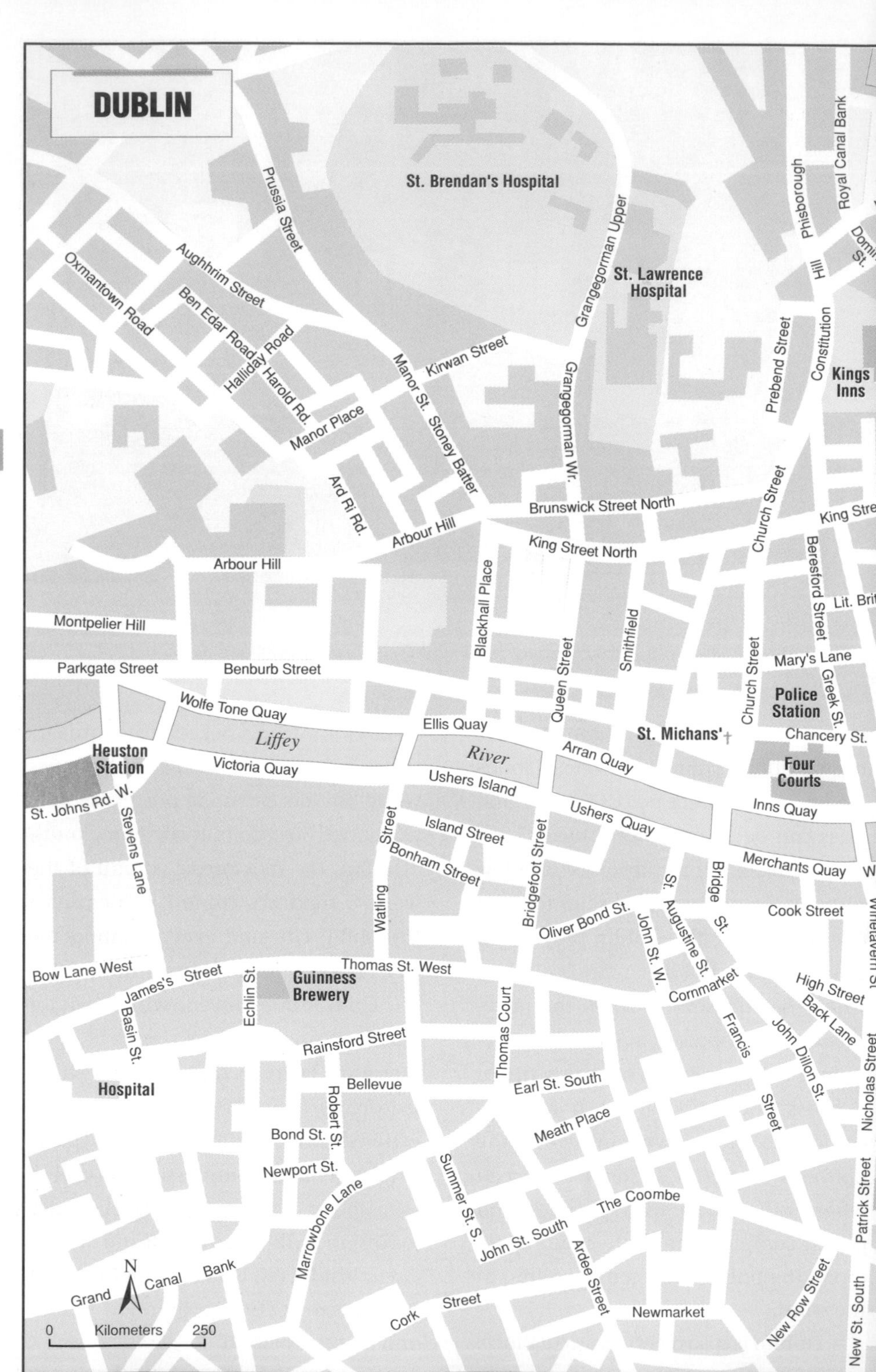
DUBLIN
St. Brendan's Hospital
St. Lawrence Hospital
Kings Inns
Prussia Street
Aughrim Street
Oxmantown Road
Ben Edar Road
Halliday Road
Harold Rd.
Manor Place
Manor St.
Kirwan Street
Stoney Batter
Grangegorman Upper
Grangegorman Wr.
Phisborough Hill
Royal Canal Bank
Prebend Street
Constitution
Ard Ri Rd.
Arbour Hill
Brunswick Street North
King Street North
Church Street
King Street
Beresford Street
Lit. Brita
Blackhall Place
Smithfield
Queen Street
Montpelier Hill
Parkgate Street
Benburb Street
Mary's Lane
Greek St.
Police Station
Wolfe Tone Quay
Ellis Quay
St. Michans'
Chancery St.
Liffey
River
Heuston Station
Victoria Quay
Arran Quay
Four Courts
Ushers Island
Inns Quay
St. Johns Rd. W.
Stevens Lane
Watling Street
Island Street
Bonham Street
Bridgefoot Street
Ushers Quay
Merchants Quay
Bridge St.
St. Augustine St.
Oliver Bond St.
John St. W.
Cook Street
Winetavern St
Bow Lane West
James's Street
Echlin St.
Guinness Brewery
Thomas St. West
Cornmarket
High Street
Back Lane
Basin St.
Francis Street
John Dillon St.
Rainsford Street
Thomas Court
Hospital
Bellevue
Robert St.
Earl St. South
Nicholas Street
Bond St.
Meath Place
Newport St.
Summer St. S.
Marrowbone Lane
The Coombe
Patrick Street
John St. South
Ardee Street
Grand Canal Bank
N
Cork Street
Newmarket
New Row Street
New St. South
0 Kilometers 250

Mountjoy Square
Art Gallery
Rotunda Hospital
St. Mary's Catholic Pro-Cathedral
Connolly Station
Bus Station
Custom House
G.P.O.
Tara Street Station
River Liffey
Bank of Ireland
Trinity College
Hospital
Pearse Station
City Hall
Castle
Civic Museum
National Library
National Gallery
Leinster House (The Dail)
Mansion House
National Museum
Merrion Square
St. Stephen's Green
Blessington St.
Upper Dorset St.
Temple Street North
Gardiner Place
West Gardiner St.
Charles St. Gt.
Portland Row.
Buckingham Street
Summerhill
Killarney St.
Amiens Street
Frederick St.
Denmark St.
N. Gt. Georges St.
Hill Street
Parnell Street
Parnell Sq.
Parnell Sq. E.
Granby Parnell Sq. West
Mountjoy St.
Dorset St.
Dominick Place
Dominick Street Lower
Kings Inns St.
Sean Mac Dermott Street
Railway Street
Gardiner Street
Corporation St.
Foley Street
Sheriff St.
Waterford Street
Marlborough Street
O'Connell Street
Talbot Street
Moore St.
Coles Lane
Denmark St.
Parnell Street
N. Earl Street
Store St.
Beresford
Henry Street
Jervis Street
Mary Street
Abbey St. Lower
Custom House Quay
Abbey St. Middle
Liffey St.
Eden Quay
Capel Street
Abbey Street
Lotts
Bachelors Walk
Georges Quay
Burgh Quay
City Quay
Strand St. Gt.
Ormond Quay
Aston Quay
Westmoreland St.
D'Olier St.
Tara St.
Gloucester Street
Townsend Street
Wellington Quay
Fleet Street
College St.
Temple Bar
Essex Quay
Essex Street
Pearse Street
Lombard St. S.
College Grn.
Dame Street
Lord Edward Street
Westland Row.
Suffolk St.
Nassau Street
Georges Street
Exchequer St.
Wicklow St.
Boyne St.
Leinster St.
Lincoln Place
Ship Street
William Street
Grafton Street
Dawson St.
Frederick St.
Denzille Lane
Upper Stephen St.
Lane
Molesworth St.
Anne Street
Chatham St.
Kildare Street
North Street
Aungier St.
Mercer St.
King Street
West
Wood St.
Peter Street
York Street
North Baggot Street
Merrion St.
Fitzwilliam Lane
Bishop Street
Kevin Street
Cuffe Street
South
East
Baggot Street

Bonny lasses of Dublin.

A Brief History

Dublin, or *Duibh-linn*, which translates as "the black pool" in Irish, describes the part of the Liffey River near where the present city is located. However, the original Bronze-Age Celtic settlement which preceded the present town was situated where an artificial ford of hurdles crossed the river and was actually the important trading road from Tara in the north to Wicklow in the south. The town which grew up at the ford was called *Baile-atha-cliath*, "the town of the hurdle ford", which is still the name used by Gaelic speakers when talking of Dublin.

Lured by Ireland's monastic treasures, the Vikings seized and fortified the settlement in AD 838. Although they never completely stopped marauding the area, Dublin's Norse rulers traded with the local inhabitants and their commercial towns became a new element in Irish life. Their power, however, declined considerably when the Irish High King Brian Boru defeated the Scandinavian allies just north of Dublin at the Battle of Clontarf in 1014. The death knell for the Vikings finally came when Strongbow and his Norman English seized Dublin in 1170, took control of the walled city and banished the Vikings to a separate colony called Oxmanstown, on the northern bank of the Liffey. Only two years later, Henry II of England declared Dublin the capital

Halfpenny Bridge, over the Liffey River, joins the north and south of the city.

of his Irish kingdom. From earliest times, the Liffey River, which cleaves the city into its north and south sides before emptying into the Irish Sea halfway down Ireland's east coast, was an important factor in the city's growth.

The Vikings used it as their main maritime artery and the river was responsible for Dublin's rapid trading growth. The first settlements were on the south bank as was the walled stronghold which later became Dublin Castle. In medieval times, Dublin was still contained within these fortified walls but after Cromwell's reconquest and the Duke of Ormonde's arrival, the city expanded to the east and then across the river to the north. From the 18th century onwards, when Dublin became the second city of the British Empire, the great Georgian developments began which still characterize the city today: handsome squares, broad roadways, and stunning public buildings.

Dublin demands at least two days sightseeing but is best seen in a week. Its sights are all within easy walking distance of each other on both sides of the River Liffey. However, since the city began on the south side, it seems more fitting to start our tour there.

South of the Liffey

Gulls screech and wheel over the Liffey which slides beneath the **Halfpenny Bridge**, a marvellous pedestrian span

James Joyce's Dublin

James Joyce, literary genius.

It seems ironic that James Joyce, 20th-century Ireland's most famous literary son, spent most of his adult life escaping from and railing against his native Dublin. Yet all his books revolved around the lives of Dubliners and were played out on the city's streets. Joyce's method of mentioning real locations and people's actual names may have incited wrath and delayed publication of his books in his day, but this is a boon for literary enthusiasts who can spend days exploring Dublin's streets in the footsteps of Joyce's characters.

The Liffey River which divides the city is a fitting place to begin the homage. Joyce's early years were spent north of the river, but his university was south of the river and he and his characters roamed extensively, as Dubliners still do today, across both banks.

From O'Connell Bridge look downstream to the far end where Stephen Dedalus, Joyce's alter-ego in *Portrait of the Artist as a Young Man,* walked alone along the shore "and felt the vast cyclic movement of the earth". To the east is the imposing **Custom House**, which Stephen used as a landmark in his early wanderings after the family had moved back to Dublin.

At the junction of Henry and O'Connell Streets, on the footpath outside Eason's bookstore, is a plaque (the first of 14) which commemorates where Leopold Bloom began his chapter-eight walk through Dublin in *Ulysses.* Every year on 16th June, known as "Bloomsday", Joyce-buffs dress up and make a pilgrimage around the path of Joyce's protagonist.

On Saturday afternoons the pedestrian mall of **Henry Street** and the adjacent **Moore Street** where hawkers still call out their wares, is redolent of the "Araby" scene in *Dubliners* when "we walked through the flaring streets, jostled by drunken men and bargaining women, amid the curses of labourers, the shrill litanies of shop-boys...".

Memories of *Dubliners*

East in Marlborough Street, is **Mary's Pro-Cathedral** where the Kearney family in the *Dubliners* cynical short-story "A Mother", used to go for Sunday mass. The streets about the cathedral used to be known as Monto, the red-light district which Joyce immortalized as "Nighttown" and where the young Stephen lost his virginity. Further north is **Parnell Street**, named after the great Irish nationalist leader, Charles Stewart Parnell, whose statue stands on the corner of O'Connell Street. His untimely death in 1891 was the subject of Joyce's poem "The Death of Parnell" which Joe Hynes gives an emotional rendering of in the *Dubliners* "Ivy Day in the Committee Room".

Nearby is the Rotunda Hospital and the adjacent **Rotunda Rooms** where concerts were held in aid of the hospital. It was at one of these performances that the saturnine loner, James Duffy, first met Mrs Sinico in the emotional *Dubliners* tale "A Painful Case". On the north side of the square, opposite Findlater's Church, there was once a cigar store where Stephen Dedalus's diary records that on 3rd April, his friend Davin asks "was it true I was going away and why". Exile, even then was Joyce's solution.

In Denmark Street is **Belvedere College**, a Jesuit day school, which still looks much the same as when Joyce was a pupil. His schooldays are vividly portrayed in *Portrait of the Artist as a Young Man*. Not least, is the incident indicative of his later life when "Mr. Tate, the English master, pointed his finger at him and said bluntly; 'This fellow has heresy in his essay'." Many old Georgian homes here are reminiscent of the "gaunt spectral mansions in which the old nobility of Dublin had roystered".

At the Jesuit **Church of St Francis Xavier**, the devout go in to say morning mass just as Joe Dillon's parents in *An Encounter* always did. North from here is **Eccles Street** where Leopold and Molly Bloom of *Ulysses* lived at No 7, now the Mater Private Hospital. Further west is **King's Inns** "where Little Chandler, clerk and would-be poet, spent his workdays" in, *A Little Cloud*. Down Capel Street at the **Gratton Bridge**, Little Chandler had a moment of poetic brilliance when he imagined that the houses along the lower quays looked like a band of tramps "stupefied by the panorama of sunset". On the north bank still stands the much-renovated **Ormond Hotel**, yet another *Ulysses* site. And further along at Inns Quay, bustling with bewigged lawyers, is **Four Courts** which Gabriel passes at dawn in *The Dead*, noticing that it "stood out menacingly against the heavy sky".

South of the River

South of the river at **College Street** is the "droll statue of the national poet of Ireland",Thomas Moore. Dubliners have long seen the connection between his poem *The Meeting of the Waters* and the fact that his statue stands above a public toilet. Joyce remarked on this same fact in *Ulysses* and a bronze plaque marks yet another Bloomsday site. Nearby is the **Bank of Ireland** where in *Protrait of the Artist as a Young Man* Stephen (actually the young Joyce) went to claim his essay prizes for "thirty and three pounds" which he spent in a "swift season of merrymaking", buying presents and taking his family and friends to the theater.

Facing College Street is "The grey block of Trinity" which Joyce in a rather maudlin way described as "set heavily in the city's ignorance like a dull stone set in a cumbrous ring". Nearby **Grafton Street** was the scene of many of Joyce's tales and the place where Stephen Dedalus met the girl student he had long fancied. "The crowd brought us together", he wrote in his diary, "I liked her and it seems a new feeling for me".

Wicklow Street, to the right of Grafton, was where "Ivy Day in the Committee Room" was acted out and **Duke Street**, to the left, was where the pub crowd from "Counterparts" decided on their next watering hole. In neighboring Kildare Street, Stephen Dedalus often studied in the **National Library** which has not changed much since Joyce's day. Students and old academics still pour over ancient tomes propped up by wooden stands.

Beside the southeast corner of Trinity at Lincoln Place, is a greengrocer's shop with **Finn's Hotel** painted on its gable. Nora Barnacle, Joyce's wife, once worked here as a chambermaid, and across the road is **Sweeney's Pharmacy** which still stocks the same lemon soap that Leopold Bloom purchased here in *Ulysses*. North from here is fashionable **Merrion Street**, lined with red-brick Georgian townhouses which look far more resplendent than in Joyce's day. Here Stephen lectured Lynch on his ideas of "beauty" in *Protrait of the Artist as a Young Man*.

Further west is **St Stephen's Green**, mentioned innumerable times in Joyce's books and the source, some academics insist, of the name Stephen Dedalus, Joyce's alter-ego. Overlooking the green on the southern side is **Newman House**, the Catholic University that Joyce attended and which features in *Portrait of the Artist as a Young Man* when Stephen has a long talk with the English-born dean of beauty, art and speculative thinking. It was at Newman House that Stephen (Joyce) came to the conclusion that art was to be his way of life and this turning point also marks the beginning of his criticism of his earlier life which was to become a hallmark of his writings.

of cast-iron which was constructed in 1816, and the start of our tour of the south side. Its official name is the Liffey Bridge but its more popular title derives from the days prior to 1919 when users had to pay a halfpenny toll. On the southern bank, walk under Merchant's Arch and into Crown Alley, part of a maze of cobbled streets known as **Temple Bar**. Clockmakers and printers' shops, the original tenants here, have now given way to music shops, rock n' roll bars, funky boutiques, wholefood cafés, bookshops and galleries. Sinhead O'Connor look-alikes loll about the **Bad Ass Café** where the shaven-headed singer once waited on tables. In adjoining **Fownes Street**, old shop-houses have been revamped into boutiques such as **Desparados** and the **Real McCoy** which specializes in "Vintage Leather and Suede from the 1950s and 1960s".

Turn left at Dame Street, one of the city's oldest thoroughfares, for College Green, once the site of the 12 m (40 feet) mound known as the Thingmote where the Vikings held their parliaments. It was leveled in the 17th century and the earth was used to raise nearby Nassau Street above flood level. Later, College Green was used as a common and in medieval days public executions took place here.

A Very Special Bank

To the left of College Green, flanked by rows of columns, is the imposing **Bank of Ireland**, which, prior to 1803, was the Irish Parliament Building. Its designer, local architect Edward Lovett Pearce never lived long enough to see its opening in 1739. The porticos and subsequent additions were constructed in later years.

After the unsuccessful uprising of the United Irishmen in 1798, parliament was forced to vote itself out of existence and the fulcrum of power switched to London. The Chamber however, still remains intact with its superb oak woodwork, an original chandelier, and tapestries depicting famous battles.

The politicos moved out of the old parliament nearly two centuries ago, and when the bank took over it was on the condition that the building could not be used for political purposes. However, the bank's wrought-iron fence near the eastern portico still serves as a soapbox for anyone with a political quibble. High above the crowd, standing aloft on a column plinth, an intent youth urges passers-by "don't walk past until you've signed our petition on racism in Ireland". It is indeed an excellent site to lobby for signatures as directly opposite is Dublin's famed **Trinity College**, the sole college of the University of Dublin founded in 1592 which boasts some 8,000 students and was one of the first to admit women from 1903.

Treasures of Trinity

Enter Trinity College with the hordes of

Trinity College sets the standards for Dublin's academic tradition.

students through the Front Arch in the 90-m (295 ft) long **facade**, built in 1752, to the quadrangle of **Parliament Square** where pigeons swirl about the manicured lawns and students rattle their bicycles across the cobblestones. Directly opposite you is the superb **campanile** (1853) and beyond it the red-bricked **Rubrics**, Trinity's oldest building which dates from 1700. To the right is the 18th-century **examination hall** which houses a gilt oak chandelier.

To the left is the **chapel**, noted for its fine plasterwork, and beside it is the beautifully restored **dining hall**. Follow the right-hand path (or the crowds of tourists) for the magnificent **library** which contains the 8th-century *Book of Kells*, the world famous illuminated manuscript depicting the four Gospels of the New Testament (see box story p.168).

To step into the aptly-named **Long Room**, Europe's largest single-chamber library, is to step into Dublin's Georgian past. It is old and musty, housing over a million volumes, many of them ancient and priceless. Light shines through waxed blinds in the window niches, creating a soft yellow glow which further enhances the Georgian ambiance. Other memorabilia include Ireland's oldest harp.

Adjacent is the **Colonnades Exhibition Gallery** and a **souvenir shop** which has a good selection of Irish books and souvenirs.

Molly Malone, who is alleged to have sold cockles and mussels in Dublin's Fair City.

Light Distractions

Leave Trinity by the same gate and turn right into Westmoreland Street for a delicious detour to the original **Bewley's Café**, a favorite hangout for James Joyce and still beloved by Dubliners today. Under *art-nouveau* stained-glass windows, beside potted palms, urbanites warm themselves by the open fire, peruse the *Irish Times*, eat their éclairs and sip the freshly-brewed coffee that has been a Dublin trademark for over a century.

Head back past Trinity into **Nassau Street** where there is a statue of Molly Malone, a street girl who is alleged to have sold cockles and mussels, at least according to the famous song, *Dublin's Fair City*.Continue, past the **House of Names**, to Westland Row, where **Pearse Station** holds the honor of being the terminus for the world's first commuter train journey which first traveled from Dublin to Dun Laoghaire in 1834. At No 21, in the same street, Oscar Wilde, the renowned and notorious homosexual playwright, was born in 1854. Further along the road at No 36 is the **Royal Academy of Music**.

Merrion Square

Head south from here for **Merrion Square** which is ringed by handsome rows of Georgian town houses. Merrion

The entrance to the ancient common of St Stephen's Green, now a public park.

Square has always housed the rich and famous and it is still a very up-market address. At No 1, lived the well-known eye surgeon Sir William Wilde, his wife Jane who wrote poetry and prose under the pen-name of "Speranza", and their precocious son Oscar. Daniel O'Connor, the great emancipist once lived at No 58; WB Yeats the Nobel prize winning poet resided at No 82, and another Nobel Prize winner, the physicist Ervin Schrodinger lived at No 65.

On the west side of the square is the **National Gallery** housing collections of the Irish, Italian, Spanish, Flemish, Dutch, French and English schools. George Bernard Shaw's statue immortalizes the playwright who bequeathed his royalties to the gallery.

Adjacent to the National Gallery is **Leinster House**, originally Lord Kildare's town house. Built in 1745, it once housed

The *Book of Kells*

The Book of Kells, an exquisite 8th or 9th-century copy of the Gospels of the New Testament.

In a strange quirk of history, the Norsemen, who plundered Ireland's monasteries from the 9th century, were illiterate and as a result they had little interest in Irish manuscripts bypassing them for the more obvious monastic treasures of precious metals. The most famous of these early illuminated manuscripts is the *Book of Kells*, an exquisite 8th or 9th-century copy of the four Gospels of the New Testament. This celebrated text is the most famous but not the most antiquated of Ireland's books as the *Book of Durrow* is reputed to be a century older.

Dating the Work

Scholars' views on the age of the *Book of Kells* vary from the 7th to the early 9th century. Tradition, however, relates that monks first worked on the manuscript in Iona in Scotland and completed it at the Abbey in Kells, County Meath, probably after the Vikings invaded the Columban monastery of Iona around AD 806, forcing the Abbot to sail to Ireland and seek refuge at Kells. Some historians, though, attribute an even earlier date to the text using the book's illustrations as proof, citing that the warriors' small circular swords date from pre-Viking days.

An 11th-century account in the *Annals of Ulster* tells of how the "The Great Gospel of Colum Cille...the principal relic of the western world" was stolen from the Church of Ceannanus. When it was rediscovered, buried under a sod of earth in Kells "after 20 nights and two months", the thieves had stripped its gold, and scholars think that this could account for the book's current discoloration and damage. From the 12th century when the austere Columban era ended, the book resided in the parish church at Kells, and in the 17th century

the Fitzgerald clan including Lord Edward Fitzgerald, the leader of the United Irishmen who was killed in the 1798 uprising. From 1925 Leinster House has been the headquarters of Ireland's parliament, comprising the *Dail* (Lower House) and the *Seanad* (the Upper House).

South of here is the **Natural History Museum**, known by city wits as "The Dead Zoo" for its Victorian collections of stuffed animals and skeletons including the extinct Irish elk.

St Stephen's Green

Take a short diversion down Mount Street

it was moved to Dublin's **Trinity College library** for safe-keeping when Cromwell with bloody thoroughness quelled an Irish rebellion. Three hundred years later the *Book of Kells* is still in residence there. The library has scarcely changed in all this time, its original interior wall-to-wall with antique books and it is a fitting final resting place for Ireland's greatest national treasure. No doubt, though, some visitors, among the thousands who troop by to peer into the glass case, are disappointed by its size, for its reputation far outweighs its dimensions. The 340 parchment pages, measuring 32½ cm (13 inches) by 23½ cm (9½ inches), contain the New Testament Gospels of Saints Matthew, Mark, Luke, and John, but what it lacks in size, the *Book of Kells* certainly makes up for in its exquisite craftsmanship.

Artistic Paragon

Written in Latin, the *Book of Kells* also contains, in addition to the Gospels, prefaces, summaries, tables of reference and a glossary. Each page, one of which is turned every month, has approximately 16 lines of Irish majuscule script. Intricate designs of interwoven ribbons, scrolls, spirals, trumpets, animals, humans, and leaf patterns are imaginatively painted in a spectrum of rainbow colors. The paints used were derived from insects and ground from precious stones such as lapis lazuli and malachite. Color illuminations decorate the starting initials of paragraphs, brackets (used to enclose words outside a line), and renowned gospel passages including the Genealogy of St Luke, the Beatitudes and the Judgement passage in St Mathew.

The ingenuity of the designs is thought to be the work of not one but several artists, who were influenced by not only their native Celtic sources, but by other European and even Oriental schools. Francoise Henry, the authoress of *Irish Art*, theorizes that the profuse animal decorations are due to contact with artists in Gaul, and other scholars even point to Eygptian influences in the portraits. Particularly exquisite pages include the masterful and intricate Eight Circle Cross, thought to symbolize the four elements; the Chi Rho page with its amazing details like the scene where cats watch mice eating a piece of altar bread; the opening page of St Mathew's Gospel known as "the book of the generation"; the full-page illumination on the first page of St Mark's Gospel; the three full-page portraits of the Evangelists; the dramatic Arrest of Christ; and the Euselian Canons, the book's opening pages which are beautifully displayed in a design reminiscent of Byzantine architecture.

The *Book of Kells* is a striking example of Ireland's venerable literary tradition, for Irish is the oldest language in Northern Europe with ancient writings still extant. It is well worth queuing to view the *Book of Kells*, (the crowds in the summer can be very large, and require patience) for surprisingly enough, although the manuscript is so incredibly old many of the letters are still reminiscent of modern Irish script and the colors are so bright, it is hard to believe that it is was written over 12 centuries ago.

Upper and around the back of St Stephen's Church to view the tree-shaded **Grand Canal**, built in 1755, which winds from Dublin through the countryside to connect with the River Shannon, in the west. This former commercial thoroughfare is now a quiet waterway overlooked by fine Georgian facades. Nearby, **Fitzwilliam Street** and the square of the same name still house beautiful examples of 18th and 19th-century architecture, complete with ornamental wrought-iron balconies.

Take Leeson Street, home to Dublin's late-night basement nightclubs, to **St Stephen's Green**, an ancient common which was a private park until the Guinness clan took over the lease, laid

Grafton Street, the bustling heart of Dublin.

out the lake and the gardens, and opened it to the public in 1880.

Joggers and a medley of people enjoy themselves among the waterfalls, flowers, lawns and statues, including one of James Joyce which stands opposite **Newman House**, part of University College, which he attended and later immortalized in his *Portrait of the Artist as a Young Man.*

The park also has a unique garden for the blind, with plants labelled in Braille. Prominent buildings around St Stephen's Green include **Iveagh House**, now the Department of Foreign Affairs, which was built in 1736; the **Royal College of Surgeons of Ireland** which was occupied by rebel troops during the 1916 uprising, together with the elegant **Shelbourne Hotel** where the front columns still show bullet marks.

Outside this Victorian-era hotel statues of Nubian slaves hold lamps aloft and top-hatted coachmen persuade tourists to take a carriage ride around the Green. To the west, **Grafton Street**, now a pedestrian mall, bustles with shoppers, buskers and street poets, and is lined with trendy boutiques and department stores such as Switzers and Brown Thomas. On nearby Johnstown's court is the stylish **Powerscourt Shopping Center.**

The National Museum

Heading north from St Stephen's Green is Dawson Street with its elegant, early 18th-century **Mansion House**, the home of the Lord Mayor of Dublin; the **Royal Irish Academy** with its world-renowned library of Irish manuscripts; and **St Ann's Church** which still retains a shelf beside the altar where bread for the poor is left, a legacy of Lord Newton's dating from 1723.

On Kildare Street, parallel to Dawson street, Leinster House is flanked by the **National Museum** and the **National Library** which have matching Victorian-style rotundas. The museum's domed foyer has a marvellous tiled floor depicting the 12 signs of the zodiac and notable collections of early Celtic antiquities, hoards of golden jewelry dug from bogs, early Viking artifacts including awls made of antlers, and treasures of

Dublin Castle, at the forefront of Irish history for centuries.

Irish art including the Tara brooch.

At the library opposite, visitors are given a pass to enter the Reading Room, the stained-glass windows of Michaelangelo and Leonardo da Vinci, are situated above the stairs *en route*.

Dublin Landmarks

Head back to College Green, then along Dame Street to Dublin's medieval center. Just beyond Sycamore Street is the **Olympia**. Built in 1870 it is the city's oldest surviving theater and has a superb baroque-style interior. A little further on, on the opposite side of Dame Street, is the **City Hall** built between 1769 and 1779. This edifice has had a chequered history it was used as a torture chamber during the 1798 rebellion and witnessed a public whipping in 1814 where nine onlookers were killed when a railing gave way. In the mid-19th century it was taken over by the Dublin Corporation whose motto in the floor mosaic of the entrance rotunda is rather ironic, *Obedientia Civium Urbis Felicitas*, ("Happy the city where citizens obey").

Turn left up Cork Hill for **Dublin Castle** (see box story p.16) which has been at the forefront of Dublin's history since the very beginning. Excavations indicate that earthworks existed here even before the 9th-century Viking fortress.

King John commanded the official building of the castle in 1204 and the

The Georgian architecture of Dublin lends an elegance to the city.

Record Tower, the original circular keep still survives. After the castle's destruction by fire in the late 17th century, much of it was rebuilt to its present dimensions.

St Patrick's Cathedral

Leave the castle by the Ship Street gate, turn south down Bride Street and into Bull Alley, site of the **Liberties Vocational School** which is part of the extensive inner-city redevelopment scheme funded by the Guinness beer clan in the early 1900s. Opposite is **St Patrick's Park** where a stone marks the site of a miraculous spring which appeared at the saint's touch. Here, Ireland's patron saint gave baptisms, and beside the park dominating the surroundings is the cathedral named after him. Although the first church to be built here dated from the 5th century, it was rebuilt in 1190 and only reached its present dimensions in the 13th century. The 43-m (141 ft) high west tower, was added still later, in 1370, and the metal spire in the 18th century. The renowned satirist, Jonathan Swift of *Gulliver's Travels* fame, was Dean of **St Patrick's Cathedral** from 1713 to 1745 and he is buried here near the western side of the nave. **Marsh's Library**, nearby in **St Patrick's Close**, was Ireland's first public library, much used by Swift and later by Joyce. The library contains around 25,000 valuable books dating from the 16th to the 18th centuries. The interior is still authentic, dating from 1701, and contains wire cages in which scholars reading rare books were once locked into.

Heading for Guinness

From the cathedral take Dean Street to **Francis Street** which is renowned for its antique shops and furniture restorers. From Cornmarket travel west past **St John's Lane Church** where the ancient Abbey of St John once stood, past the **National College of Art and Design** which was once a distillery, past the classical facade of **St Catherine's Church** and into Crane Street, for the **Guinness Brewery**. Famed for its stout, seven million glasses of which are guz-

The Custom House, Edan Quay, restored to its 18th-century glory.

zled worldwide every day, the brewery which was founded by Arthur Guinness in 1759 is Europe's largest and the world's greatest beer exporter. At the visitor's center and the Hopstore there are films and displays and free samples of the famed stout.

Towards the Liffey

Return to Cornmarket and detour down Bridge Street for the **Brazen Head**, Dublin's oldest pub which dates from 1668.

Nearby on High Street is **St Audeon's**, one of Ireland's oldest churches. On the river side is **St Audeon's Arch** built in 1215, the sole surviving gateway of the old city. Opposite the church, along Back Lane is **Tailor's Hall**, Dublin's last remaining guildhall (a medieval hall where a fraternity of craftsmen met to protect the rights of their members). The building contains fine examples of early 18th-century windows, and a handsome musicians' gallery. The building is now the headquarters of the National Trust for Ireland.

On the corner of Winetavern Street, dominating the block, is **Christ Church Cathedral**, originally constructed in wood for the Viking king of Dublin, Sitric Silkenbeard, in 1038. The Anglo-Normans rebuilt it in stone in the 12th century and further renovations took place in 1562. In the crypt, Dublin's oldest building dating from Strongbow's time (his tomb is also in the cathedral) which once served as "tippling rooms for beer and wine", there is a mummified cat chasing a rat, among other oddities.

North of the Liffey

Starting on the north side of the Halfpenny Bridge, head east along the riverbank to **O'Connell Bridge**, reputed to be as wide as it is long. The bridge is named after the great Catholic emancipist Daniel O'Connell, also known as "the Liberator", who is immortalized by a nearby monument and also by Dublin's widest thoroughfare, **O'Connell Street** which runs north from here.

O'Connell street has seen its fair

Caught in the traffic of O'Connell Street.

share of troubles and suffered damages during the 1916 Rising and the 1922 Civil War. Lined with monuments to Ireland's great leaders, it still plays host to petitioners and politicos who parade along the paved and tree-lined central mall.

Make a short detour downriver from here to Eden Quay, site of the magnificent **Custom House**. Designed by the London architect James Gandon in the 1780s, troubles plagued the building from the beginning. Opponents of the scheme forced the architect to carry a sword for his own safety. The site was unstable and much later during the Civil War it was badly destroyed by fire. However, restoration work carried out in 1926 and 1986 has reinstated the building to its former glory.

Entertainment on O'Connell Street

Just north of here is Abbey Street, home of the renowned **Abbey Theater**, founded early this century by WB Yeats and his friends in order to stage the works of Irish playwrights. Plays by Synge, Yeats, O'Casey and Shaw which debuted here were not without controversy. Synge's *Playboy of the Western World* caused riots in 1907 and more disturbances followed O'Casey's *The Plough and the Stars* because the Irish flag shared center stage with a whore. After the old theater was gutted by fire a new replacement was built in 1966.

Back on O'Connell Street, **Eason's bookstore** on the corner of Abbey Street is worth a good couple of hours browsing as it has a huge collection of books on Irish literature, mythology and every other conceivable Irish subject. Nearby west of Abbey Street adjust is lively **Moore Street** where fruit, flower, and vegetable stalls abound; carts pulled by draft horses still survive here. Moore Street was named after Henry Moore, the 18th-century Earl of Drogheda, after whom nearby Henry, Earl and Drogheda (O'Connell) Streets are also named.

Symbols of the Republic

Back on O'Connell Street, the austere, battle-scarred **General Post Office** holds a special place in the hearts of all Irish folk as it was here that Patrick Pearse, James Connolly and their Irish Volunteers made their headquarters during the 1916 Easter Rising. The rebels proclaimed the Irish Republic here but they were forced to flee after a week's shelling by the British resulted in the Post Office being gutted. The aftermath of the insurgence, when 15 leaders were executed, changed the public's apathetic mood to country-wide agitation, resulting in an independent Ireland six years later. Nearby, at the Henry Street junction, now a pedestrian mall lined with department stores, boutiques and eateries, once stood the 41-m (134 ft) high Nelson's Pillar, a city landmark and a British symbol which was blown to pieces on the 50th anniversary of the uprising, in 1966.

Parnell Square

The well-stocked and very informative **Tourist Information Office**, a must for all travelers, is further up O'Connell Street, on the right. Behind here, on Marlborough Street, is **St Mary's Protestant Cathedral**. Built in impressive Greek-Doric style in 1825, the church is famed for its Palestrina Choir where the renowned tenor John McCormack started his singing career.

Parnell Square, the city's second oldest square (St Stephen's is the oldest) was originally known as "The Barley Fields", then Rutland Square, after the reigning viceroy, before taking its present name after Charles Stewart Parnell, the great, misunderstood politician who is commemorated by a monument at this junction.

In the late 18th century, Parnell Square and the surrounding area was a prestigious address for prominent politicians and religious leaders. Some of Dublin's fanciest homes were once sited here including Charlemont House, now the **Municipal Gallery of Art** which takes turns in housing the superb Hugh Lane Impressionist Collection with London's Tate Gallery. This unusual situation came about because Lane, a famous Irish collector and connoisseur, drowned with the sinking of the *Lusitania* liner in World War II before signing the will which bequeathed the paintings to Dublin. The **Dublin Writers' Museum**, nearby, with memorabilia and many rare manuscripts of Dublin's renowned writers, is in the revamped Georgian houses at Nos 18 and 19. Next door is the **Abbey Presbyterian Church**, commonly known as Findlater's Church after its merchant patron.

The Rotunda & Remembrance Park

On the east side of Parnell Square is the **Rotunda Hospital** built as a maternity hospice in 1757. Its magnificent chapel is decorated with carved mahogany pews and columns and a superb stucco ceiling. Attached to the hospital is the **Gate Theater** where James Mason and Orson Wells made their acting debuts, and adjacent is the **Rotunda Room** where events were staged in aid of the hospital including readings by Charles Dickens. In the center of Parnell Square is **Remembrance Park**, in memory of the martyrs who fell in the Easter Rising. "O generations of freedom remember us, the generations of the vision", is poignantly written in Gaelic by the bronze sculpture of *The Children of Lir*, a legend which tells of four children who transformed themselves into swans.

Architectural Highlights

East, along Denmark Street is **Belvedere College**, immortalized by its most famous pupil James Joyce in *Portrait of the Artist as a Young Man*. The school still looks the same as Joyce's description and its beautiful ceilings by the master of stucco Michael Stapleton, can easily be viewed from the street when the rooms are lit in the evening. In the surrounding streets of Great St Georges, Gardiner Place, Gardiner Street and Mountjoy Square, there are many fine examples of classical Georgian architecture. However, compared to the southside with its streets of well-cared-for townhouses, the north is a study of contrasts. Some homes have been lovingly restored while others are empty and dilapidated. However, much of the area is now being revamped and many of the old Georgian homes on **Upper Gardiner Street** have now been refurbished into comfortable and elegant bed-and-breakfast establishments.

Two early 19th-century churches are also found in this vicinity. **St George's Church** in Hardwicke Place has a spire copied from St Martin's-in-the-Fields, London, however it is no longer in use as a church. But the Jesuit **Church of St Francis Xavier** in Upper Gardiner Street, is always full of worshippers. The interior is superb with coffered ceilings, fine woodwork and 19th-century oil paintings.

Courts & Mummies

Follow Parnell Square West, past the Dublin Wax Museum into Dorset Street Upper and then head left into Henrietta Street, which is now run-down but was once a fashionable address. Ahead is the **King's Inns**, designed as a residence and study-center for barristers by Gandon, of Custom House fame, in 1795, but finished by his protégé in 1816. From Henrietta Street, follow King Street North and turn into Church Street for **St Michan's Church** which is renowned for its vault containing some excellently preserved 17th-century mummified bodies said to have inspired Bram Stoker's *Dracula*. It was founded by the Vikings and was Dublin's only northside parish church for half a millennium. Other fascinating items housed here include an organ reputedly used by Handel while composing *The Messiah*, and Dublin's only "Penitent's Stool".

Northern Landmarks

Around the corner in cobbled Bow Street is the **Irish Whiskey Corner**, the headquarters of the Irish Distillers, which holds demonstrations, films and free samplings. Continue down Bow Street to Arran Quay by the Liffey River. To the right is **St Paul's Church**. Built in the mid-19th century it contains the first set of bells hung in an Irish Catholic Church since the reformation.

Towards the city center beside Inns Quay is another Dublin landmark, the impressive **Four Courts** which houses the law courts. Its great domed roof dominates this end of the river as does the architect Gandon's other architectural gem the Custom House, to the east. Anti-treaty forces took over the building at the start of the 1922 Civil War and after a two-month siege, a three-day battle with government forces almost destroyed the building, which although superbly restored today still wears battle scars on the portico columns.

Returning to the Liffey

Spanning the Liffey, west of Four Courts, is **Father Mathew Bridge** which is where the original hurdle ford crossed the river, the original *Ath Cliath* (hurdle ford), where Dublin first began. From here, walk back along Ormond Quay to **Gratton Bridge**, the city's second oldest river crossing where the street lamps made of wrought-iron are shaped into mythical creatures.

Further along this quay lined with antique shops and second-hand bookstores is **The Winding Stair**, a wholefood café and bookshop which has great food and wonderful views of the Liffey and the Halfpenny Bridge, where our Dublin tour began and now ends.

Dublin Environs

From the rocky headland the view sweeps northward, along the harbor-studded coast where the silvery beams of sunlight streaks the Irish Sea, where raucous seabirds nest on vertical cliffs and below seals cavort in the green-blue surge. It seems a world away from the hustle of the city, but the celebrated harbor and headland of Howth is only a quick hop away from Dublin, on the north suburban train line.

Rhododendrons, ubiquitous in Dublin's environs.

As well as spectacular sea views, this northern region, within a day's drive from the capital, offers a wealth of other attractions from the mystic Celtic heartlands of the Boyne Valley to the Danish town of Drogheda, through quaint villages and past antiquities too numerous to mention.

Spectacular Howth

Named after the Danish *hoved* for "head", the summer

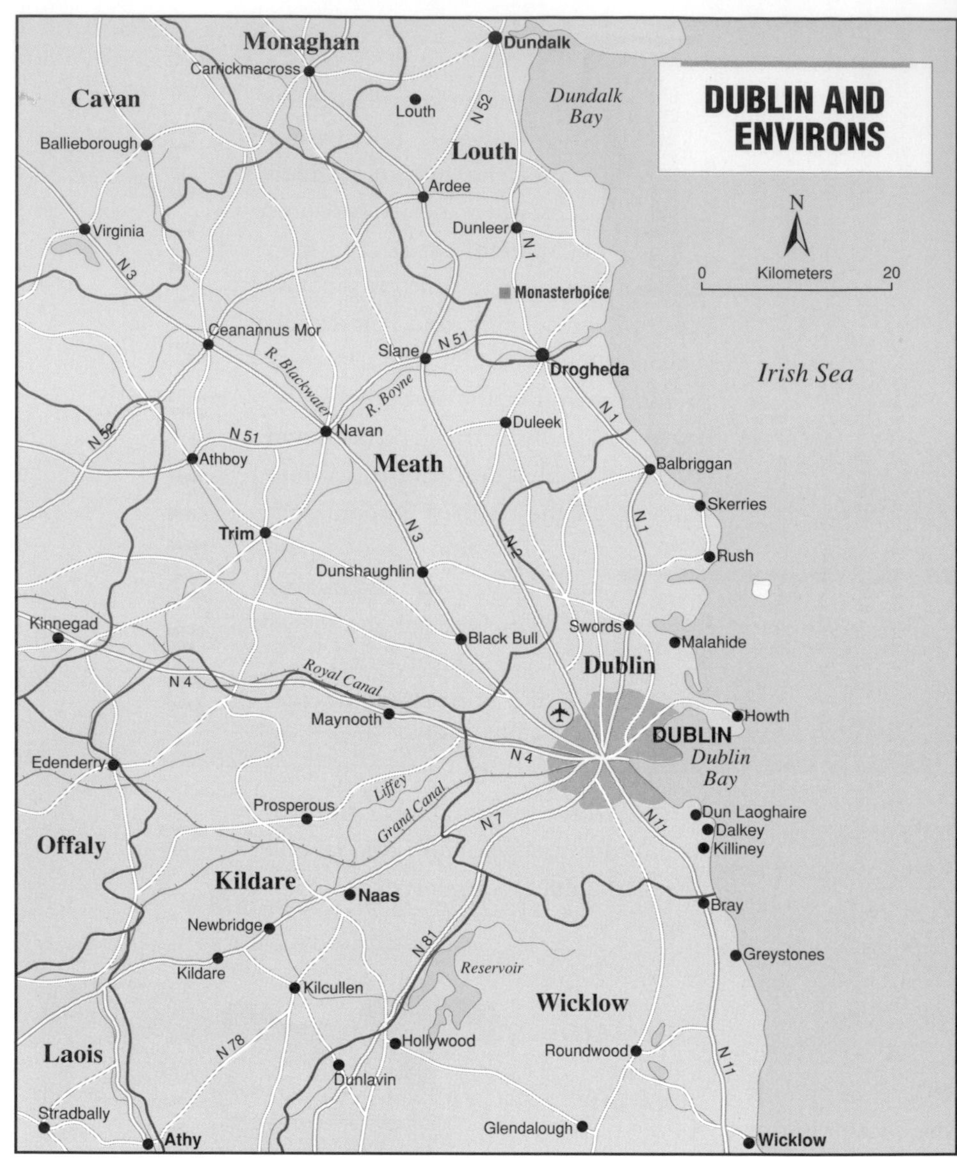

resort and fishing port of **Howth**, 14 km (9 miles) northeast of Dublin, was where the celebrated writer WB Yeats lived from 1880-83. His residence, the white-washed, stone **Ballscadden House**, at the start of the cliff walk, has a plaque inscribed with his immortal words: "I have spread my dreams under your feet. Tread softly because you tread on my dreams".

It is easy to imagine the romantic poet being inspired by the views from his old home and from nearby **Howth Head** which rises 171 m (560 ft) above

Howth Harbor, a popular holiday area.

sea level. While walking around the hour-long trail, past the flowering gorse and the rugged cliff terrain, the hiker feels akin to another writer, HG Wells, who was reputed to have remarked that this vista was "one of the most beautiful in the world".

Howth Harbor, built in the early 19th century as the principal port for the steamer service from Wales, prickles with aluminium yacht masts, evidence of the town's summer popularity, and bustles with fishing boats. In 1914 the yacht *Asgard* berthed here while gun-running for the Irish Volunteers. Behind the port are the old stone shops of the town center which house art galleries, trendy restaurants and fish-and-chips cafés. The 13th-century **St Mary's Abbey** and the adjacent **Ye Olde Abbey Tavern**, renowned for its traditional music nights, are nearby. Above the town are winding streets with elegant homes and manicured gardens where well-heeled Dublin commuters reside.

Offshore, accessible by launch from the East Pier, is the island known as **Ireland's Eye** on which are remains of a 6th-century church and a ruined **martello tower**. From Howth railway station, walk away from the town for **Howth Castle** which is situated along the road to the golf club. Grey and austere, with zigzag-style battlements, and ringed with old pines where rooks circle, the castle commands a superb position overlooking Dublin Bay. The interior is closed to the public but the

Howth Castle commands a superb position overlooking Dublin Bay.

grounds and the nearby **Transport Museum**, housed in an old cattle shed, are worth a look.

Keep walking past the castle up the hill to the **golf club**, where crowning the rise behind the clubhouse is the rhododendron garden immortalized in James Joyce's *Ulysses*. It is wild and untamed with windswept pines and boulders with a Japanese-garden feeling to it. Among the riotous pinks of the rhododendrons which flower from mid-March to June, are ancient stone dolmens and a tomb, which according to legend is the resting place of a Celtic princess. The coastal views from the top of the hill south across Dublin Bay and north to the fishing village of Portmarnock, are quite spectacular.

Malahide & Donabate

Further north along the suburban DART line, is neat and trim **Malahide** well known for its castle and winner of the 1990 "Tidy Town" competition. With its commanding battlemented towers, **Malahide Castle** has a glorious history and was the residence of the Talbot clan from the 12th century until 1975 when it was turned over to the Dublin County Council.

The council now run the castle as a tourist attraction complete with guided tours through the portrait-studded rooms and a model railway which is very popular with children. Medieval banquets can even be organized on request in the

12th-century Malahide Castle had a glorious history and was once the residence of the Talbot clan.

15th-century Great Hall.

Malahide Castle's most famous owner was Richard Talbot who was given the title of Earl of Tyrconnell by England's King James II, who made him head of the army in Ireland. Two years later he was made James's viceroy and angered the Protestants by handing out high offices to Catholics and re-examining land titles.

He even persuaded King James to revoke the land settlement of Cromwell who somewhat ironically had remarked during his tenure at Malahide Castle

The Howth Peninsula stretches from the north of Dublin to the isolation of Howth Point.

(the only time when the Talbots were not in residence during the last 700 years) that only here would he tolerate living on Irish soil. After James's forces were defeated by William of Orange's army at the Battle of the Boyne, fought just north of here in the Boyne River Valley near Drogheda, the Earl of Tyrconnell fled to France and the Protestants once again assumed power.

At **Donabate**, 6 km (4 miles) further north, accessible by both suburban trains and buses, is **Newbridge House**, the former residence of the Archbishop of Dublin, built in elegant, mid-18th-century Georgian style. Now run as a historic site by the Dublin County Council who conduct tours and run a craft shop there, the mansion became famous in the 1960s as the site where the movie *The Spy Who Came in from the Cold* was shot. Apparently before the filming Newbridge House had no electricity.

The adjacent **Traditional Farm** is well worth a visit to see how Ireland's farms were run in the Georgian era. Both the historic house and the traditional farm are open every day except Monday.

Drogheda

A millennium ago during Viking days, **Drogheda**, further up the coast, was Dublin's rival, but unlike Howth, the town's name was not derived from the Danish but comes from the Irish for "the

The 13th-century Lawrence Gate dominates the main street of Drogheda.

bridge of the ford" which was where the ford crossed the River Boyne. This ancient settlement still retains the **Millmount**, a prehistoric Norse mound, and it exudes a decidedly medieval air with its crooked streets, old fortifications including the 13th-century **Lawrence Gate**, one of Ireland's best-preserved town gates and the **Magdalen Steeple**, the only remnant of the Dominican Friary which dates from the same era.

On West Street is the Victorian-style **St Peter's Church**, built to commemorate the martyr Oliver Plunkett, whose head is still preserved and displayed in a shrine at the church. Plunkett, who was the Archbishop of Armagh and was later canonized, was executed in London for high treason in 1681.

The charges against Plunkett were trumped up; he was meant to have plotted to assist French forces in overthrowing the English government. His trial was held in England to make sure that his supporters were not around to sway the course of justice which was biased by the emotional hysteria prevailing at the time. Plunkett was canonized in 1975.

Drogheda also had the misfortune of playing an ignominious role in Cromwell's policy of "frightfulness" in Ireland, and except for Wexford, south of Dublin, no other town suffered such terrible casualties. No priest was spared and by Cromwell's own admission "I think we put to the sword altogether about 2,000 men".

The passage graves of Newgrange, one of Europe's greatest prehistoric structures.

Newgrange Burial Chambers

It seems fitting that in the historic **Boyne River Valley**, just inland from Drogheda where the Orange triumphed over the Green and where Cromwell laid his curse, is also the site of one of Europe's greatest prehistoric structures, the great **passage graves of Newgrange**, described by the writer Robert Kee as being "the earliest personal signatures of an Irish identity". Constructed by pre-Celtic peoples around 3,000 BC, these stone graves covered by a circular mound 13 m (44 ft) high, were the spacious burial chambers for tribal chieftains. They are decorated with mystical patterns of concentric whorls which were carved by Stone Age masons before iron tools were invented, the designs are still unsolved. The ceiling of the great chamber which is over 6 m (20 ft) high, is corbel-vaulted and it was built with remarkable engineering ingenuity; the rising sun at the winter solstice shines through a small aperture and illuminates the furthest end of the passage grave, the only time of the year when this extremity is lit with sunlight.

Known in Irish as ***Brugh na Boinne*** (The Palace of the Boyne), this auspicious burial chamber contains the grave of Aonghus, the God of Love. According to legend he was the son of Boand, a water goddess from which the River Boyne is named, who mated with Dagda, the great God.

Great Monasteries & Manuscripts

Just north of Newgrange, 10 km (6 miles) from Drogheda, is **Mellifont Abbey**, the remains of Ireland's first Cistercian monastery which the brotherhood founded in 1142. Inside the original perimeter walls are a church and a square tower, and a two-storey, octagonal lavabo where the monks took their ablutions.

Turn off the same northwest road from Drogheda for **Monasterboice**, an early Christian monastery founded in the 5th century and renowned for its decorative stone high crosses, including the 5 m (17 ft) high **Muireadach Cross**, which was carved in the 10th century. Soaring behind the cross is a round tower which like others across Ireland was built as a lookout and place of refuge from the marauding Vikings who ransacked the coast from the 8th century. When the alarm was sounded, the monks would shelter in the tower by pulling the ladder in after them.

Monasterboice flowered during the Gaelic Golden Age when Ireland was the guiding beacon for European Christianity during the Dark Ages. Irish scholars set down their history and culture in magnificent illuminated manuscripts like the 8th-century *Book of Durrow*, and Irish scholars traveled extensively through Europe contributing greatly to Ireland's knowledge of monasteries on the continent.

The Book of Kells (see box story p.168), the most famous of all Ireland's illuminated manuscripts, was unearthed at **Kells**, further west of Drogheda in the forested **Valley of the Blackwood River**

The Hill of Tara, the coronation site of the ancient Celtic kings.

where there are still remains of **St Columcille's**, a monastery dating from the 6th century. In **St Columba's Church**, visitors can view a copy of the famed book which has resided for centuries at Dublin's Trinity College.

Heading Back to Dublin

Heading back to Dublin from Drogheda, stop over at the picturesque village of **Slane**, overlooking the Boyne River. History has it that on nearby **Slane Hill**, St Patrick confronted the pagans and lit his pascal fire at Easter in AD 433. A ruined 16th-century church marks the spot where Ireland's patron saint proclaimed the land for Christianity and the views from the hill across the Valley of the Boyne are well worth the climb. At turretted **Slane Castle**, which has been renovated since a fire destroyed much of it in 1992, is a grassy amphitheater which has played host to summer rock concerts including those of Ireland's U2, Bruce Springsteen and Bob Dylan.

Further south in County Meath, turn off at **Navan** for one of Celtic Ireland's most famous sites, the mythical **Hill of Tara** (see box story p.22). The most influential of the five original kingdoms of Ireland, Tara was the place where coronations of the ancients took place and where the great assemblies of warriors and leaders, known as *feis* were held every three years. In modern times it was the venue in 1843 for one of the

"Liberator" Daniel O'Connell's mass Monster meetings when millions of people turned out to oppose the Corn Laws. These days a statue of St Patrick crowns the hill and all that is left of the mythical days of yore are some cryptic granite carvings.

Trim, 8 km (5 miles) from the Hill of Tara, offers yet another castle and plentiful ruins. The ruined **Trim Castle**, built in the 12th century and covering less than 1 hectare (2 acres), lays claim to being the largest Anglo-Norman castle in Ireland. Nearby, is the **Yellow Steeple**, a ruined abbey built in the 14th century.

Dublin's Southern Suburbs

In the south of the Dublin conurbation are a number of pretty villages by the sea. Part of the city of Dublin, they can be reached by taking the spectacular coast road or the DART train from Dublin.

Dun Laoghaire, the port town where a large percentage of visitors disembark at at the Sealink ferry terminal from Hollyhead in Wales, is often not seen at its best when one arrives tired out from the voyage and often a little nauseous after a particularly rough crossing. Take time to recuperate and then revisit Dun Laoghaire (pronounced "dunleary"), which boasts beautiful coastal scenery and a pleasant Georgian main street, fronting a harbor full of boats enclosed by long stone piers which extend out into the Irish Sea. Dun Laoghaire's **National Maritime Museum** features an optical instrument from Baily Lighthouse, Howth.

At **Sandycove**, the southern promontory of the bay, is a martello tower, now known as the **James Joyce Tower**. Immortalized by the writer in his monumental novel *Ulysses*, he apparently stayed here in 1904, the stone tower is now a museum of sorts for its native son who had such a love/hate relationship with his homeland, once referring to it as "the old sow who eats her farrow". Memorabilia celebrating Joyce is on display and there is an interesting bookshop. The tower is open from 1000 to 1700 hours, from April to October and adult admission is IR£1.75.

The coastal pathway which winds 5 km (3 miles) from Dun Laoghaire, through the picturesque village of **Dalkey** to **Killiney Bay**, affords stunning sea views and a chance to breathe in fresh salty air. Dalkey, a popular resort town, was a prominent port in the Middle Ages. Offshore is the bird sanctuary of **Dalkey Island**, accessible by boat from **Coliemore Harbor**, where there is a ruined **Benedictine church** and a **martello tower**. Further south is the seaside village of **Bray**, where the young James Joyce lived as a boy before going off to school in Kildare. The **Bray Heritage Center** tells the story of Bray's history with old photographs, making for an interesting stopover, especially for James Joyce nostalgia.

County Wicklow

Often referred to as "The Garden of Ireland", the scenic hills and valleys of Wicklow County, home to some of the country's best known gardens, mansions, and historic monasteries, have been for centuries Dublin's favorite country retreat. Although the region can be covered in a daytrip from the capital, most visitors will definitely feel like spending at least two days, for the region has a subtle charm that entices folks to linger. An extract from JN Synge's *Prelude*, speaks of Wicklow's charm:

The idyllic gardens of Mount Usher.

> Still south I went and west and south again,
> Through Wicklow from the morning till the night,
> And far from cities, and the sights of men,
> Lived with the sunshine, and the moon's delight.

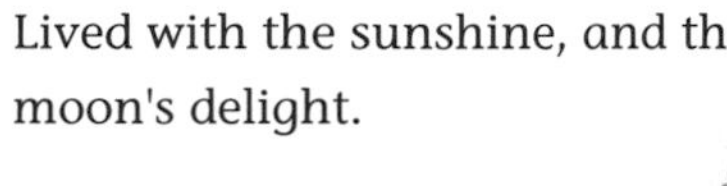

Great Houses & Gardens

Just outside of Bray, where County Wicklow begins,

County Wicklow where blossoms abound in the summer.

turn off the coastal road for **Enniskerry** and the nearby gardens of **Powerscourt** located in a superb setting overlooked by the nearby Wicklow Mountains. The 18th-century "great house" which once commanded over these gardens, was burnt down in the 1970s. Magnificently landscaped, with manicured lawns and Georgian statuary, the gardens are at their delightful best during spring and early summer. Nearby Spectacular **Powerscourt Waterfall** descends from heights of 90 m (295 ft).

There are a number of other famous gardens and "great houses" in Wicklow which are open to the public and often included in theme tours entitled "Ireland's Great Gardens", which for garden-lovers are well worth looking into. Allow yourself some time to appreciate these garden wonders. Turn off at **Ashford**, south of Bray on the coast road, for **Mount Usher**, a 8-hectare (20-acre) area of parkland and gardens on the River Vartry, famed for its exotic trees, flowers and shrubs.

Russborough, south of Blessington on the inland border of County Wicklow, also has delightful grounds, but is best known for its Albert Beit art collection which contains works by the great masters including Goya, Reubens, Vermeer and Velasquez. Built in the mid-18th century for the Earl of Miltown, this Palladian-style mansion boasts the longest frontage of all Ireland's "great houses", measuring 213 m (700 ft) from end to end.

One can walk for hours in the mountains with only sheep for company.

Wicklow & the Wicklow Mountains

Wicklow comes from a Viking name, but the older Irish name for the region was *Kilmantan*, "the church of Saint Mantan", who was a disciple of Patrick's. An old tale recorded in the ancient annals tells that when St Patrick tried to land in Wicklow, an enraged pagan struck Patrick's disciple with a stone, knocking out his teeth and from then on he was named Mantan, which means "the toothless one" in old Irish.

As a perfect complement to the gardens and mansions of the area is the backdrop of the Wicklow Mountains, which range from Bray to Arklow. Formed in the Ice Age, they are actually a series of granite hills, averaging around 610 m (2,000 ft) high, swathed in gorse and heather and slashed by sparkling rivers which tumble through deep ravines carved by ancient glaciers. It is a place of remarkable solitude, apart from the tourist coaches that flock here in summer, but even then it is easy to escape the crowds, for the highlands' villages are few and far between and beyond them you can walk for hours with only sheep for company.

The best way to immerse yourself in the Wicklow Mountains is to hike the 113 km (70-mile) long **Wicklow Way** which runs from **Marlay Park** in the Dublin suburb of Rathfarnham to **Clonegal** in County Carlow. This government-sponsored pathway runs along the crest of the mountains, passing **Mt Lugnacullia**, the republic's third highest peak, and the rugged Devil's Glen. In clear weather, from the top of the trail at the 610-m (2,000-ft) high **White Hill**, it is possible to see the Welsh mountains. It is rugged country, sparsely populated, and it is easy to see how these mountain strongholds were capable of hiding the O'Toole and the O'Byrne clans who harassed the British with their cattle raids in the 16th and 17th centuries. Maps of the trail can be obtained from the Dublin or Wicklow tourist offices, and there are a number of hostels within walking distance from the track.

The ruins of Glendalough Monastery which once housed 5,000 monks.

The Glendalough Valley

Glendalough, pronounced "glen-da-lock", situated in the heart of the Wicklow Mountains, is an enchanting valley reached from the village of Laragh at the the end of a winding road through Wicklow Gap. Nestled in the valley are two lakes, after which Glendalough is named, and a ruined 6th-century monastic settlement surrounded by pine forests. Founded by St Kevin, who apparently slept in a tree before the monastery was built, Glendalough in its heyday housed 5,000 monks, and its cathe-

Country air and ruddy health in the Wicklow Mountains.

dral, now in ruins, was the second largest in Ireland.

The remains of several churches are scattered around the valley, but the most dominant and best preserved architectural survivor is the round tower with its conical roof that soars $33^1/_2$ m (110 ft) above the graveyard. "Anti-Viking towers", they were fittingly nicknamed by the writer Thomas Keneally, for when the Vikings attacked the monasteries to plunder their treasuries, the monks would scamper up a ladder to the stone safety of the tower, dragging their ladder after them. Saint Kevin, a kinsman of the Leinster Kings of Tara, is immortalized by **St Kevin's Cross**, a stone high cross in the graveyard which incorporates both a crucifix and the circular symbol of the sun, apparently to bring more pagans into the fold by combining the symbolism of both the old and new orders. At **Kevin's Bed**, an austere cave high above the lake, the saint is said to have been propositioned by a lustful woman. His anchorite training prompted him to hurl her into the rapids below, prompting this cynicism from a contemporary writer: "What a destiny it is to love or desire one whose life belongs to the Most High God!"

The power of a name is shown in even more unlikely titles like the St Kevin's Bus Service which runs to Glendalough from Dublin's St Stephen's Green. Busloads of tourists, backpackers, and daytrippers converge on the valley during the summer season, when the tourist office shows films of monastic life and guides visitors around the ruins.

However, despite the commercialism Glendalough still manages to preserve a marvellous air of tranquility. Superlatives come easily to the tongue as Thackeray himself enthused, "I do not know if there is any tune about Glendalough

Lough Tay, one of the many gems of the Wicklow Mountains.

but, if there be, it must be the most delicate, fantastic, fairy melody that ever was played".

Hostel accommodations are available at Glendalough, but the neighboring village of **Laragh** has a host of bed-and-breakfasts, a rustic hostel and snug little tearooms.

Wicklow

Wicklow, the county's largest town of the same name, overlooking the Irish Sea, is a good base for exploring the coast and the hills. The tourist office is in **Market Square** which still hosts fruit and vegetable stalls. At the Grand Hotel end of Main Street, is a 13th-century **abbey and friary**, and nearby Market Square is the unremarkable ruins of **Black Castle**, although the scenic seascapes and views of the neighboring countryside from the castle are superb.

A path leads around the promontory to a lighthouse, and according to local legend this cliffside trail was where the supernatural figure of a young woman appeared during the fierce storms in 1922 when houses and ships were wrecked by the mountainous seas whipped up by the gale-force easterly winds.

So the story goes, she was the spirit of the west wind who ran back and forth along the path until she appeased the east wind by sacrificing herself from the cliffs.

A cheerful welcome is always provided by the many bed-and-breakfast homestays.

Every year on 24th October, in commemoration of this strange event, Wicklow hosts the **Festival of the Winds** to honor the girl who saved their town from the sea's destruction.

Beaches & Ravines

From Wicklow, the coast is studded with sandy beaches, like well-known **Brittas Bay** famed for its giant crabs, all the way to **Arklow**, 24 km (15 miles) distant. Northwest of Arklow where the Avonmore and Avonbeg rivers meet, is the **Vale of Avoca** which is believed to have inspired the Thomas Moore song *The Meeting of the Waters*. Further north, surrounded by the Avondale Forest Park is the birthplace of Ireland's greatest nationalist politician, Charles Stewart Parnell. Now a museum, the Georgian "great house" of **Avondale** commemorates its misunderstood and heroic former occupant.

Continue north and take the Roundwood road from Ashford to the **Devil's Glen**, a steep gorge where the River Vartry plunges 30 m (100 ft) into the chasm. Hiking trails meander about the surrounding rugged ravine country, and there is a hostel at the glen where travelers can put up for the night. For those who like a taste of adventure, the locally-based **Tiglin Adventure Center** runs weekend courses on kayaking, canoeing, mountaineering and rock-climbing.

Wexford to Cork

Hurtling down the motorway between Dublin and Cork is the most popular route for tourists still caught up in a frantic "do a place" pace. However, for a relaxing alternative that is far more in keeping with the Irishness of travel, why not take the coastal route which winds past sandy bays and verdant fields, through the historic Danish ports of Wexford and Waterford, past Ardmore with its round tower and Youghal with its clock tower, and other innumerable towns and villages all with their own specialities and quirks, to Cork, the republic's bustling rival to Dublin.

Blarney Castle, built in 1446, is famous for its Blarney Stone.

The Villain of Ferns

From Arklow, on the Wicklow coast, head south to Gorey in County Wexford, then forsaking the coastal road take the main road to the quaint village of **Ferns**, its size belying the fact that it was once the capital of Leinster. Named from the Irish

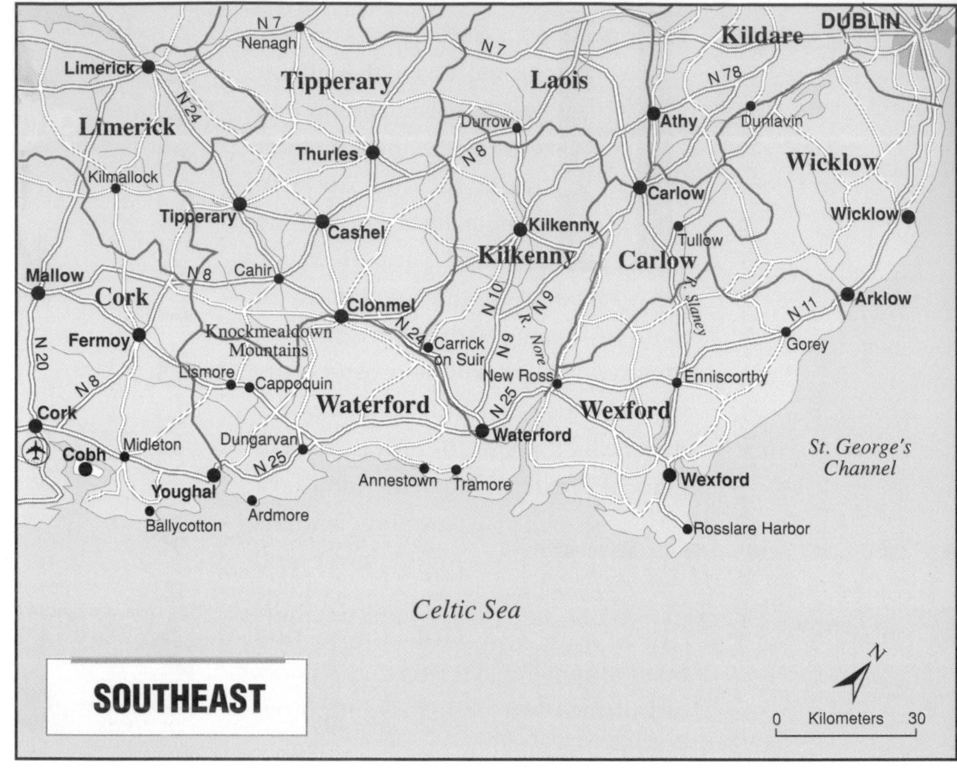

Fearna, meaning "a place abounding with alder trees", Ferns boasts an impressive 12th-century **castle** with circular towers, but it is better known for its landlord, the notorious Dermot (Diarmait) MacMurrough than for its architecture. He was the villain responsible for bringing the Normans to Ireland, a crime that has tainted his name ever since.

It all came about in 1166 when a dynastic struggle saw MacMurrough lose his throne, so he went to England, rounded up some Norman barons and came back with them, clad in armor, to successfully reconquer Ferns, and from there to take Wexford and Waterford and change the face of Ireland forever. MacMurrough got his come-uppance, though, at his first wedding anniversary when his high-born wife, Chelsea of the Willows, whom he had kidnapped from England, drugged his wine and burnt him to death with a log from the fireplace. The splendid circular chapel in the abbey was apparently built by his wife in atonement for her crime, although in popular opinion she was well justified to put one of Ireland's most famous traitors to the torch.

The Martyrs of Enniscorthy

Picturesque **Enniscorthy**, 13 km (8 miles) further south, straddles the River Slaney,

A restaurant in Wexford town, honoring Commodore John Barry, the father of the US Navy.

its historic center huddled around the 13th-century **Enniscorthy Castle**. As though to make amends for MacMurrough's mistakes, the men of County Wexford, and particularly of Enniscorthy, are now best known for their heroic role in the uprising against the British in 1798. The rebels took Enniscorthy, then set it on fire before setting up camp on nearby **Vinegar Hill**. The historical writer, Robert Kee, describes it as not really being a camp but "a place where thousands of men and women who had been terrorized by the troops in the countryside round about gathered in confusion to tell each other their sufferings and clamor for revenge". At the camp there was a picnic atmosphere, rustled cattle were cooked up "in great copper pans", musicians were playing on instruments which had been looted from the Protestant houses, and bedding down on Wilton carpets, also part of the loot. The rebels held off as long as they could until they joined the long list of Irish martyrs in the bloodbath known as the Battle of Vinegar Hill.

Over two centuries later, the men of Enniscorthy still showed their mettle against British rule by joining the Fenian Easter Rising of 1916, and taking over the town for a week before they too were routed. The 1798 Uprising and other significant events in County Wexford's history are well documented at the museum inside the castle which also houses the tourist office. Enniscorthy is not all musty history, however, for every year in the first week of July, the town erupts for the fun and frolic of the **Strawberry Fair**, when the fair maidens of the county vie for the title of Strawberry Queen.

Wexford

Wexford town, shows its history in its geography and its architecture. Named "the harbor of the mud flats" by the Vikings, Wexford was the first town to fall to the Normans when they landed at nearby Baginbun and marched on the town. According to a firsthand account by Gerald the Welshman, who accompanied the Normans, when the townsfolk "saw the lines of troops drawn up in an unfamiliar manner, and the squadron of knights resplendent with breastplates, swords and helmets gleaming" they burned the suburbs and withdrew inside Wexford's fortified walls. Although the population resisted the might of the Normans prevailed as the popular ditty goes:

> At the creek of Baginbun
> Ireland was lost and won.

Wexford has certainly had its share of woes as it also holds the dubious honor of being the town most massacred by Oliver Cromwell, whose soldiers ran amok, killing at least 2,000 inhabitants in his 1649 rampage. Little wonder that the Wexfordians reacted as they did during the 1798 rebellion.

Jonathan Swift's sarcastic remark that in Wexford "they say the cocks and dogs go to sleep at noon, and so do the people" may have rung true in the 18th century, but not today, as the town bustles with locals and tourists and is filled to the rafters every October and November when Wexford hosts its **Festival of Opera**, a major European musical gathering renowned for its eclectic and unusual operatic offerings. At the quay, where a statue immortalizes John Barry, native Wexfordian and the founding father of the US Navy, fishing boats bob at anchor, and narrow streets, a Norman heritage, wend their way up to Wexford's town center.

On North Main Street, a statue depicting one of the peasant rebels of the 1798 Uprising, marks the **Bull Ring** where the medieval amusement of bull-baiting used to be staged. At the **Selskar Abbey**, a staircase leads to the top of a tower offering scenic views of the town and harbor. During Lent in 1172, England's King Henry II stayed at the abbey in atonement for killing Thomas à Beckett. **Westgate**, nearby, is the only original tower left of the Norman fortifications.

Wexford Environs

Travelers fond of theme parks and most children will enjoy the **Irish National Heritage Park** at **Ferrycarrig**, 3 km (2 miles) north of Wexford town, where replicas of Bronze Age graves, dolmens and a full-size Norse ship, trace the history of Ireland from the Stone Age to the Vikings. Adult admission is IR£2 and the park is open daily from March to November.

Six km (4 miles) south of Wexford is **Johnstown Castle**, a 19th-century Gothic mansion, renowned for its gardens which are especially delightful during autumn when the deciduous trees are a riot of reds and golds. The adjacent **Irish Agricultural Museum**, only open

19th-century Johnstown Castle, renowned for its delightful gardens.

in summer, shows Irish farming through the ages.

Wexford is a popular destination for travelers arriving from England and France as ferries ply to both countries daily from **Rosslare Harbor** connected to town by the N25. Further south is **Our Lady's Island** where pilgrims come every year from mid-August to early September, in memory of a supernatural sighting of the Madonna, in years past. More tangible sights on the island include a ruined **Augustinian Priory** and a **leaning tower** which locals maintain leans even more than its famous Italian counterpart. Further southwest at **Kilmore Quay**, boats ply, weather permitting, to the uninhabited **Saltee Islands**, the republic's largest bird sanctuary, home to thousands of puffins and razorbills.

Continuing westwards around the coast two historic promontories jut into the Irish Sea: **Baginbun Head**, where ramparts built during the 12th-century Norman invasion can still be seen and **Hook Head** where Cromwell deliberated as to whether to take Waterford by Hook Head, or from Crook, on the other side of the bay, unwittingly coining the phrase "by hook or by crook".

Heading north on the Waterford road, stop over at **Dunbrody Abbey**, a ruined Cistercian abbey built in 1190. Further north, outside of New Ross, is the **John F Kennedy Park**, an arboretum of thousands of trees, in memorium to this US president whose ancestors came from nearby Dunganstown.

Waterford, known throughout the world for its exquisitely cut crystalware.

Waterford City

Waterford city, capital of the county of the same name, takes its name from the Viking for "west fiord" but it is also known by its old Irish name of Port Lairge. Both a historical and industrial city, the latter is provided for by Waterford's most famous attraction and export, Waterford crystal.

The best views of the city can be had at the top of **Reginald's Tower**, which almost 1,000-years-old, was named after the Viking King Sigtrig's son Ragnvald. The tower is located at the end of the quay. Nearby is the 9th-century **St Olaf's Church**, another tribute to the city's antiquity although most of it dates from Norman times and an 18th-century restoration.

Viking artifacts unearthed during recent excavations are on display at the nearby **Waterford Heritage Center**. Much of the old city is built on Norman foundations recalling the days when Dermott MacMurrough gave his daughter Princess Aoife of Leinster, as a bride to Strongbow, after he had conquered Waterford. This event, seen as giving Ireland away to a foreign power, was depicted as a symbol of the country's oppression, all the way to the present century.

On the Cork road, 3 km (2 miles) from town, is the **Waterford Crystal Factory**, the city's biggest tourist attraction. Fascinating tours which show how

The Waterford Crystal showrooms.

crystal is produced from the raw glass to the finished glittering, polished product, are run five times daily and buses run direct from the city to the factory.

Founded in 1753 by the Penrose brothers, the company became famous for its crystal glassware but was forced to close down in 1851 due to high taxes on the imported raw products. The nationalist, Joseph McGrath restarted the factory in 1950, and today the world-renowned company employs 3,000 people. The prices of products sold in the factory's gallery may astound you, but a quality item can take weeks to cut with its distinctive honeycomb and diamond pattern. The city has throughout history had strong connections with Europe and has a prospering container port.

The Road to Cork

Due south of Waterford is the resort town of **Tramore**, its Irish name meaning "great beach" being totally justified. Past pretty Annestown and Dungarvan, take a detour to **Ring**, an isolated Irish-speaking area far from the other Gaeltacht areas, where the pubs are enlivened by traditional musicians.

At **Ardmore**, southwest of Ring, is Ireland's most perfect **Round Tower** said to have been built in a single night by St Declan who arrived here in AD 402, preceding even St Patrick, to convert his fellow countrymen to the true faith. Nineteenth-century excavations in the base of the $29^1/_2$ m (97 ft) high tower unearthed two skeletons which had been covered for centuries under layers of stone and cement.

Colorful **Youghal**, a seaport on the road to Cork, makes for an excellent overnight stay. Interesting old shops crowd its narrow lanes, a long strand of sandy beach makes for pleasant bathing and strolling, the quay is the jump-off spot for exciting shark-fishing excursions and straddling the main street is Youghal's most famous landmark, a remarkable **clocktower** built in 1771, which is still wide enough to accommodate the town's traffic. Every summer the town hosts the **Walter Raleigh Spud Festival** with dancing, cooking contests and road-racing among the festive events. Sir Walter, sent to Youghal in 1579 to assist in the subjugation of a

The Mohan Falls Valley, County Waterford, beautiful walking territory.

rebellious lord, was rewarded rather lavishly, even by Elizabethan standards, with a tract of 18,000 hectares (45,000 acres) of confiscated land.

Known as **Myrtle Grove**, Raleigh's oak-panelled residence, recently opened to the public, was where, according to legend, he planted Ireland's first potato. As if this was not historic enough, Raleigh is also credited with smoking the first tobacco ever brought to Ireland, under a yew tree in the arbor, one of the same trees that the town, meaning "yew wood", was named after. In more recent history, Youghal, pronounced "yawl", was used as the backdrop for John Huston's film version of *Moby Dick*.

Other interesting diversions on the road to Cork, include the fishing village of **Ballycotton** which has excellent sandy beaches; **Cloyne**, a typical County Cork town, where a statue by the hurling field immortalizes the great hurler, Christy Ring; and **Cobh**, overlooking Cork harbor, where so many emigrants, willing and unwilling, took off for greener pastures never again to see the emerald fields of their native land. Splendidly surmounting the port is **St Colman's Cathedral**, a magnificent testimony to Pugin's design and the Gothic revival, and probably the last building that the emigrants saw of Ireland as their boats left Cork harbor. Arrayed across the harbor front, in the shadow of the cathedral, are pastel-hued guesthouses with attic windows all gazing seawards, the last windows of Ireland.

Cork

Cork, Ireland's second biggest city with a population of 140,000 has a decidedly contemporary, and even continental air, the latter probably influenced by its proximity to France; daily ferries ply to Roscoff and weekly to Le Havre, as well as a boat service to Wales. Named from the Irish, *Corcach* meaning "marsh", Cork grew up around a monastery built on the edge of a marsh by St Finbarr in the 6th century. Waterways still dominate the city center, which the natives call "the flaat o' deh city", situated on an island in the River Lee. The poet Edmund Spenser described it as:

Who knows what you might find in the intriguing second-hand shops along the back-streets of Cork.

Kissing the Blarney Stone

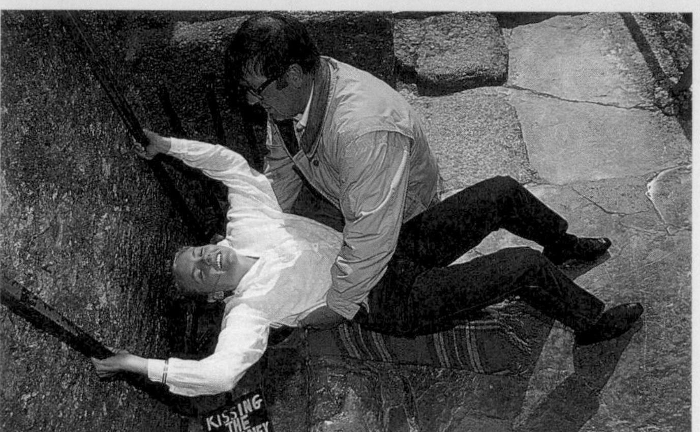

Kissing the Blarney Stone is supposed to endow eloquence, so the legend goes.

"I can hardly wait to see Mick do that!" exclaimed the raucous-voiced, obese tourist, while looking at snapshots of visitors bending backwards in order to kiss the **Blarney Stone**. Mick, was just as overweight as his wife, but they did not intend to miss this unique opportunity to acquire the art of blarney, the biggest attraction of Blarney Castle.

The *Oxford Dictionary* defines "blarney" as "empty or flattering talk", adding in parenthesis that the expression originates from Blarney, a castle in Cork. Believe me, if you spend any time there listening to the nonsensical talk of tourists and guides alike it is not hard to understand that it was here that the saying originated. Even trying to sift through the myths and legends as to how the Blarney Stone legend began is difficult enough. There are two rival tales which share top billing. The first is that Queen Elizabeth I apparently annoyed by the Lord of Blarney's "fair words and soft speech" coined the phrase, and the second is that the stone was given as a gift to the King of Munster by a witch he had saved from drowning. And it was she who first mentioned that anyone who kissed the stone would be granted eloquence thereafter.

Blarney Castle

Probably the first thing that strikes visitors to **Blarney** (a 20-minute bus ride from Cork), after parting with the admission fee and maneuvering past the tour buses and souvenir stalls, is that the castle itself is far from grandiose, particularly if you have done the rounds of far more monumental edifices like Kilkenny Castle. But then most visitors come for the stone and the blarney, and not for the building. Cormac MacCarthy, the High King of Munster, built the present structure in 1446 but it was the third castle to be constructed on the site, replacing

The spreading Lee, that, like an
island fayre,
Encloseth Cork with his divided
flood.

Indeed, the city still retains a watery feel for you can walk its length without leaving the river. Wander down the spacious **Grand Parade** to the River Lee, where stone bridges arch across its waters, and the spires of **St Finbarr's Monastery** reflect in its waters. Stroll along Western Road to **Cork University**, a 19th-century Gothic revival of stone corridors and spacious lawns, where willows drape over the river. Some

the wooden one from the 10th century and a stone structure from the 13th century.

In spring before the crowds become asphyxiating, when the blossoms are just coming out, the walk up to the keep across a bubbling brook and past splashes of purple heather and yellow daffodils, is quite enchanting; another of Ireland's many garden greats. Walk through these extensive gardens which obscure the castle from the village, to the base of the castle where the search begins. You will probably spend some time looking for the famous stone if you do not see the sign which points upwards. Follow the sign and the other tourists up a spiral staircase which winds up the keep, past stuffy little rooms and miniature lookouts to the roof where the esteemed stone is situated.

A Dizzy Kiss

Reaching the castle's battlements a giddy sight will be revealed to you. A magificent view across the green lawns and surrounding countryside stretches before you, but below is a sheer drop. You may be horrified to discover that it is in this precarious place that the stone is situated. This is indeed not a task for sufferers of vertigo.

In order to kiss the stone and thus acquire the gift of Blarney, you have to lie back head-first with your head slightly lower than your body, a rather nauseous feeling, and press your lips against the stone. An assistant is on hand to keep you steady through the ordeal.

Although as advertised, "There is no charge for kissing the Blarney Stone", the assistant is accompanied by an opportune photographer who swoops down like a vulture upon the tourist prey. The tourist attraction suffered somewhat with the world-wide AIDS epidemic, but such speculations have been quashed by scientists; you cannot catch AIDS from the Blarney. The legend lives on.

The ruins of Blarney Castle seen from the castle's giddy heights.

of the original thoroughfares like **St Patrick's Street** were once rivers, hence their winding nature; the **South Mall** was built over a canal.

If you do happen to be in Cork during a predictably wet winter, or during the time of the equinoctial gales, it is easy to be reminded as Sean O'Faolain is in his turn-of-the-century *An Irish Journey* that "Cork is a seaport and the sea at our door". In those days the "floods rise, the streets are sometimes submerged, and the winds from the ocean tear into the cup of the valley of the town". But, then, just as quickly, the sky will clear, the clouds roll away and Cork is re-

An aerial view of Cork City.

vealed at its best, particularly when a late afternoon sun paints a golden wash over the rows of houses that rise in tiers in the hills above the north of the city.

Cork Culture

The Vikings and the Normans all found Cork a great place to trade and during the 17th century European merchants flocked here to trade in salted fish, meat and butter. Not much of Cork's ancient history survives, there are a few token historical sights like the tower of **St Anne's Shandon market** with its three-tiered red-and-white tower, and the **Cathedral of St Finne Barre** with its Gothic gargoyles and griffins, the cathedral contains a canon ball which was fired in the seige of the city in 1690 and which was lodged in the old church on the same site. The charm of Cork lies however, more in its culture and ambiance than in mere tangible monuments.

Opposite St Anne's is the **Shandon Craft Center** where artisans work on and display crystal-ware, ceramics and weavings. At Emmet Place, in the city center, is the **Crawford Municipal Gallery** with its fine collection of Irish art, and on Tobin Street, off South Main Street, the **Triskel Arts Center** displays contemporary artworks and has an interesting bookshop as well as an auditorium. Check the tourist office for what's happening at the **Opera House**, which apart from operas stages drama, jazz,

Colorful residences in Cork town.

and variety shows. Other big events include the **International Film Festival** and the **Guinness Jazz Festival**, both in autumn, and the summertime **International Folk Dance Festival** held at nearby Cobh.

Accommodations & Ambiance

Accommodations are no problem in Cork, except perhaps in the peak season. **Western Road**, which runs parallel to the Lee and the university, is lined with a rainbow-colored assortment of bed-and-breakfasts and guesthouses, all seemingly engaged in a competition as to who has the prettiest facade. There are primroses and daffodils in window boxes, net curtains fluttering in bay-windows, at Carbery House, Antoine, Killarney, St Kilda, and dozens of other look-alikes. Down a side lane, where graffiti announces that "Pink Floyd Lives", evidence of Cork's youthful approach to life is **Fitzgerald Park**, a serene garden with statuary, a little lake, and beds of fragrant hyacinths.

The **Cork Public Museum**, a square Georgian affair, offers rooms full of Cork history. Outside the museum is however more inviting where old men in woollen caps and overcoats sit chatting and taking in the spring sunshine on the museum garden's benches. Somehow, the scene seems to sum up the aura that is Cork, better than any dry historical site.

The Golden Vale

South of Dublin, the inland route across County Kildare, County Kilkenny and into County Tipperary, is known as the Golden Vale. Named after the lush verdure of its countryside, this area was throughout history a great drawcard for invading forces as a place where they could graze their horses and cattle throughout the year. This is the area where Ireland is perhaps at its greenest best.

The Rock of Cashel was a pagan site before being sanctified by St Patrick.

Geologically the area is a rolling limestone plain dotted with rivers, lakes and bogsides and covered with a deep green grass. Not surprisingly sheep farming is a mainstay of the economy, but it is the area's horses that are of international repute. In the Golden Vale, nothing is sacred when it comes to horse-racing. As you travel through the countryside in white-fenced riding schools furry ponies graze in shockingly green pastures. Just outside of Kildare town **The Curragh** has been a horse-

A local man, leaning on a post-box and watching life go by.

racing venue since Celtic times and is still the place where all the nation's greatest horse-races are held including the Irish Derby. Also near to Kildare town is the **National Stud**, where all the nation's top stallions are housed.

Kildare to Kilkenny

A bus Eireann leaves from Busarus, Dublin, traveling the route of the Golden Vale to Kilkenny; whether you choose this bus or travel by car it will be a memorable journey. **Kildare town** (there are frequent buses from Dublin) was once the site of a monastery founded by St Brigid; the **Cathedral of St Brigid** still stands in her memory. Building work on the cathedral began in 1229. At pretty **Naas**, 32 km (20 miles) from Dublin, where a Gothic steeple dominates the town and where traditional shop fronts house expensive establishments like Benetton, it is obvious that the horse-flesh business is taking good care of the economy of this town.

The N9 road continues from Naas to **Kilcullen**, a charming village situated over a bubbling stream. Take the N78 road from Kilcullen past umber-colored fields that are raked as neat as a Japanese rock-garden and stone "great houses" flanked by yellow gorse and daffodils, all the way to Athy.

In **Athy town** a fine narrow main street flanked with Georgian-style shops winds down to a 16th-century tower beside the River Barrow. Continue on bus 56 or 83 or drive on the N78 towards Kilkenny stopping by at **Castlecomber**, a pretty town planned and built to a classical design in 1636.

Kilkenny City

Billed by tourist brochures as "Ireland's Medieval Capital" or "Marble City" because the limestone with which the city is built resembles polished marble, Kilkenny does not disappoint. From the dining-room windows of Fennelly's Guest House in Parliament Street, one can look across the road to the somber 18th-century **Courthouse** made of the famed "marbley" limestone. Kilkenny is a medieval town, much more so than Dublin which is of course such a Georgian city and even more so than Galway. This impression is not only fortified by so many stone buildings dating from those times, but by the fact that the Middle Ages was Kilkenny's greatest era. Although it was known as the Kingdom of Ossory from the 2nd century, Kilkenny really came into prominence with the arrival of the Anglo-Normans at the end of the 12th century. Accompanying King Henry II in 1171 came Theobald Fitzwalter, later to be given the title of Chief Butler in Ireland, and the first of a long line of Butlers who were to rule Kilkenny from their Wagnerian castle for centuries.

Although it is really a town, locals still refer to Kilkenny as a city in honor of its illustrious past when it was at the fulcrum of Anglo-Irish politics and parliament as can be seen from the *Statues of Kilkenny*, a system of apartheid-type laws that were passed in 1366, prohibiting Anglo-Normans from dressing, talking and marrying Irish. However, by the time the laws arrived there had been so much inter-marrying that they were considered farcical. When the Great Rebellion broke out in 1641, the Old Irish and the "old foreigners" (the Anglo-Normans) of Kilkenny formed the Confederation of Kilkenny, and for eight years the city acted as the capital of a united, cohesive Ireland, "the impossible dream", until it was killed by the reality of Cromwell.

Kilkenny City by the River Nore is a maze of medieval streets and lanes linked at both ends by the two great bastions of power, the castle complex and the monastic complex. Opposite the courthouse is the equally somber **Rothe House**, once a Tudor merchant's residence and now the museum, library, and genealogical center of the local archeological society. All along this busy main street, between the gray-stone antiquities are quaint pastel-colored shops and cafés. Also on the main street is the 13th-century St Mary's church which is now the **Church of Ireland Parish Hall** and the ***Tholsel*** (City Hall) built in 1761. Off the main street wander down Butter Slip into St Kieran's Street to **Kyteler's Inn** which has faithfully watered Kilkenny Town since 1324. The Inn's former proprietress and namesake, Dame Alice Kyteler, fled the country when she was charged with witchcraft and heresy leaving her maidservant Petronilla to be burnt at the stake.

Kilkenny's Irishtown

The castle is Kilkenny's high point so it is probably best to reserve this sight until last and tour Irishtown first. The area is called Irishtown because it was here that the native inhabitants lived during the Anglo-Norman heyday when apartheid denied them residence within the castle walls.

At the bottom of the town, beside the river, is **St Francis Abbey** in the grounds of **Smithwick's Brewery**, a unique combination of the Irishmans' love of liquor and religion. The brewery, built on the site of a 12th-century Franciscan monastery runs a tour through its modern factory which John Smithwick founded in 1710, and the ruined abbey where according to the brewery brochure "those holy men of yester-year allowed themselves the distraction of brewing a light ale".

Treasures of Kilkenny Church.

Climb the walled streets up the hill for the gray and forboding **St Canice's Cathedral**, dominated by its 31-m (101-ft) round tower which dates from the 10th century. Sacked by Cromwell who stabled his horses inside, the cathedral is named after the saint who built a monastery on this site 14 centuries ago. Cainneach, whose name was anglicized to Canice but is pronounced "Kenny", is not only immortalized at the cathedral but his name is the title of the city and county as Kilkenny means "the church of Saint Canice's". Another famed religious seat is the 13th-century Dominican **Black Abbey** with its marvellous stained-glass windows where eight friars perished during the Black Death of 1348. Friar Clyn ended his own testimony, "I leave parchment to carry out the work if perchance any man survives...", and a different hand recorded his death.

Kilkenny Castle

One of Ireland's most splendid feudal edifices, **Kilkenny Castle**, dominates the defensive end of town overlooking its natural moat, the River Nore. The castle grounds which have been recently restored, involve a woodland walk, a lake and formal terraced gardens. In the woods huge old trees are swathed in ivy and daffodils burst into bloom at their feet.

Inside the castle which was the stronghold of the Butler family from the 14th century until recently, walk past Gobelin tapestries and smaller rooms to the castle's highlight, the Long Gallery. The gallery is lit by a huge skylight which runs the length of the room. The ceiling beams are fantastically painted with medieval maidens and heraldic designs and the roof struts are carved with the heads of mythological creatures. The walls are bedecked with more huge tapestries and one entire wall is given up to 43 portraits of the Butler family, from the late 17th century when the Butler Duke of Ormond was the Viceroy of Ireland up till 1935 when the last Butler left for America. When the family emigrated all the household contents were auctioned and the paintings and family heirlooms were scattered all over the world. The castle was left empty for 30 years, then when the sixth Marquis returned in 1967 he gave the castle to the city for IR£50. Since then the city has been trying to trace the castle's lost contents and buy them back to restore them to their true home.

Kilkenny Castle, one of Ireland's most splendid feudal edifices.

The last Marquis and his wife who lived in the castle immortalized in oils, were apparently big spenders and lived it up until their fortune was finished. The present Marquis who lives in Chicago is a retired librarian in his 90s who was born in England—the Marquis returns every three years for the Butler reunion but when he dies he will probably be buried here at the castle.

Opposite the castle is the renowned **Kilkenny Design Center** where a show-

The Rock of Cashel

Intricate carvings adorn the inside of the Round Tower of Cashel.

Caiseal, the Irish name for Cashel, means "a bulwark", and what an apt description it is indeed for this citadel-topped hill which rises 91 m (300 ft) above the farmlands of the Golden Vale. Commanding an unparalleled defensive situation, the Rock of Cashel is often known as St Patrick's Rock, after Ireland's patron saint who once preached here. The rock was an important fortress from many centuries ago. Conall Corc, founder of the kingship of Cashel in the 4th century, was a descendant of the semi-legendary Eoghan who gave his name to the royal seat of the Eoghanacht who ruled over southern Ireland as the Kings of Munster, like the O' Neills of Tara did over the north. Not until the 9th century did the Eoghanacht acknowledge the supremacy of Tara, and even after the royals were ousted by the Dal Cais in the 10th century, Brian Boru and his clan were still calling themselves the Kings of Cashel.

King Cormac MacCarthaigh Chapel

The **Round Tower**, the Rock's highest (28 m/ 92 ft) and most antiquated edifice, was built around the turn of the 12th century when Muircheartach O'Briain handed the fortress to the church, a cunning move as by doing so he effectively deprived his foes, the Eoghanacht, of their traditional kingly base. Three decades later, King Cormac MacCarthaigh built the **chapel** that still bears his name.

Features like the tympana carved with beasts over the doorways, the twin towers and the arcading were previously unknown in Irish church architecture and historians point out that this shows both Norman and Germanic influences, as do the names of two of the monk-carpenters, Conrad and William, who are listed in the annals.

Beautifully designed, the chapel was far in advance of its time. The chancel arch has human heads carved into it and the entire vaulted arch was once brilliantly colored in white, yellow, deep red and blue, of which small traces still remain. Originally found near the north of the cathedral, a splendid carved sarcophagus, dating from the same era and often regarded as that of King Cormac, is now preserved inside his chapel.

St Patrick's Old Cathedral

Although other buildings preceded it, the

room tempts visitors with outstanding silverware, ceramics, woollen and linen wares. In the old castle stables at the back is the government-backed **Crescent Studios** where many of the arts and crafts are produced.

present cathedral with its 12 m (39 ft) high walls, was built in the 13th century possibly by Archbishop MacCeallaigh who founded the town's Dominican Friary in 1243. Later additions like the transepts and the central tower are attributed to Archbishop MacCearbhaill, the founder of Hore Abbey, and William Fitzjohn who walled Cashel town around 1317. The Hall of the Vicars Choral and the castle which was the archiepiscopal residence were probably built by Risteard O'Eidhin who held the See from 1406-40.

Legend has it that Gerald, the Earl of Kildare, burned the cathedral at the end of the 15th century and by way of explanation to King Henry VII he said that he put it to the torch as he thought the archbishop was inside it. Historians, these days, though, cite the lack of burnmarks on the limestone as proof that this could have been a tall story, or at the best a very minor fire.

In the early 16th century the Fitzgerald and the Butler clans both had their coats of arms carved on the castle walls as family members held the bishopry from 1504-25. After the Reformation the notorious Miler MacGrath held the See until he died at the ripe old age of 100 and was buried in the cathedral wall where the tombstone still bears the epitaph composed by him:

The Ode of Miler Magrath, Archbishop
of Cashel, to the passer by:
Patrick, the Glory of our Isle and Gown,
First sat a Bishop in the See of Down,
I wish that I succeeding him in place
As Bishop, had an equal share of Grace,
I serv'd thee England, fifty years in Jars
and pleased thy Princes in the midst of Wars;
Here where I'm placed I'm not; and thus the
case is,
I'm not in both, yet am in both the Places.
1621.

He that judgeth me is the Lord,
Let him who stands, take care lest he fall.

Poignant Magnificence

The Rock was witness to its share of tragedies, not least, during the uprisings of 1647 when 20 men of the cloth burnt to death in the castle vault when Inchiquin's soldiery stormed the citadel. When the enemy had advanced upon the town the people fled to the Rock where they were slaughtered by the hundreds. After this, although the cathedral remained in use until well into the 18th century, the buildings of the Rock began to gradually decay despite repairs in the mid-17th century. The death knell, though, came in 1748 when the title of Cathedral was granted to **St John's Church** in Cashel town, effectively ending the reign of St Patrick's upon the Rock.

The ruined and roofless cathedral is graphically depicted in an etching from Bartlett's *Scenery and Antiquities of Ireland* dated 1842. But there is a certain splendor and a haunting melancholic mood in the artist's impression which gives a far more powerful impression of the Rock than any modern-day photograph can hope to convey. Extensive restoration works have been carried out from the 1860s, and in 1975 the Hall of the Vicars Choral was signalled for an overhaul as Ireland's part in the European Architectural Heritage Year. Even up till the present day, scaffolding still shows that the revamp of the Rock is far from finished.

In the high season, tourists swarm over the ancient citadel, its base is packed with tour buses, the entire complex glows under its nightly spotlighting, but on a cold March day, under a sullen sky, with few visitors, the Rock looks almost as enticing as it does in that old etching, unrestored and uncommercial, and somehow much more authentic.

Southeast of Kilkenny town is **Jerpoint Abbey**, the ruins of a 12th-century Cistercian monastery near Thomas-town on the River Nore. The ruins are some of the finest in Ireland and they are enlivened by an interest-

Kilkenny Castle's owners grace the walls of its galleries.

ing visitor's center. Nearby on the Castlecomer road north of Kilkenny, are the unique limestone formations of the **Dunmore Caves.**

The Kilkenny to Cashel Road

Take the N76 road out of Kilkenny towards Clonmel. Along the way are yet more green fields and a beautiful wooded pass in the Comeragh Mountains. From the outskirts of Clonmel take the N24 to **Carrick-on-Suir** a town dominated by the ubiquitous church steeple, and where, in the riverside park a Madonna shrine is ringed with purple and yellow pansies.

The town is surrounded by green square fields edged with hedgerows and the ridges of the hills are covered in pines. Drive past the neat, thatched-roof, white-walled showroom of **Tipperary Crystal** and a bright-blue pub called "Ikes and Mikes" welcomes you for refreshment. The town's straight-faced old Georgian "big houses" are beautified by the surrounding scenery.

Travel westwards out of Carrick-on-Suir this time into **Clonmel town**. Clonmel is Tipperary's largest town and is an excellent base for exploring the area with a number of interesting things to see.

The **Museum and Art Gallery** has a large collection of local works and nearby is the 17th-century **Main Guard,** a large garrison house which is being

A colorful presentation in Kilkenny town.

restored. The **Old West Gate** of the city still survives girdling the main street. Other antiquities include the Post Office which is now the excellent **Post House Bookshop**, the perfect place for a browse. **St Mary's Catholic Church** is a 19th-century creation.

The Rock of Cashel

Due west of Clonmel is **Cahir**, another attractive South Tipperary town dominated by a well-preserved Norman castle on the River Suir which surrendered

The well-preserved Norman Castle of Cahir nestles beside the River Suir.

to Oliver Cromwell in 1650. Head due north from here to the famed **Rock of Cashel**, whose rugged citadel is a ubiquitous sight on Irish place-mats and other souvenirs throughout the emerald isle. The reality is no less impressive. As you enter the outskirts of Cashel town The Rock emerges in all its splendor looming out of the fields, a better site or more natural defense one could hardly imagine. This historic hill was a kingly site for centuries before Ireland's patron saint made his celebrated visit here in the 15th century.

At The Rock, there are parking lots for fleets of buses, evidence of the high-season madness that descends on Cashel's famed citadel, but if you wander across the fields to **Hore Abbey** an old Cistercian ruin set in the emerald fields only a half-mile walk away, you will be left to the company of the rooks, half a dozen bleating sheep and the beauty of nature. The last of the Cistercian houses to be built in Ireland during the medieval times, Hore Abbey was founded by monks from Mellifont in 1272.

These days the roofless ruin is flooded in light but for the monks it must have been an austere and gloomy place as the original had but few windows. But the view of St Patrick's Rock with its great walled complex would have been just as splendid, and from this direction it looks like the castle and tower have been formed from the very rock of the hill, so well do they merge

Lovely Hore Abbey, a haven of tranquility.

with their surroundings.

At the Rock of Cashel itself, a splendid vista of the town and the surrounding fields of the Golden Vale opens up before you. Allocate at least half a day to wander around the extensive ruins. The Rock is often known as St Patrick's Rock, after Ireland's patron saint who once preached here. For many centuries before this Cashel was a pagan fortress (see box story p.218) founded by Conall Corc in the 4th century AD.

Highlights of the rock are the 12th-century **Round Tower**, **Cormac's chapel**, the **Cathedral of St Patrick** and the **Hall of the Vicars Choral**. The chapel has a series of fine carvings and its architecture betrays Norman and Germanic influences.

Cashel Town

In Cashel town itself the main street has a very attractive range of traditional shop-fronts. There are a number of craft workshops and a small museum. Capitalizing on such a renowned tourist attraction Cashel is not short of gift shops or accommodations. The **Cashel Palace Hotel** on Chapel Lane, once a palace of the Church of Ireland, is a particularly fine place to stay with its original oak-panelling from the 18th century, the food and drink is also exquisite. The **Diocesan Library** in the Cathedral precincts contains one of Ireland's greatest collections of 16th and 17th-century books.

The Far Southwest

It would be an understatement to say that just about everyone *en route* to Kerry takes the main road from Cork to Killarney leaving Ireland's southern extremity to its lonely splendors. It is not due to a dearth of attractions, quite the opposite, for the region boasts spectacular coastal and mountain scenery, seaside resorts, and historical sites aplenty, but it probably suffers from a lack of tourists because it is merely off the beaten track and is too quiet. However, for a traveler seeking solitude this loneliness is more of an attraction than anything else.

The wild beauty of the gardens at Glengarriff, County Cork.

Kinsale Food & History

A newcomer to **Kinsale** at the height of the season, would however, definitely think the forgoing description of the far south was erroneous as County Cork's most popular seaside town is hardly quiet during the summer months when the population

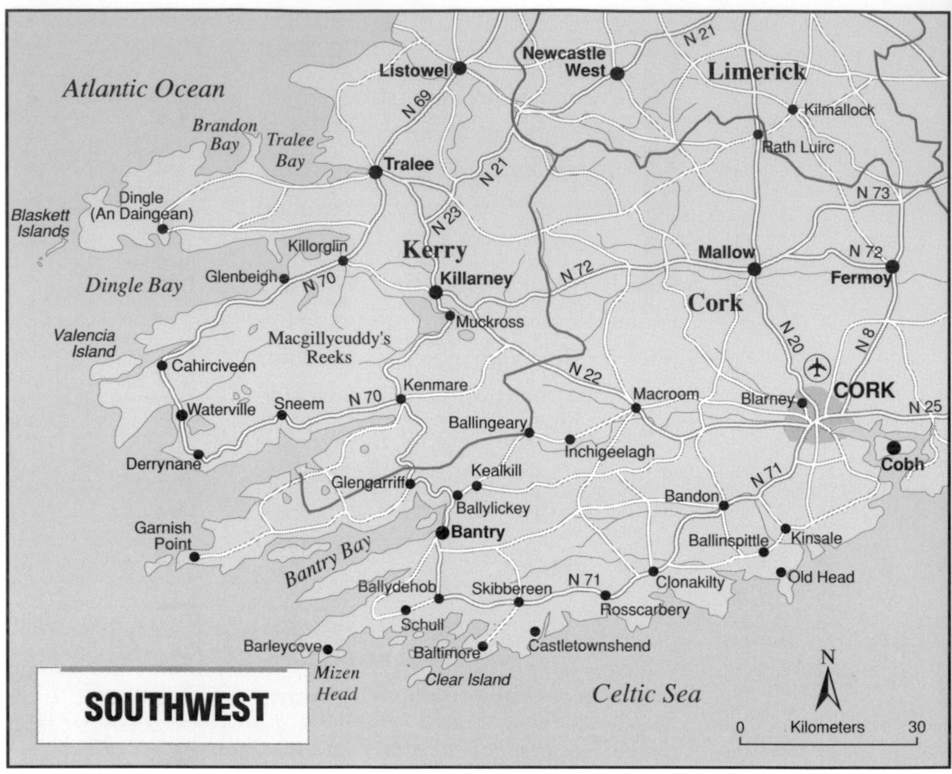

expands sixfold and the town lives up to its reputation as the gourmet food capital of the nation. As a renowned center for deep-sea fishing, fresh seafood is the obvious speciality at Kinsale's famed group of restaurants known as the **Good Food Circle**, and food freaks converge on the town during October for the annual treat of the **Gourmet Festival**.

Food, though, is not what the seaside town was originally famed for, but a historic battle. Kinsale was where the decisive English victory occurred in 1601 which precipitated the "Flight of the Earls", when the cream of Ireland's Gaelic aristocracy fled in exile to the continent, effectively ending the old order. Although, the last of the great Irish chieftains, Hugh O'Neill, whom Queen Elizabeth I had titled Earl of Tyrone, was groomed in Renaissance England he chaffed at the way England was settling Protestants in his native Ulster and together with his neighboring chieftain Hugh O'Donnell they rose in arms against the colonialists.

In September 1601, when a massive fleet of Spanish ships sailed into Kinsale harbor to help with the uprising, Tyrone and O'Donnell marched south to meet with their comrades-in-arms, as did Lord Mountjoy and his British forces who routed the Irish at the Battle of the Yellow Ford near Kinsale. The Spanish did not even get to enter the fray. It was to take another three centu-

The harbor at Kinsale, County Cork's most popular seaside town.

ries before the Irish were to again raise their flag in place of the Union Jack. At **Charles Fort**, on the easterly side of Kinsale Harbor, the remains of ruined Elizabethan fortifications are all that lingers of this historic event. Other historic sites in town include the 12th-century **Church of St Multose**, named after the town's patron saint; **Desmond's Castle**, a symbol of British tyranny; and the 17th-century **Regional Museum** in the Courthouse.

Along the Coast Road

Ballinspittle, southwest from Kinsale on the coast road, came into national prominence in 1985 when at a roadside grotto a statue of the Madonna was seen to be rocking back and forth. Although scientists were sceptical of the claims, the faithful still visit the shrine in the hope that they too will witness a sacred vision.

Continue west to **Timoleague** where St Molaga founded a Franciscan monastery extensive ruins of which still survive. Just outside of town are the **Castle Gardens**, a riot of blooms in spring and summer where travelers can pick their own berry fruits in season. Set in the forest a 20-minute walk from Timoleague, is the budget-priced and amiable **Lettercollum House Hostel** where backpackers can put up in a marvellous Victorian "great house".

Clonakilty, the largest and liveliest town in this part of County Cork, is best known for its nearby beach, **Inchydoney** which boasts the best sands on the coast. Music and mime crowd the town's airways and pavements in August at the annual **Murphy's All-Ireland Busking and Street Entertainment Festival**. One kilometer north of Clonakilty is **Templebryan** where a ruined stone church dates from Celtic times and history buffs might take a look at the downtown regional museum in Western Road.

The real pleasures of West Cork, though, are the simple ones like downing a Guinness in a local pub, feeling the salty breeze on a cliffside walk, or even watching a game of road bowls where traffic takes backseat when a "bahling contest" is in full swing. Along a road near Clonakilty a road sign advising "Slow Village Ahead" had been defaced by a local wit to read "Go Slow or You'll Miss the Village Ahead".

From Clonakilty, travelers can choose either the scenic high-country road which heads north to Enniskean and then west through Dunmanway and the rugged Shehy Mountains to

Bantry, or take the coastal route via Skibbereen.

On the Skibbereen road, 16 km (10 miles) from Clonakilty, is **Rosscarbery**, where visitors can see the medieval remains of a **Benedictine monastery** and the ruins of **Derry House**, the birthplace of Charlotte Payne-Townshend, the heiress, who married George Bernard Shaw in 1898 after nursing him through an illness. Their apparently celibate marriage lasted 45 years until Charlotte's death in 1943. Winner of the 1925 Nobel Prize for Literature, Shaw, visited Derry House in 1905 where he worked on his celebrated *Captain Brassbound's Conversion*, a play about follies masquerading as duty and justice. Derry House burned down in 1921.

Skibbereen & Offshore Islands

Skibbereen, surrounded by magnificent countryside, is the jumping-off place for Ireland's most southerly sights. While "Skibb", as the locals call it, is nothing special, the town does host a "must-see" fair every summer when **Welcome Home Week Festival** metamorphosizes the sleepy town into a riotous hub of merrymaking. If you can not make it to this annual event, Skibbereen also hosts a weekly Friday-afternoon **market** when the local farmers descend upon the town, not as frantic as the festival but just as memorable.

Thirteen kilometers (8 miles) south

A quaint bar in the quiet town of Skibbereen.

is **Baltimore**, a tiny hamlet, once the stronghold of the piratical O'Driscolls whose namesakes still gather every June to elect their clan leader. Artists flock to the wild coastline for the spectacular ocean views particularly from **The Beacon**, a cliffside lighthouse a mile from Baltimore.

For such a small place there is a wealth of history. In the 1920s, local boatmakers constructed the *Saoirse*, the Irish ship to first circumnavigate the globe. In the 17th century Baltimore suffered from the indignity of being raided by an Algerian pirate band who ravaged the town and sold their captives in Africa's white-slave markets. The notorious event is immortalized by a local pub and a bed-and-breakfast

From Baltimore there are many scenic directions to take in the magnificent South.

(B&B) named **The Algiers Inn**.

Ten kilometers (6 miles) out of town is **Lough Hyne**, a peaceful salt-water lake. Baltimore's most popular destination is however, the **Cape Clear** and **Sherkin Islands**. Boats ply to Ireland's most southerly islands from both Baltimore and Schull, further west in the aptly-named Roaringwater Bay.

Cape Clear Island, with its miniscule population of 160, is a cultural oddity as it is one of Ireland's last surviving pockets of Gaelic culture. Irish-language students converge on the island every summer as do ornithologists to study the seabirds from **Cape Clear Bird Observatory**.

Traditional dancing is often held in Cape Clear during the summer and tourists can put up at either the hostel with great seascapes or at a handful of B&B's which offer home-cooked bread or scones to tempt lodgers to stay longer. Sherkin Island, closer to Baltimore, is not quite as incredibly Irish as its Gaeltacht neighbor but much of its native botany has a longer pedigree than that of Ireland's, having vanished from the mainland eons ago. Other attractions include a ruined **Franciscan Friary** and sharing the *craic* (camaraderie) at the local pub.

From **Schull**, a port renowned for its offshore fishing, the coast winds down to the nation's most southerly extremity, **Mizen Head**, where sheer cliffs, often fog-shrouded, signal land's end. Backtracking to Ballydehob, the road to

The spectacular coastline at Bantry Bay, County Cork.

Bantry heads due north through desolate and rugged countryside around **Mt Gabriel** offering superb views of Dunmanus Bay.

Bantry

Bantry, or *Beantraighe* in Gaelic, is named after *Beann* (pronounced "ban"), a son of the 1st-century Ulster king, Conor MacNessa, whose tribe first settled in the region. As though this pedigree is not old enough, an ancient manuscript actually cites Bantry as the location where Ireland's first settlers put ashore led by a grandson of Noah. The Irish, though, remember Bantry for a more recent event, albeit 200 years ago, when the great Wolfe Tone arrived at the head of a fleet of 35 French ships to liberate Ireland or in his words to "break the connection with England, the never failing source of all our political evils and to assert the independence of my country".

It must have been a stirring sight to see the fleet sail into one of Europe's greatest and deepest bays, their decks swarming with troops fresh from a triumphant revolution in France. But what could have been a victory, later described as one of the most dangerous moments in English history, turned into failure when the weather turned foul and gales and storms prevented the ships from landing. It would have been easy pickings had the troops been able

Entrance to the magnificent Georgian, Bantry House.

to get ashore as there were only a handful of British troops stationed there and the way was clear for an easy march to Cork. But it was not to be. When Wolfe Tone sailed out with the French after they had been trying to land for a week his remark that England had not had such an escape since the days of the Spanish Armada has been immortalized as one of the truisms of history.

Bantry House, a magnificent Georgian "great house" and the town's architectural high point, commands a marvellous view over the bay. When the French fleet were trying to land, the owner organized the local yeomanry as a resistance force. Although they never saw action he was given the title Lord Bantry by the relieved English administration. His descendant, the second Earl of Bantry was into more frivolous pursuits, evidenced by his collection of *objects d'art* which are presently on display at Bantry House which charges admission to view the house and grounds.

Glengarriff & Environs

On the other side of the bay is **Glengarriff**, the jump-off spot for the starkly beautiful and isolated **Beara Peninsula** dominated by the **Caha and Slieve Miskish mountain ranges**. Sea mist swirls about tiny stone cottages set in this awestruck scenery where rocky fields are bordered by fuchsia hedges, and the coast is a frenzy of glacial up-

Perfect peace in Glengarriff.

heavals. In Glengarriff itself, a beautiful villageset in a glen, George Bernard Shaw wrote his play *St Joan* from the 19th-century **Eccles Hotel**.

A short boat ride from Glengarriff is **Garinish Island** where a man-made garden, by the name of **Ilnacullin** was created early this century by transporting soil from the mainland to this barren isle. The garden is renowned for its formal Italian-style landscaping and its exotic collection of plants and shrubs. There are splendid views from the Grecian Temple and old martello tower.

Before Glengarriff, on the Bantry road, take the inland route to **Gougane Barra**, one of Ireland's most hauntingly beautiful lakes set in an amphitheater of hills. It was here that Saint Finbarr, the founder of Cork, lived on an island in the lake where he founded an oratory, and as legend has it, battled with a water monster. The lake is also the source of the River Lee which winds 72 scenic km (45 miles) past the ruins of abbeys, castles and monasteries from Gougane Barra to the sea at Cork. J J Callanan wrote of the lake in his 18th-century ode;

> There is a green island in lone
> Gougane Barra,
> Whence Allua of songs rushes forth
> Like an arrow;
> In deep Valley Desmond a thousand wild fountains
> Come down to that lake, from their
> home in the mountains

Killarney & the Ring of Kerry

There is something quite magical about Killarney despite the profundity of tourists who flock here during the summer months. The popularity of the region has everything to do with its superb setting, in the unspoilt southwest, beside the picturesque Lakes of Killarney, backed up by Ireland's oldest national park and with the dramatic backdrop of the country's highest peaks, the **Macgillycuddy's Reeks**, which are often dusted with snow.

Genteel transport at Muckross House.

Killarney Town and Outskirts

Travelers are nothing new for **Killarney**, which means "The Church of Sloes" in Irish, for it was developed as a resort town back in the 18th century by the Earl of Kenmare. A visiting surveyor in 1756 remarked that "the curiosities of the neighboring lake have of late drawn great numbers of curious travelers to visit it". A century later Killarney's tourist

A mural on a cottage in Killarney.

industry was given a further boost when Queen Victoria came to stay in the town and the road which linked the town with Cork and Limerick was finished.

As the surrounding countryside is the real attraction for visitors to Killarney, the town itself, crammed with B&Bs, hotels, cafés, restaurants, souvenir shops and other tourist traps, is often overlooked.

However, if you are an observant tourist with a little bit of time in your hands, there are plenty of interesting sidelights to see around the town before you even start exploring beyond. Beware however of Killarney traffic which can run into jams in the town's small narrow streets. The town is something of a regional center as well as the base of many tours to the Ring of Kerry.

A good start for an exploration of the town is the **tourist office** in the Town Hall on Main Street. Behind here is an old **Holy Well** which legend has it "jumped" across the road from **St Mary's Church** on the other side. Walking away from downtown you will notice Killarney's trademark, the horse-drawn "jaunting cars" driven by loquacious "jarveys", awaiting customers for rides to Muckross Demesne, the heart of the national park.

On the outskirts of Killarney town to the left of the turnoff to Muckross is **Brewery Lane** with its old stone cottages once owned by brewers. Further up East Avenue Road is the **Railway Station** and the **Great Southern Hotel**

The spectacular Ring of Kerry is encompassed with flowers.

built in 1854 to accommodate the swell of tourists with the coming of the railway. Brendan Behan, the renowned and outspoken playwright, was said to have remarked on one of his visits that he knew the hotel well, "Didn't I paint and decorate it with my father", recalling the time, not so far into the past, when he had had trouble making ends meet.

On nearby Park Road, the main Cork road is a statue by Seamus Murphy, the well-known sculptor, to Kerry's poets of the 17th and 18th centuries, one of whom was Pierce Ferriter who was hung here during the British rule. Dubbed **Martyr's Hill**, this part of town was where 17th-century public executions took place.

Opposite is the **Franciscan Friary**, founded by monks who were forced to take to the mountains to say their Mass during the Penal Laws of 1697. On their return to the town in 1780 they built the friary, the present building however dates from the mid-19th century. The friary does however still contain some outstanding carved altars and there is a fine Harry Clarke stained- glass window over the main entrance.

Head back to town via College Street and make a detour around the old cobbled lanes behind Plunkett Street where some of the old stone houses have been painted with murals, really more like *trompe l'oeil* of old-time Irish folk leaning from the doorways and windows. The **Artist's Gallery** on Plunkett Street has an interesting collection of Irish

Muckross Abbey, near Killarney, was founded in the 15th century.

landscapes. The Celtic Twilight Gallery on **Brewery Lane** has a collection of Celtic paintings and drawings. **The Studio** on Town Hall Street has another collection of Irish scenes.

Wander through Plunkett Street's old arch to **Market Cross**, the original center of town. Take time out here to visit the quaint bookshops and cafés all housed in traditional shopfronts, then follow New Street to **Cathedral Place** and **St Mary of the Assumption Cathedral**. This splendid Gothic-Revival cathedral, designed by Pugin in the mid-19th century, has marvellous stone work in the Nave, intricate wood carvings in the Lady Chapel and excellent stained-glass windows. The Cathedral was recently renovated.

Muckross Demesne

Leaving Killarney travel 6 km (4 miles) out of town to **Muckross Demesne**. Muckross Demesne is the site of the 19th-century **Muckross House** which is now a **Kerry Craft Museum and Demonstration Center**. **Muckross House Gardens** are magnificent in spring with their magnificent azalea and rhododendron displays.

Ruined **Muckross Abbey**, at the entrance to Muckross Demesne, is wellpreserved and was founded by the Franciscans in the mid-15th century. Closer to Killarney, a pleasant 3-km (2-mile) walk from town through a road, which skirts moss-covered by forests,

The museum at the spruce, picture-postcard town of Sneem.

will take you to picturesque **Ross Castle** beside Lough Leane. In the summer boat trips leave from the stone jetty and the lake is a hive of activity, but in early spring the scene is quiet and tranquil and the traveler can wander the lake shore in absolute solitude.

The Ring of Kerry

The Ring of Kerry, Ireland's famed scenic route, begins and ends in Killarney. The route takes the N70 road circling the Inveragh Peninsula, and covers 175 km (108 miles). "The Ring" as it is popularly known, is a favorite with cyclists but it is a challenging route taking in mountains and tortuous roads with the rewards of spectacular scenery and communion with nature. If you do decide to cycle "The Ring" and do not have your own bicycle, you can hire one from the many cycle rental shops in Killarney. The best route is the anti-clockwise one towards Glenbeigh, since traveling south of Killarney involves a rather strenuous uphill route. It is also possible to travel the route by bus; a service runs regularly from Killarney in the summer months stopping only for photo-stops, but it is a relaxing alternative. Cycling the Ring of Kerry at a steady pace takes around three days. The cost of bicycle hire is IR£15 per person for three days; you must leave your passport behind by way of a guarantee.

Killarney to Glenbeigh

The road from Killarney to Killorglin *en route* to Cahersiveen is a thin shoulderless one. Edged by hedges there is little room to pull in for oncoming traffic and the Irish drive along it like it is an expressway. To the left the flanks of snowy peaks are mottled with yellow gorse while in the Shamrock-green fields, a color peculiar to Ireland, ponies still wear their winter coats and long fleeced sheep skip about with pink and green dye painted on their rumps. Skirting the River Laurie you arrive at **Killorglin**, a typical Kerry town full of character. Perched on a hillside, the town is famous for its **Puck Fair**, held from 10th-12th August every year. The festival

St Mary's Cathedral, Killarney, Pugin's masterpiece.

probably originated from a pagan harvest festival but the centerpiece of the festival – the crowning of a mountain goat as "King" of the fair, commemorates the time when Killorglin's goats are said to have saved the town from Cromwell's bloody hand. The fair is in true Irish style accompanied by a free-flow of Guinness. The nearby ruins of **Conway Castle** date from the 12th century.

Continue out of Killorglin on the main road towards Glenbeigh. The snow-peaked caps of the region are now behind you but the hills are still high and rocky with fields trimmed with stone fences. The paddocks are rougher now and saturated with water.

Glenbeigh is a very attractive village backed by high hills which have been replanted with pines giving it a Swiss non-Irish look. The village offers spectacular views over Dingle Bay where farmlands with almost vertical fields drop to the sea. On the outskirts of the town are the **Glenbeigh Towers** built by the eccentric Lord Headley in the 1860s. The architect's work was something of a disaster and the so-called "castle" fell to pieces around 1922. This delightful fishing village makes a good base for walking and climbing in the area. Walk out of the village for splendid views of the "Glenbeigh Horseshoe" a spectacular show of mountain splendor. Forest walks begin from the Rossbeigh road.

Glenbeigh comes alive every July when its Flapper (horse) races take place.

Mottled mountains, rustic gems on the coast of Kerry.

An old railway snakes around the cliffs nearby, unfortunately for tourism it was closed in 1961.

Kells Bay to Cahersiveen

Continue along the coast to **Kells Bay** a picturesque fishing village. Magnificent vistas as far as the Blasket Islands open up before you on this tortuous road. The bay is an excellent spot for bathing. Sheep graze in the nearby mountains, right up to their summits. Farmers clamber the hills with their sheepdogs looking for sheep that have gone astray.

After Kells Bay the road turns away from the coast to **Mt Knocknadobar** where a holy well at 691 m (2,267 ft) is the mecca for local pilgrims. From the mountain the road descends steeply into an idyllic valley of green geometric fields, a scene of amazing fertility compared to the barren uplands behind you.

In the valley lies **Cahersiveen town**, most famous for being the home town of "The Liberator" Daniel O'Connell. The appropriately large **O'Connell Memorial Church** commemorates the great local. Nearby, **Carhan House** where O'Connell was born is open to the general public. This area is a true example of unspoilt Ireland and it is worth spending a night experiencing real Kerry character which you will often hear being discussed and joked about throughout Ireland. A ferry runs daily in summer from Cahersiveen to Valencia Island.

Skellig Michael

The jagged rocks of the Skelligs, favored by birds and monks.

On a clear day you can see the **Skelligs** (Irish for "rock") rearing from the sea off the storm-lashed coast of southwest Kerry. These precipitous, jagged crags are renowned internationally for their great breeding colonies of stormy petrels, puffins and other seabirds, and Little Skellig, instantly recognizable by its covering of snow-like guano, is the world's largest gannetry housing around 22,000 pairs of gannets. It comes as a surprise, however, to anyone viewing these isolated rock islands which seem totally off-limits to human habitation, that birds were not always the only dwellers here as for 600 years, from the 6th to the 12th centuries, one of the crags known as **Skellig Michael** actually supported a monastic settlement.

Legend has it that the monastery was started by the leper, St Finian of Clonard, the instigator and most famous practitioner of penitential monasticism. Indeed if he was looking for solitude and a place where God was close at hand, he certainly chose his site well.

"The magic that takes you out, far out, of this time and this world", was how the noted playwright George Bernard Shaw described Skellig Michael, and for those lucky visitors today who manage to time their journey with calm seas, a rare occasion in these notorious waters, Shaw's remark is just as poignant.

Penitential Solitude

Weather permitting, boats make the one-and-a-half-hour journey to the cathedral-shaped rock from Knights Town on Valencia Island, or from the mainland ports of Portmagee and Derrynane. It is only a 45-minute journey from **Ballinskelligs** which boasts the ruins of an off-shoot monastery of the Skelligs. This town is the nearest port to the islands and the historical departure point for medieval pilgrims. The voyage itself, often through a turbulent ocean, offers fantastic views of the Kerry coast and the

Waterville & the Coomakista Pass

Leaving Cahersiveen on the N70 towards Waterville, stop by for a view of **Knights Town** on Valencia Island where white-faced houses and shops reflect in the still waters of the Portmagee Channel. All the hills in this region are a patchwork of greens and browns crotcheted with the dark gray of stone walls. Peat stacks are found outside most houses – a good source of fuel, plentiful

bird and fish-life around the islands is prolific.

From the landing, visitors mount 600 stairs which were carved from the steep cliffside by the early monks as part of their austere training to bring them closer to the faith. The steps wind past the stations of the cross, including a stone known as the **Wailing Woman**, a well-known medieval pilgrimage route, to the monastery which stands 150 m (492 ft) above the sea. Fashioned from stones are beehive-shaped huts where the monks lived and the ruins of a church and a boat-shaped oratory. Adventurous souls can climb another 61 m (200 ft) higher to **Christ's Saddle**, the summit of the island, where the views of Little Skellig and the far-off coast are breathtaking.

Named after St Michael, who together with St Patrick expelled snakes from Ireland, Skellig Michael was one of many isolated monasteries, including Iona in Scotland, which was founded by Irish monks in the 6th century. They favored the penitential form of monasticism which some historians say closely paralleled pagan traditions which focused around the bones of the dead. The monks' beehive-huts were constructed around reliquaries. The monks endured their austere lives on Skellig Michael eking out an existence while the Vikings plundered the mainland and even attacked this remote outpost a number of times during the 9th century. They never succeeded in wiping out the monastic settlement which held on until the 13th century. By this time though austerity had became unfashionable in the church, Skellig Michael was abandoned and the monks went to live at nearby Ballinskelligs leaving their isle to the the birds, adventurous pilgrims, and now to the tourists.

in this area. The roadside is flanked by rows of fuchsia hedges which are a wonderful sight in spring.

The scenic road continues to the seaside resort of **Waterville**, overlooking Ballinskelligs Bay. The town was once a famous Victorian and Edwardian resort and a favorite hideaway for Charlie Chaplain. There are rows of old guesthouses along the coast, some have been renovated and others are vacant, staring out forlornly at the sea. The town is a popular angling center celebrated every July in the **Salmon and Trout Festival and Regatta**. There is an 18-hole golf course, the **Waterville Golf Club** and fine sandy beaches. The **Arms Hotel** has a selection of Charlie Chaplain photographs in its foyer.

From Waterville it is all uphill to the top of the **Coomakista Pass**. Across the panorama of stone-fenced fields and white-washed farmlands over the bay and out into the Atlantic are the jagged rocky outlines of the **Skellig Islands**, famous for their gannetries and a monastic settlement where monks once lived way back in the 5th century (see box story on "Skellig Michael" p.242). The islands can be reached by boat from either Ballinskelligs, Cahersiveen, Knightstown Harbor or Waterville. Continuing up the Coomakista Pass, the road seems to snake upwards forever, the fields giving way to great rocky outcrops which lie about obliquely as if they had been cast up by some giant hand. Cast in concrete, holy Mary crowns the parking bay at the top of the pass where the wind can be extremely blusterous.

On the other side of the pass the countryside is much less arable than it is on the other coast and the hills are all striated with gold and wheat-colored rocks. There are a great number of desolate stone cottages and it is not hard to see why it would be very hard for anyone to eke out a living from this windswept, forbidding place. The countryside is however enlivened by a profusion of golden flowering gorse.

Derrynane House & Sneem

South of Waterville, on the Southern side of the Coomakista Pass Derrynane House and National Park are situated in spectacular scenery. **Derrynane House** was for centuries the home of the O'Connell family who are remembered in various artifacts and personal relics. The O'Connell's most famous son was the 19th-century "Liberator" Daniel O'Connell. The 128 hectares (320 acres) of parkland offer spectacular coastal views. West of Derrynane are the white sands of **Castlecove**, an excellent place to take a dip. "Ireland's only beach bar" which is situated here, is shut until Easter.

Sneem on the southern coast of the Iveragh Peninsula, the winner of the 1987 "Tidy Towns Contest", is balm for the soul. There is a stone bridge which spans a cascading river, a bright red museum with cartwheels on the walls and heaps of restaurants. The quaint town is a well-known angling center so it is a good place to eat seafood. There are also pleasant sandy beaches in the vicinity. The two squares in the town, Chaim Herzog and Ceabhaill O'Dalaigh, are named after the Dublin-born president of Israel and a former president of Ireland, respectively.

Parknasilla to Kenmare

Leaving Sneem the N70 road undulates *en route* to Kenmare. The wind is quelled by fine forests of pine making this a very tranquil region. You can enjoy pleasant

A 15th-century castle perched on the summit of Cape Douglas, Kerry.

walks through these forests at Parknasilla where there are also good beaches and safe bathing. The area is dotted with pretty stone cottages where in the spring-time primroses and violets bloom under the hedgerows. At **Blackwater Bridge**, the Blackwater River plunges down a gorge overhung with pines.

Kenmare town situated where the River Roughty opens up into the Kenmare river, is a refreshing town. The main streets of the town built by the Marquess at Landsdowne in 1775 are wide and prettily lined with limestone

These jaunting cars will enable one to take the slow road to Killarney.

houses. The awesome Derrynasaggart Mountains form a spectacular backdrop to the town. Surfing equipment is for hire off the pier and there is a 9-hole golf course.

Towards Killarney

Leaving Kenmare your journey around the ring has almost ended. The road ascends steeply to **Moll's Gap** where the scenery becomes somewhat barren. Carry on to **Ladies' View** another view-point offering a sensational panorama. From here you have a birds-eye sighting of the lakes to the west of Killarney: Lough Leane, Upper Lake and Muckross Lake.

To the north of Upper Lake is the peak of Purple Mountain which stands at 835 m (2,739 ft). Descending the pass you will find yourself beside the waters of **Lough Leane** in **Killarney National Park**. Near to Muckross House (see p.238) is the **Torc Waterfall**, one of Ireland's greatest, you can climb a foot-path to the top for a stunning view. From the Torc Waterfall head north along the N71 and back into the crowded, bustling city of Killarney which makes every other town on the Ring of Kerry seem deserted.

Having completed the Ring of Kerry, you will surely never forget its green, unspoilt beauty, eternal hills, sleepy towns and hospitable locals, sights and sounds of the real undiluted Ireland.

Lost to the world at Lough Leane.

The Dingle Peninsula

Thrusting into the Atlantic, the Dingle Peninsula, in the northwest of County Kerry, is Europe's most westerly outpost. Dramatic mountains rear above white-washed cottages set like pawns on the chessboard-like fields and along the sea-drenched coast deserted bays and beaches beckon the traveler to linger. The region is peppered with the ruins of monks' hermitages and prehistoric remains, and in the lonely Irish-speaking villages, known as Gaeltacht, the Irish language is still the lingua franca.

Beachcombers on the sands at Inch.

Tralee to Dingle

From Tralee, the peninsula extends westwards 48 km (30 miles) to Slea Head, and roads creep along both the north and south coasts, cleaving the Slieve Mish Mountains

In the lonely villages of Dingle, folks are warm and friendly.

through spectacular passes. **Tralee,** memorable mainly for its song-connection *The Rose of Tralee,* makes a good starting point for a journey along the Dingle Peninsula. As Kerry's commercial capital, Tralee lacks the appeal of other more aesthetic towns in the region but it boasts plenty of accommodations, good pubs and eating establishments, marvellous summer theater at **Siamsa Taire Theater**, Ireland's national folk theater and the riotous **Rose of Tralee International Festival** held every August.

Leaving Tralee by the northern route, head due west around the shores of **Tralee Bay** where **Castlegregory** beckons with long sandy beaches. Looming to the south are the **Slieve Mish Mountains** where walking trails climb lofty **Mt Caherconree**, which at 827 m (2,713 ft) offers fantastic vistas stretching all the way to the Mouth of the Shannon on the Clare coast from an Iron Age stone fort which still survives near the summit. After **Stradbally's** sandy shores keep on until you reach Ballyduff and turn off for **Cloghane** with its even more impressive beaches on **Brandon Bay**. Austere **Mt Brandon**, patriarch of the ranges of the same name, looms 953 m (3,122 ft) above Cloghane. A steep ascent to the summit begins from this village at its base, but the classic climb to the peak, known as the **Saint's Road**, built by St Brendan himself, begins from near Kilquane on a different road north of Dingle. Cresting

Kilmalkedar Church, made famous by St Brendan.

the 418-m (1,371-ft) high **Conor Pass**, too tortuous for tour buses, the countryside spreads out in a startling panorama in all directions.

Dingle

Dingle, the westernmost town in the European Community, where the next parish is Boston, USA, runs on tourism but still retains much of its own unique character. The sounds of uillean pipes and tin whistles drift from no less than 54 pubs and there is even a resident dolphin called Fungi who lives in the bay. Rent a boat to view him or even a wetsuit for a close encounter. Seafood restaurants abound as do plentiful accommodations including an 18th-century mansion which now serves as a hostel offering horseback riding.

Dingle's high summer season is punctuated with festivities like the **Dingle Races** and the **St Brendan Festival** which features *curragh* (lathe-and-canvas or leather canoe) races. It was in one of these traditional craft which still ply Brandon Bay and other Dingle inlets, that St Brendan and his fellow monks made their legendary 6th-century journey across the Atlantic. Recorded in the medieval *Navigation of St Brendan*, the adventurers sailed in search of an earthly paradise, and after 40 days of battling sea monsters and viewing a floating mountain "the color of silver, harder than marble, of substance of the clearest crystal," actually an iceberg, they came to a sea which "had thrice 50 islands, and some thrice the size of Eire". Was it the Caribbean or Newfoundland? And were these Irish monks the first Europeans to sight the Americas? The questions remain unanswered.

The Saint's Road

To view the site where Kerry's patron saint first pushed off on his epic journey take the road from Dingle north to **Brandon Creek**. On the way, energetic travelers can take time off to climb the Saint's Road to the top of Mt Brandon where the remains of St Brendan's oratory still survive. Pilgrims make the ascent every year on 16th May, the saint's

Accommodations are very homely in this hospitable part of Ireland.

feast day, but it is a difficult and sometimes dangerous climb.

The entire region is awash with reminders of the saint. Apart from a head, bay, village, mountain, peak and creek named after him, there is also a host of legends, and most, like the following, are almost as fanciful as his epic voyage.

One such legend is that one Easter Sunday atop the mountain, Brendan forgot his prayer book which was back at Kilmalkedar Chapel, a good 10 km (6 miles) as the crow flies. As the tale relates, the crowd was so dense that the word was passed through the crowds back to the base of the mountain and then to a messenger who retrieved the holy book. When he brought it back to the mountain the prayer book was passed hand over hand all the way to St Brendan at the summit altar. The present **Kilmalkedar Church** in Romanesque style with a corbelled stone roof dates from the 12th century, though the inscribed Ogham (Celtic alphabet Stone), sundial and cross are from a much earlier era.

For even more impressive antiquities, head further west past Ballydavid on Smerwick Harbor and take the turn at Murreagh for the **Gallarus Oratory** at Ballynana, Ireland's finest extant early-Christian oratory. The oratory which dates from the 7th or 8th century, was built by Christian masons who used no mortar in the dry-rubble walls which are still weatherproof today.

The desolate Blasket Islands offer dramatic scenery.

The Blasket Islands

In the far west of the peninsula, accessible by road from Dingle, is **Slea Head** where sheer cliffs plunge into the Atlantic at Ireland's western end. Here the fields are like postage-stamps, encircled by stone walls, one way in which the farmers could clear the rocks from their fields. Just east of the head near Fanan, on hills overlooking the sea, are beehive-shaped huts, like an Irish version of the Eskimo's igloo, built by 6th-century monks seeking wisdom in isolation. Nearby, is the spectacular promontory fort of **Dun Beag**.

At the village of **Dunquin**, just north of the headland, boats ply to the desolate **Blasket Islands** encircled by hundreds of dangerous rocky outcrops, a peril for shipping. The last of the islands' inhabitants left for the mainland in 1953, but not before their traditional way of life was preserved for posterity by three local authors and their books: Tomas O'Crohan's *The Islandman*, Maurice O'Sullivan's *Twenty Years A-Growing* and Peig Sayer's *Peig*. **Great Blasket**, the largest island about 6 km (4 miles) long by 3 km (2 miles) wide, is the most accessible, with daily boats making the run from the mainland. Attractive, in a wild untamed way, **Great Blasket** offers dramatic scenery and a good chance of viewing seals and puffins. Stone walls and ruined cottages are testimony to the hard, traditional life-

Kerry Place Names and their Meanings

History, geography, legends and religion are all intimately bound up in Ireland's place names, particular in County Kerry, which still retains many of its original Irish names which were not as anglicized or corrupted as those of the east coast where the English presence was much more formidable. Many names go under a multitude of different spellings as ancient Irish was difficult to express in English letters, however, true to the Kerry spirit, there are no hard and fast rules and often two or more spellings are equally acceptable. Deciphering place names can also be a great way to start to learn how to speak Gaelic as many root words, like *inis* (also spelt inish, ennis, and inch) meaning "island", or *dun* for "fort" or "kingly residence", often precedes the name. Dunbeag on the Dingle Peninsula then translates as "the little fort" (*beag* means "little").

Improving Your Gaelic

County Kerry's ancient name is derived from *Ciar* (pronounced "keer") one of the sons of Maev, the Queen of Connaught, who ruled around the 1st century AD. His descendants, known as the *Ciarraidhe* (pronounced "Keery"), held the territories west of Abbeyfeale, which is still on the border between Limerick and Kerry, and the region became known as *Ciarraighe* or Kerry, as it is today.

Killarney, unmistakably the most famed town in Kerry, has more than one legend as to how its name came about. *Cill* (pronounced "Kill"), meaning a church, is the same in both versions. The most popular translation is "the church of the sloes" supported by the fact that there are a number of sloe woods around the town. Another interpretation, though, is that it was one of a trinity of churches, Killaha (Church of Aha) in the east of town, Killarney (Church of Airne) in the south, and Killagi (Church of Agi) on the Kenmare road, which were founded by three sisters and named after them.

Innisfallen, the scenic isle and abbey of the same name in Killarney's lower lake, or Lough Leane, is written as *Inis-Faithlenn* (pronounced "Fahlen", a man's name) in Irish, and means the "island of Faithlenn". Overlooking the same lake is **Ross Castle**, and is not as many people would presume named after its owner, but for the *ros*, or peninsula, on which it stands. **Muckross**, which gives its name to the nearby Middle Lake, a 19th-century mansion and its famous gardens and abbey, translates as "the peninsula of the pigs", and **Torc Mountain** which overlooks the lake and the Torc Cascade which pours down from it derives its name from a similar theme "the mountain of boars".

The **River Laune** which flows into Killarney's Lower Lake means "the elm-producing river", and the mountain at its source **Carrauntoohil**, Ireland's highest peak, translates as "the reversed reaping hook". This odd name comes from the jagged shape that the mountain shows from the Killarney side where the teeth-like ridges appear to be on a convex edge. *Tuathail* (pronounced "thoohil") actually means "left-handed", but it can also mean something which is the opposite to its original position; and *carran*, is the "reaping hook".

Catthair, anglicized and pronounced "caher", means a "circular stone fort", and forms the prefix for a number of Kerry place names. **Cahersiveen**, a western town on the Ring of Kerry, means "the stone fort of Sabina" (a woman's name from the Irish *Saidhbhin*) and **Cahirconree Mountain** near Tralee takes its name from the 1st-century stone fort of Curoi

style that was the islanders' lot until halfway through this century.

When the sun shines on the green fields, and the sea and skies are bathed in a bright azure it is easy to imagine that life in the Blaskets could have been idyllic, but when the weather turns foul and the fogs creep in, it brings to mind lines from Robin Flower's *The Western Isle* describing the night-passage to the

MacDaire which still survives on the peak.

A Spanish Connection

Valencia Island, off the west of the Iveragh Peninsula, was named by the Spanish who settled here after losing their famous battle to Sir Francis Drake. Its original title which is still used by its Irish-speaking populace is *Dairbhre*, pronounced "Darrery", meaning "a place producing oaks". South of Valencia are the **Skellig Islands**, sheer-sided crags that thrust from the sea, which derive from the obvious Irish name for "rock", *Sceilig*. The port opposite the islands is **Ballinskelligs** or *Baile an Sceilig*, "the town of the rock". Further east, overlooking the sea, is **Derrynane**, home of the "Great Liberator" Daniel O'Connell. Derrynane's name is anglicized from the Irish *Doire-Fhionain* which means "the oak grove of St Finan", and must derive from the 6th century when the saint was at his most active.

Dingle, on the peninsula of the same name, sounds like the noise a bell makes, but its name came from Dingin, a form of *Daingean* or "a fortress", and was shortened from the original Dingle-I-Coush, the stronghold of its ancient chieftain, O'Cush. **Ventry**, a well-known beach to the west, comes from the Irish meaning "white strand", and the **Slieve Mish Mountains** that dominate the Dingle Peninsula derive from the Irish *sliabh*, pronounced "sleeve" for "mountains" and *mis* was a girl's name.

Other meanings of Kerry place-names include **Tralee**, "the strand of the Lee"; **Scartaglin**, "the thicket of the glen"; **Reask**, "a marsh"; **Lough Guitane**, "the lake of the little boat"; **Coomnagoppul**, "the hollow of the horses"; and **Cloghan**, "a row of stepping stones".

isles; when "on the slippery quay, Men talked, a rush of Gaelic never-ending", and the *curragh* (leather boat) was "A frail skin rocking on the unquiet water". During the passage the men sang a

A charming little white-washed cottage.

song to the rhythm of the oars about a maiden "barefooted under rippling tresses", who was the spirit of Ireland, who answered them by saying:

"Men have died for me, men have still to die."
The voice died then, and, growing in the darkness,
The shape of the Great Island
Rose up out of the water hugely glooming,
And wearing lights like stars upon its brow.

Monuments of the Ancients

North of Dunquin, on the western promontory of Smerick Harbor, is **Dun An**

Slea Head, Ireland's most westerly point.

Oir, a Stone Age fortress which translates as "The Fort of Gold". Here, in 1579, an army of 700 Irish, Spanish and Frenchmen led by the rebellious Fitzmaurice Fitzgerald, defied the might of the Elizabethan administration. Even the blessings of the Pope did not help Fitzmaurice whose valiant attempts to free his country from Protestant rule ended in his army being slaughtered, a massacre that historians saw as a prelude to the later decimation of Munster in 1583.

Returning from the fort, follow the

Dick Mack's Pub, Dingle Town.

main road to the turnoff for **Riasc**, an early Christian monastic site which was excavated in the 1970s. Remains of walls and foundations have been exposed along with carved standing stones etched with symbols and curlicue patterns. All in all, along the mainly western part of the Dingle Peninsula there are an extraordinary number of stone remains and from Dun Beag to Slea Head there are apparently around 500 cave dwellings, standing stones, forts and beehive huts.

Another place of interest on the peninsula is the ruined keep of **Minard Castle** which was destroyed by Cromwell's troops in 1650. The castle overlooks Dingle Bay and is perched just above the tideline of aptly named **Boulder Bay**. At Anascaul take the shoreline road to the famed **Sands of Inch** which stretch 5 km (3 miles) across the mouth of Dingle Bay. Iron Age people lived here in the sand dunes and there are still remnants of their occupation.

Simple Dingle Pleasures

Unhurried, the Dingle Peninsula is not a place for travelers in search of the bright lights. Its pleasures are simple, an evening spent drinking, listening to the village fiddler, cycling along the *bohareens* (the Dingle name for country roads), and just taking in the dramatic, untamed beauty of Ireland and Europe's last westerly outpost.

Limerick & The Lakelands

Shamrock-green fields, as level as a billiard table sweep from one horizon to another where vast cloudscapes, unimpeded by mountains, dome overhead. There are castles, manor houses, abbeys and monasteries and picturesque market towns, but most of all there are a disproportion-ate number of waterways, lakes and canals all drained by the mighty River Shannon which for 259 km (161 miles) runs through the center of Ireland. Often overlooked by tourists, other than fishermen and boating enthusiasts, much maligned Limerick and the country which extends northward from there through the Shannon Valley boasts far less touristy trappings than say Kerry or Galway. At the hub of the rich agricultural areas, the area is not as reliant on tourism as other less fertile regions and this makes the mid-west a great place to go touring if you do not want to run into a lot of folks toting cameras and

Bunratty Castle, Limerick's most renowned attraction.

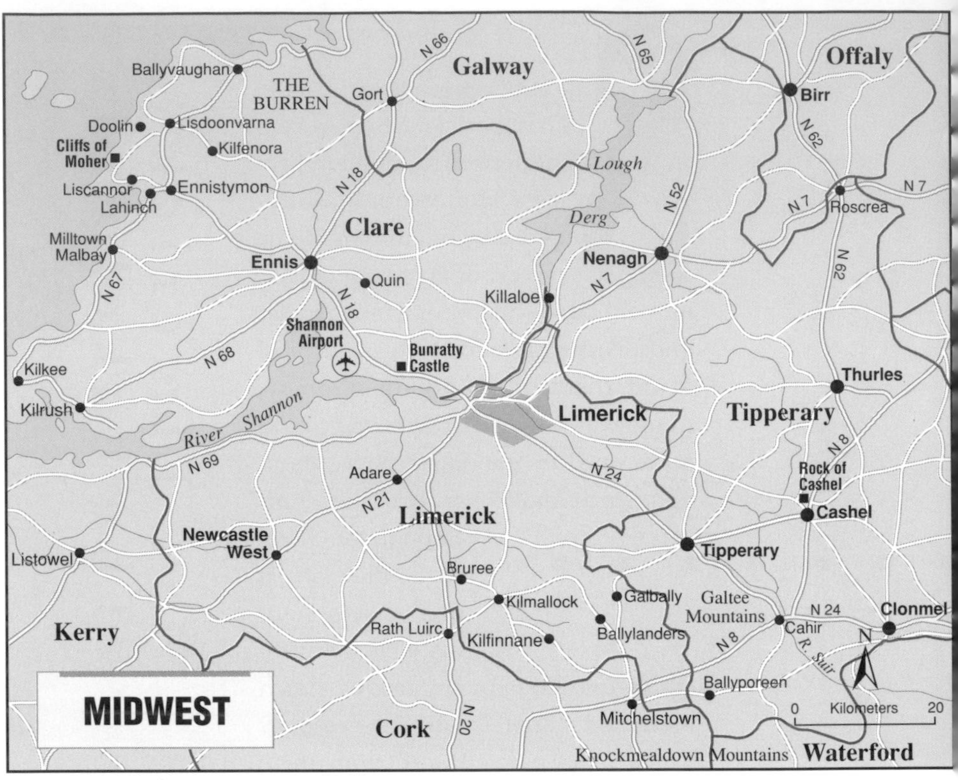

getting on and off tour buses. Middle Ireland is often referred to as the "real Ireland" as compared to other more renowned places where the line between what is "real" and what is put on for the tourists is less sharply defined.

Limerick

Limerick, on the "hit list" of most tour guides, certainly lacks a scenic backdrop, but on the other hand, there is nothing that is instantly off-putting about Ireland's fourth largest town apart from its gray and colorless appearance. Located only 24 km (15 miles) from **Shannon Airport**, the hub of many domestic and trans-Atlantic flights, Limerick was founded by the Vikings and later seized and destroyed by the High King Brian Boru. In keeping with Limerick's low-key reputation, its name is hardly romantic being a corruption of the old Irish *Luimnech*, meaning "bare spot of land".

After William of Orange's decisive win at the Battle of the Boyne, his general Ginkel moved west to the Shannon where victories in battle at Athlone and Aughrim further strengthened their hand and decimated the power of the Irish Catholics. After a gallant defeat, which would be symbolically remem-

In memory of the Treaty of Limerick, which heralded a mass emigration of Catholics.

bered for centuries after, the Irish under Sarsfield were forced to surrender and the **Treaty of Limerick** was signed by both parties. Although it was meant to protect the interests of those Catholics who stayed behind, thousands of fighters later known as the Wild Geese left for France rather than live as second class citizens in their own land. The treaty is remembered in Limerick as a "symbol of betrayal and deception". A memorial stone still stands in the town where Sarsfield surrendered in 1691 and the 13th-century **King John's Castle** near Thomond Bridge still shows battle scars three centuries later.

At the 12th-century **St Mary's Cathedral**, now a Protestant church, there are beautiful carvings on the choir stalls and the 85-m (280-ft) steeple of the 19th-century **St John's Cathedral** is Ireland's highest. Limerick's streets boast elegant Georgian houses dating from the 18th century when England went on a building spree in Ireland's urban centers, and one of these on **Pery Square** now serves as the Hostels International hostel.

The city's youthful population swells during the college season due to the close proximity of the **University of Limerick**, a kilometer out on the Dublin road. At the university's **Hunt Museum** there is an excellent display of early Celtic and medieval collections and the unique **National Self-Portrait Collection**.

Bunratty Castle & Folk Park

Bunratty Castle, Limerick's most renowned attraction, is located 13 km (8 miles) from town on the airport road rather incongruously perched among industrial estates and motorways. Magnificently restored in the 1960s with original furnishings and stained-glass, this medieval stronghold dating from 1450 was the fief of the O'Briens who controlled this part of Munster during the 16th and 17th centuries. Bunratty is no dull museum, however, as it also hosts real medieval banquets where visitors can not only enjoy the splendid castle atmosphere but can feast and make merry to the strains of authentic

Thatched-roof cottages are common in the delightful town of Adare.

madrigals.

At the **Bunratty Folk Park**, (see box story p.266) adjacent to the castle, are full-size replicas of original Irish country homes including the thatched-roof Shannon Farmhouse which was removed stone-by-stone from the runway of Shannon Airport before being reconstructed at Bunratty. For many travelers, this step back in time is particularly rewarding as the interiors are faithfully reproduced with household items, some of which are still found in off-the-beaten-track cottages.

Adare & Desmond Castle

Adare, on the River Maigue, only 16 km (10 miles) south of Limerick on the road to Killarney, serves as a reminder of how pretty a town can be after the neutrality and concrete of the nearby city. Even the most jaded of travelers would have no problem making a pit-stop here where thatched-roof houses, a rarity in the rest of the country, even appear in Adare's main street. The 19th-century Earl of Dunraven was responsible for the town's current appearance.

Adare's history, however, goes back centuries and is all centered around the picturesque ruins of **Desmond Castle**. Known in Irish as *Ath Dara*, "the ford of the oaks", this stronghold originally the seat of the O'Donovans, was seized by the Normans and in 1227 was taken by the Earls of Kildare, the powerful Fitzgeralds, who held it until 1534 when it was forfeited by the Crown and leased to the Earl of Desmond. Gerald, the Fitzgerald's most famous member, the 16th Earl, rebelled against English rule and their lands were confiscated in the Elizabethan era. Scattered about the castle and its parklands are the monastic and castellated ruins of this powerful dynasty, including a 14th-century Augustinian priory and a 15th-century Franciscan friary.

Old ladies in tweeds and cardigans peddle their bikes on country roads south of Adare where in the early spring sunshine entire families are digging up the umber-colored earth for their summer gardens. Parked in a lay-by off the main road are a convoy of caravans, home to Ireland's original "traveling people", who used to take to the road in horse-drawn caravans which are now rented by modern-day travelers in search of the "real" Ireland. Kids and dogs mill about while the women sit chatting in the

Adare Manor, one of Ireland's many "great houses".

doorways of their caravans, completely oblivious to the traffic roaring by.

Historic Attractions

Newcastle West, further south from Adare, beside a stream in the midst of lush farmlands, is another attractive town with old stone walls and a ruined castle. From here, take the loop road through Dromcolliher to Rath Luirc (formerly Charleville) and on to historic **Kilmallock** on the River Loobagh.

Kilmallock was once a walled town, but today only the **Blossom Gate** survives of the original four entrances. Killmallock's other impressive antiquities include a **Dominican priory** dating from the 13th century, a Norman **castle** and the medieval **Church of Saints Peter and Paul**.

Heading north to Limerick stop over at the scenic village of **Bruree** with its old water mill on the River Maigue and a **museum** named after its most famous inhabitant Ireland's first President, Eamonn de Valera, who went to school here in his youth.

Lough Gur, halfway between Limerick and Kilmallock, has been settled since neolithic times, evidenced by the dolmens, stone circles and Stone-Age houses which have been unearthed around the lake's shores. Travelers interested in pre-history can visit the **Tourist Center** which displays a reproduction of a Stone-Age dwelling.

The great 6th-century monastery of Clonmacnois.

Along the Shannon

North from Limerick, the vast waterlands of the River Shannon and its attendant necklace of glittering lakes are best explored by hiring a river cruiser, a great way to beat the crowds and venture into Ireland's heartland by the backroads, or in this case by the waterways. From Killaloe, 22$^1/_2$ km (14 miles) north of Limerick, the Shannon is navigable for 241 km (150 miles) through the counties of Tipperary, Clare, Galway, Offaly, Roscommon and Longford, to Carrick-on-Shannon in Leitrim, only 32 km (20 miles) from the border of Northern Ireland. At least 10 different companies hire motor cruisers on the Shannon (enquire at tourist offices for details) and these can be picked up at the major towns along the way.

From **Killaloe**, where the 13th-century **St Flannan's Cathedral** houses the celebrated **Thorgrim Stone** carved with both Viking and Celtic scripts, the rivershore expands to **Lough Derg**, rimmed with lakeside villages such as **Mountshannon** at the foot of the Slieve Aught Mountains. Explore **Holy Island**, with its ruined monastery, and on the outskirts of the village is **Beal Boru**, an earthern fort which some historians think may have been the 11th-century stronghold of the High King Brian Boru. After Lough Derg, the river wends its way through the first of its six locks to **Banagher**, a popular jump-off spot for

Bunratty Folk Park

Lifestyle and tradition at the Bunratty Folk Park.

In rural Ireland, only a few generations ago, stone cottages with thatched roofs, warmed by the open hearth of a peat fire, were the norm rather than the exception. Traveling around the countryside, today, there are still many traditional homes, but as the nation modernizes, their numbers are thinning, and these days many locals would rather live in a cement bungalow and leave the thatched-roof homes for the tourists.

For the visitor with not enough time to explore country roads in order to find original dwellings, or even for travelers who are interested in rural life before electricity and television made its mark, the **Bunratty Folk Park** at Bunratty Castle, just outside of Limerick, is the place to go. The Folk Park offers a unique opportunity to see at first hand all the different types of houses that were once prolific across the land and which are preserved as a microcosm of Irish country life in the late 19th century.

The **Shannon Farmhouse**, a rectangular stone building with a thatched roof, the first to be re-erected at the Park, was moved from its original home on the runway of the nearby Shannon Airport. Its idiosyncracies include a flight of steps beside the chimney which lead to a storage loft, a perch over the door where the rooster slept so that his crowing would wake the family at dawn and an efficient and inexpensive alarm clock. Under the kitchen is a bedroom with a unique "covered-car bed" which provided privacy for a loving couple in a large household. Lined with wooden boards on three sides and the ceiling, the bed was snug and safe from prying eyes when the front curtain was drawn.

The **Mountain Farmhouse** came from the Sliabh Luachra, the highlands where Kerry, Cork and Limerick counties meet. Compared to the Shannon farmhouse which would have supported about 12 cows, the mountain farm would have only fed half this herd on a larger acreage, but with far less arable soil. However, the farmer would have supplemented his income by peat cutting which was readily available in this region. The children slept, warm and secure, in an open-fronted loft above the kitchen, and the flagstone floor of this cottage was part of the bride's dowry when she joined the mountain farming family.

Far simpler is the two-room house of a **Cashen fisherman** which originally came from the south bank on the mouth of the River Shannon. Because of its proximity to the sea, this house utilized driftwood for much of its

cruises along the Shannon. Continue on to **Shannonbridge** where true to its name an arched bridge crosses the river. Take a break from the river here and board the fascinating 45-minute railway tour of the **Bog of Allen**.

framing, and the planks and beams would have once been used as timbers on some ill-fated sailing ship that went down off the west coast. The nautical touch is apparent on the ceiling which is made of white-washed canvas, and the bedroom furniture of solid timber crafted by a local boat-builder who also turned his hand to household joinery.

A farmer-fisherman from western Clare once owned the **Loop Head House**, built of stone with wooden interior walls between the rooms and a high ceiling with exposed beams, which is now fashionably known as "a cathedral ceiling". The four-poster bed in the upper bedroom was made by a craftsman from Kerry, who would have sent his handiwork across the Shannon by sailing boat, a journey of only half an hour as opposed to the cross-country trek which took all of two days.

The most prosperous home in the Park is the **Golden Vale Farmhouse**, which would have boasted at least 40 hectares (100 acres) and have been worked by laborers and servants as well as the owner's family. The spacious kitchen was the only floor with flagstones, the others being of wood, and the wide open hearth even had a crane for lifting heavy pots and a bellows operated by a wheel. The parlor, with its chaise lounge, framed portraits, floral wallpaper, and knick-knacks displayed on polished sideboards, followed a fashion dating from the 18th century, and was the showpiece of such a prominent farmer's house. However, it was seldom used by the family who preferred the warm intimacy of the kitchen hearth. Strangers or government officials were often entertained in the cold parlor but it was considered an insult to entertain close friends there. Woe betide a visitor though who made the mistake of sitting down, without being invited, in the master or mistress's chairs which were often at either side of the hearth, as this was considered the height of bad manners.

The laborer's humble abode, the **Bothan Scoir**, is in direct contrast to the landowner's comfortable dwellings consisting of only one room with an earthen floor, a bare hearth and just the bare necessities needed for living. Close by is the **Byre Dwelling**, which unlike most of the above, has been extinct in Ireland since the start of the century. In these homes the cattle lived at one end and the people at the other with a drain across the center of the floor to differentiate the areas and also to absorb the cows' droppings. On the side of the hearth was an outshot-bed, a curtained alcove with a bed usually used by a grandparent who could comfortably lie down while still enjoying the company of the family at the hearth. Other interesting features include a "falling table" which folded up against the wall when not in use, and feather dusters made of goose wings.

The **Moher Farmstead** from the famed cliff country of Clare, is made entirely of stone which was an excellent use of this prolific building material in a region where wood was a rarity. The walls, roof and floors are all of cut stone which is even used in lintels, benches and shelves which in other areas would have been made of wood.

As well as the different types of farmhouses, there is even an original village at the Bunratty Folk Park, complete with gas lights in the streets, and the pub is authentic in every detail right down to the liquor advertisement on its walls. However, many of Ireland's villages still look much like this one, as old-style shopfronts are preserved along with Irish names and lettering on signboards, especially in the Gaelic-speaking areas of the west.

Time marches on and fashions change, but it is interesting that much of the old-style furniture not so long ago considered worthless, like the household goods in the Bunratty houses, are now fetching outlandish prices at antique auctions. Luckily, though, there are places like the Folk Park which can preserve a little bit of life in the "good old days".

After Shannonbridge, the river world is a vast vista of marsh and reeds, everything built by man is kept away from the river and out of flood danger, for the Shannon has a way of enlarging itself up to 10 times wider during floods.

A patient local lass.

Birdwatchers can spot gray herons, kingfishers, cormorants and curlews, and the fishing here is excellent.

At **Clonmacnois**, the riverside scenery is enlivened by the towers of this great 6th-century monastic complex which during its heyday attracted pilgrims from all over Christendom. Its name, though, pre-dates Christianity as it is derived from the Irish for "the meadow of the sons of Nos", a Celtic tribe whose territory included Clonmacnois. Visitors can moor their cruisers at the jetty and potter about the round towers, the ruins of a cathedral, several churches and a castle, and admire the beautifully-incised stone **High Crosses** and hundreds of inscribed grave slats and sepulchral stones.

Athlone

Athlone, on the main Galway to Dublin road, sits astride the River Shannon before it mushrooms into Lough Ree, and announces its presence downstream by glimpses of its mosque-like twin domes of **Saints Peter and Paul Church** which appear and then disappear at each bend in the river. The town jetty is now patrolled, following some cruiser break-ins, so Athlone is a good, safe place to leave the boat to do some explorations and soak up Midland life at a local pub.

Athlone Castle has been guarding the town's strategic riverside location since the 13th century as the resident museum's display indicates and was the scene of fierce fighting during the Williamite wars of the late 17th century. The town's other claim to fame is located off Mardyke Street, in **The Bawn**, where an inscription marks the birthplace of Ireland's greatest tenor, John McCormack.

The Northern Shannon

Lough Ree is a mecca for fishing, boating and water-ski enthusiasts, but it can become rough in foul weather and cruising boats are advised to cross these open waters during early morning hours before the winds come up. Boating instructions also point out the advisability of tackling the lake in the company of other cruisers, but even in high season this is sometimes a tall order for the Shannon is a big river and river cruising is really only in its infancy; bliss for travelers who want to avoid the crowds. After the wide-open vistas of Lough Ree, the river narrows again at **Lanesborough** and country life is again revealed with stone houses nestling in the hillsides and cows grazing in the lush green pastures of the Midlands.

After three more locks, the market town of **Carrick-on-Shannon**, another popular jump-off spot for cruiser holidays, is reached. In June, the town lets off steam with its annual **Community and Arts Festival**, a three-day extravaganza of jazz bands, street theater and unabashed merrymaking, but for the rest of the year it appears a fairly typical Midlands town. Named after an ancient weir which crossed the river, Carrick-on-Shannon is also a popular base for exploring the northern lake country including enchanting **Lough Key Forest Park** 6 km (4 miles) from town on the Boyle road. In spring, riotous rhododendrons color the 33 islands which make up the park, and on one of these is a ruined abbey.

Once the stronghold of the McDermott clan, the islands and the surrounding environs were confiscated by the Crown in the 17th century and were then given to Sir John King whose family controlled the park from their mansion in nearby Boyle until the late 1950s when the government took over. Walking trails meander through the beautifully maintained forest park which boasts some giant cedars and conifers and a chance to spy some native wildlife such as deer, badgers, red squirrels and otters. At **Boyle** there is a superb **Cistercian abbey** dating from 1161, and east of Carrick-on-Shannon is **Lough Rynn Estate**, the former home of the Earls of Leitrim. The estate has a walled garden and a turret house.

Further east are more lakelands around Mullingar: **Lake Derrabvaragh**, home of the mythical Children of Lir who were turned into swans; **Lough Leane** renowned for its oysters; and the lakeshore town of **Fore** where a 7th-century monastery is famed for its seven wonders including a saint encased in stone.

From Cavan town in the county of the same name, hundreds of lakes stretch all the way to the Northern Ireland border, offering great fishing and towns where tourists are a rarity. In **Cavan town** itself visit Cavan Crystal where you can see glassblowing and glass being cut.

whose pioneer work in
modern Gaelic literature included
short stories best known of which
is M'Asal Beag Dubh. born Galway
died Dublin October 1928
The Old Galway Society

Clare to Connemara

Oliver Cromwell was far from enamored of the country west of the River Shannon with its stony fields, bogs, and rugged mountains. It was a world apart from the inviting lush meadows of the Midlands and the East, and he showed his distaste when meting out punishment to the Irish chieftains who had opposed him, by giving them the choice of going to "Hell or Connaught". Historically, though, this attitude to the West which was shared by all of Ireland's conquerors, served in the long run to preserve the original Irish culture and language, unlike in the East where lifestyles and dialogue became more homogenized and anglicized. From Clare, through Galway

Padraic O'Conaire, the great 20th-century storyteller, is immortalized in Galway.

The famed Cliffs of Moher tower above the Atlantic Ocean.

and Mayo Counties, there are more Gaeltacht (regions where Irish is still spoken) than anywhere else in the country. Traditional music still flourishes, the towns are few and far between, the scenery is unspoilt and spectacular and the pleasures of life are found in more simple things: the smell of a peat fire, the taste of a Galway oyster, the play of light on a Connemarra peak and the sound of a foot-tappin' fiddler in a quaint Doolin pub.

Ennis

On a map, **Ennis**, Clare's largest town (16,000 inhabitants) looks like the hub of a bicycle wheel with spoke-like roads radiating from it to every corner of the county. Limerick 32 km (20 miles) and Shannon Airport 26 km (16 miles) are to the southeast, the towns of the Shannon estuary to the southwest, the coast and cliffs to the west, the Burren to the north, and the lakelands of Lough Derg to the east.

A neat, compact town with tight streets and tall shophouses, Ennis is an unremarkable place but makes a pleasant stopover. Sights include the statue atop a pillar in the center of town of **Daniel O'Connell**, who successfully brought about Catholic emancipation while he was an MP for County Clare, and in front of the courthouse is a bronze replica of **Eamon De Valera**, Ireland's prime minister for more than two decades, who began his career here. On Abbey Street is the 13th-century **Ennis Friary** with its decorative 15th-century McMahon tomb. Apart from these historical artifacts, Ennis is best known for its traditional music and step-dancing which culminates in the lively annual **Fleadh Nua festival** held every May.

The Cliffs of Moher

Head southwest of Ennis for **Kilrush**, a market and port town on the Mouth of the Shannon, known for its good traditional pub music and nearby 168-hectare (420-acre) **Kilrush Woods**. Kilrush is only just under 5 km (3 miles) west of **Killimer** where the Kerry/Clare ferry docks are situated, and is a good stopover point for travelers coming direct from Kerry, bypassing both Limerick and Ennis. Directly to the west on the Atlantic coast is the resort town of **Kilkee**, where Victorian-style guesthouses contemplate the sea and where the **Pollock Holes** offer good bathing and scuba-diving. Further north past sandy beaches is **Milltown Malbay**, home of the **Willy Clancy School of Traditional Music** which celebrates with a music-fest during July, when Ireland's best known musicians flock here.

At **Lahinch**, another resort town popular with bathers and golfers, turn off for Clare's famed **Cliffs of Moher** which tower up to 183 m (600 ft) above the roaring surf of the Atlantic. For spectacular views, which on clear days encompass the Kerry Mountains and the Aran Islands, climb to the roof of **O'Brien's Tower**, built in 1835 as an observation point. Five kilometers (3 miles) to the south is **Hag's Head**, named after a *mal* (a witch or hag) who drowned in Mal Bay to the south. *Moherruane*, an ancient fortress of the O'Connor clan, once stood on this headland and this is how the cliffs derived their name. For the most fantastic view of all, walk north from O'Brien's Tower to a survey marker atop a bare hill where the vista stretches from Connemara in the north to Mt Brandon and the Blasket Islands in the south. Up the coast at **Aill Na Searrach**, is an extremely precarious cliff edge; no doubt a tempting route for a member of the Oxford Dangerous Sports Club, but not for the average tourist.

Musical Doolin

Detour to tiny **Doolin**, mecca for music-lovers and Ireland's best known traditional musicians. Three of the town's taverns have won nationwide acclaim for their music sessions, and during the summer, locals and travelers alike join a pub crawl which lasts until the wee hours. Every second house in the village seems to be either a hostel or a bed-and-breakfast (B&B), but Doolin's popularity is at such a high that intending visitors are advised to book ahead even during the off-season – perhaps it was that *Time* magazine write-up. Past the pastel shopfronts, walk to the pier for fresh seafood bought direct from the fishermen, and for ferry rides to Inisheer, the closest and smallest of the Aran Islands. (See p.280.)

The Burren

Lunar landscapes come into view as we head into the northwest corner of Clare. From a distance, this strange world of fissured limestone, known as **the Burren**, (see box story p.278), appears to be completely devoid of vegetation, but look closer and the clefts hide an amazing array of wildflowers and ferns which are at their colorful best during early summer. **Lisdoonvarna**, in the center of the Burren, came into prominence in Victorian times when health-conscious visitors flocked here for its mineral

A local girl at festival time.

springs and vitalizing spa waters. Sulphur baths and massages at the spa complex are a great way to energize bodies suffering from jet-lag or antiquity-viewing overload. Or if you are on the lookout for a loving mate, head here in autumn for the annual **Matchmaking Festival** which has been resurrected from an old harvest-time fair when bachelor farmers came to town to look for wives.

Further north, near Ballyvaughan is spectacular **Ailwee Cave**, once the haunt of prehistoric bears, with an underground river and waterfall. Entry is through an aesthetic limestone building which serves as the tourist center and has won architectural awards for the unique way it blends with the Burren's environment. South of here, at Kilfenora is the **Burren Display Center** where displays highlight the botany, geology and history of the region.

South of Lisdoonvarna is **Corofin** where the **Clare Heritage Center** is a must for visitors interested in their Irish roots. Meanwhile at nearby **Dysert O'Dea Castle** there is a fascinating **Archeology Center** where the stone monuments of the Burren are explained in detail.

County Galway & City

Into Galway County, where youths practice hurling in a field walled in stone and children fly kites in the blustery Atlantic winds. At Gort take the turnoff

WB Yeats's home at Thoor Ballylee.

Tranquil Galway harbor belies the fact that this is one of western Ireland's busier ports.

to **Thoor Ballylee** to view the Norman tower, picturesquely sited beside a millstream, that the poet WB Yeats lived in during the 1920s while he wrote *The Winding Stair* and *The Tower*. He paid IR£35 in 1916 for the ruined tower, which today refurbished with his original furniture, is open to paying visitors.

Just under 5 km (3 miles) away is **Coole Park**, where Yeats spent his summers with Lady Gregory, writer and patron of the Irish literary revival. His beloved wild swans still adorn the lake and although the house is no longer

The Roman Catholic cathedral seen from the blue waters of Galway Bay.

there, the **Autograph Tree** still survives, carved with the intials of George Bernard Shaw, Yeats, Sean O'Casey and Ireland's first president, Douglas Hyde.

Gray stone walls embrace emerald fields, clouds like mare's tails race across a sky, azure and unpolluted, and a great empty bay flares out to the east, we have arrived in **Galway**; western Ireland's largest city. A center for music, art, theater and traditional Gaelic culture, Galway is a lively, casual place boasting half a millennium of history. Founded by the Anglo-Normans in the 13th century, the city was run by 14 powerful families (Athy, Blake, Bodkin, Browne, D'Arcy, Dean, Font, French, Kirwan, Joyce, Lynch, Morris, Martin, and Skerret), known as the "Tribes of Galway", until the mid-19th century, and some of their old merchant houses still remain in the meandering narrow streets of the old city.

Located where the River Corrib flows into Galway Bay, the city is best seen on foot, starting at its center **Eyre Square** which borders on to the grassy square of **Kennedy Park**, named after the late US President who visited in 1963. A modern steel sculpture in the center of a fountain depicts the sails of the now obsolete Galway hooker, though you probably would not recognize the resemblance at first glance. Beside it Padraic O'Conaire, the great 20th-century storyteller, is immortalized in stone, and nearby is the 17th-century **Browne Doorway** which once adorned a rich merchant's house.

Summertime in Galway town.

Head downhill along William Street to the corner of Shop Street for **Lynch's Castle** (now a bank) which is the best surviving example of the fortified townhouses which the great merchants' families lived in during the 16th and 17th centuries. Stone gargoyles and details, reminiscent of Iberian design, are indicative of the flourishing wine trade which formerly existed between Galway and Spain.

Turn up Abbeygate Street for more memories of this powerful family at the **Lynch Memorial Window** where legend has it the term "to lynch" first originated. Apparently it derived from a 16th-century occasion when the mayor, James Lynch FitzStephen, was forced to hang his son for murder when there were no other takers for the job. The Lynch family tomb is in the **Collegiate Church of St Nicholas** on nearby Lombard Street, which dates from the 14th century, and is where according to another legend, Christopher Columbus stopped to pray before leaving Europe's shores on his historical voyage into the unknown west.

Meander through the adjacent winding lanes and streets like Shop, High and Quay Streets, which are crowded with traditional shopfronts housing pubs, cafés, boutiques, book stores, arts and crafts galleries, where buskers serenade the passers-by on Galway's left bank. **Spanish Arch**, beside the River Corrib at the bottom of Quay Street, is the last surviving 16th-century town gate and beside it in the Town

The Burren: Land of Limestone

Haunting desolation in the Burren.

A story is told in North Clare of a girl who had lived all her life beside the stony fastness of The Burren. On her first journey from home she apparently fainted when she saw her first tree near Castlebar, as she thought that it was a giant. A reasonable assumption for someone who was born and bred in such a treeless realm. Even the Cromwellian armies were taken aback by this barren, rocky region, for it was at The Burren, that Ludlow, one of Cromwell's generals made the now-famous remark that there is "not enough timber to hang a man, not enough water to drown him, nor enough earth to bury him".

Measuring around 260 sq km (100 sq miles) in area, this geographical marvel is a series of low, undulating limestone hills known to geologists as karst. Situated in the northwest corner of County Clare, bordered in the north by Galway Bay, and in the west by the Atlantic, it is Europe's youngest landscape formed by glaciation in the last Ice Age, a mere 15,000 years ago, the Burren is very immature by terrestrial standards. The entire region is limestone, and all the geological features of this type of country, like subterranean streams, swallow holes, caves and turloughs are found here, as are an incredible variety of flowers which vary from alpine to Mediterranean species, and are the main reason why it is such a popular destination for visitors.

Flowery Splendor

To call the Burren a pavement, or as some travel writers have penned, "Ireland's Pavement", is incorrect. The surface is actually the summits of countless canyons which have over the centuries eroded into the limestone plain. It is in these gryks, where the rainwater filters down, that the

House, is the **Galway City Museum**.

On the other side of the river is the **Claddagh**, once a thatched-roof village of Gaelic-speaking fishing families, which gave its name to the famous Claddagh ring, still a popular Irish wedding ring, which has its roots in Celtic times and features two hands clasping a heart. Wooden fishing boats lie on the seaweed-thick shore like beached whales and the famed mute swans congregate where tourists are throwing bread into the water.

Walk upriver from O'Brien's Bridge to the **Salmon Weir**, where from mid-spring to mid-summer shoals of this tasty fish can be seen waiting to make their way upstream to their breeding

Burren's flora thrives, protected from the salty Atlantic winds, and nutrified by miniature pockets of soil formed where the limestone has been broken down by the elements. Rare flowers, which are endangered elsewhere in the British Isles, like the creamy-hued mountain avens, blue gentians, scarlet-colored bloody cranes-bills, and orchids by the acre, grow here in abundance. Pocketed into crevices are Hart's tongue ferns, and honeysuckles snake through the stony clefts. Some flora which thrive here even consist of species which are usually considered to dislike limestone soils. Apparently, flowers grow so abundantly because of the warm, moisture-laden winds of the Gulf Stream which sweep across the Burren, warming the limestone which in turn heats the soil. Another reason why flowers thrive is that the reflections from the ocean and the pale gray-colored rocks make for incredibly strong light, vital for a plant's health.

The Marks of Man

Inhabitants began settling in the Burren around 5,000 years ago when geologists say the region was covered with pine forest. This tree cover was later stripped for farming leaving the lunar landscape which survives today. Among the rocky fastness are wedge-shaped burial chambers, the final resting places for Bronze Age folk; and there are remnants of Celtic ring-forts and dozens of ruined churches dating back to the 12th century. Although the marks of man, are but a scratching on the vastness, but people still do eke out an existence on the Burren. They graze their cattle on the higher hills during winter because the soil is warmer than in the valleys. Life, however, has always been tough here, and with lamb and wool prices in the doldrums, many people are moving off the land to the towns and cities. Tourism, though, has brought new hope and it is now The Burren's biggest industry, although it has scarcely made a dent in the landscape.

Cave-Land

Over the ages, other elements have had much more of an effect on the limestone. The continual hammering of rainwater and salt spray have eroded the rock into a maze of subterranean passages. Most of these are too small for exploration, some are well explored by expert speleologists, but only one, the **Ailwee cave**, discovered by a local sheep herder in the 1940s, near Ballyvaughan, is open to the public. A low-roofed corridor worn smooth eons ago by percolating water opens up into a lofty chamber, about 24 m (80 ft) high, and from a fissure in the roof of the cavern a veil-like waterfall descends to the floor. The Burren is a special place, not just because of its geological significance, or the fact that it is a botanists' paradise, but because of something more difficult to describe, a spiritual, mythical feeling best expressed by Tom Mooney a local poet who described it as "not a place but a presence".

grounds in Lough Corrib. Nearby, dominating the skyline, is the copper dome of the contemporary-styled **Catholic Cathedral** with its magnificent stained-glass and tile work.

Galway's other well-known sights include the **Nora Barnacle House** at the Bowling Green where visitors can peruse memorabilia of James Joyce and his Galway-born wife, and **Salthill**, a rather tacky seaside resort with a pleasant beach. Every July the festive **Galway Races** are held at **Ballybritt**, 6 km (4 miles) from the city and in this same month is the **Galway Arts Festival**. Later in the summer is the **Bucking Festival** and at the end of September is the gourmet's choice, the **Oyster Festival**.

The bogs of Connemara are set against the region's eternal mountainscape.

The Aran Islands

Twenty-four kilometers (15 miles) away, and seeming like a lot further in both space and time, are the **Aran Islands**, barren limestone isles which soar like ramparts above the surging surf of the Atlantic. Renowned for their Irish-speaking inhabitants steeped in traditional ways, their incredible stone-walled fields, and their dramatic scenery, the Aran Islands offer the visitor a unique experience. Ferries run frequently from Galway, Rossaveal and Doolin, and light planes make frequent trips from Galway's Carnmore Airport.

Inishmore, the largest island, sculpted with beaches and cliffs, and patchworked with tiny fields fenced with stonewalls, contains one of Europe's most superb prehistoric edifices, the 4,000-year-old circular stone fort of **Dun Aengus** which perches atop a 91-m (300-ft) high cliff. The famed Aran sweaters are knitted on Inishmore by Siobhan McGuiness who knits them from fleeces which she has carded, spun and washed herself.

Inishmaan, the middle island, is less commercial and as a result the islanders here live a more traditional lifestyle. The islands were immortalized by JM Synge who wrote a number of books on the islands and the play *Riders to the Sea*. Synge lived on Inishmaan for part of the year from 1899 to 1902, learnt the language and recorded his impressions

The simple home of country folk, near Spiddal.

and stories of a lifestyle that is all but vanished today. Synge found that the people were clever, agile and resourceful. *Curragh* boats (made of leather or hide) are still produced and the island is renowned for its traditional music and dance. There is no road traffic here and the cliffside walks are particularly appealing.

Inisheer, the smallest island, is famed for its summer Irish-language school, the tiny ruined **Church of St Kevin** where pilgrims say mass each year on the Saint's Day, and its miniature stonewalled fields where wildflowers bloom in summer. The island's **Folk Museum** has an interesting collection of photographs and **O'Brien's Castle** situated on a rocky outcrop, is one of Inisheer's features.

Connemara

Remote Connemara, in County Galway's west, has arguably Ireland's most spectacular scenery. Bordered by Lough Corrib in the east and the Atlantic to the west, Connemara's moorlands, bogs, lakelands and forests are set against the distant backdrop of the **Maumturk Mountains** and the **Twelve Pins** range. The coastal route out of Galway heads through the coastal resort towns of Salthill and Barna to **Spiddal**, the start of Connemara's Gaeltacht (note the Irish-language road signs), which hosts an annual regatta with *curragh* races. Further north, near Costelloe, the brown and green boglands are backed by the towering cones of the Twelve Pins.

However the most picturesque and shortest route to Clifden, unmistakeably Connemara's prettiest town and its lively hub, is the inland road through Moycullen to Rosscahill where a turn-off leads to the 16th-century **Aughnanure Castle**, stronghold of the warring O'Flahertys. Continue to **Oughterard**, a pretty village and fishing center for nearby Lough Corrib. Across the lake is the scenic

Kylemore Abbey, part of Ireland's best known scenery.

village of **Cong**, location for the John Wayne movie, *The Quiet Man*, and the luxurious **Ashford Castle**, now a hotel with a prestigious guest-register which includes the former US president Ronald Reagan.

From the crossroads town of **Maam Cross**, famed for its monthly cattle fair, the scenery is at its most splendid. A vista of lakes and moorlands opens out with a dramatic mountain background described by Thackeray as, "One of the most wild and beautiful districts that it is ever the fortune of the traveler to

examine...".

Take a detour to **Ballynahinch Lake** guarded by barren mountains where hunting lodges and castles are set in seclusion along the shoreline. Attractive **Ballynahinch Castle** nearby is now a hotel and one of its former residents, Richard Martin, nicknamed "Humanity Dick", was the founder of the RSPCA (Royal Society for the Prevention of Cruelty to Animals).

Clifden & the Kylemore Valley

In its alpine location, overlooking Clifden Bay and backed by rugged highlands, **Clifden** is one of Ireland's most scenic towns. Characterized by its twin church spires and an old-style downtown, travelers use Clifden as a base for exploring the surrounding countryside, whether by car or on foot, and there are a number of good restaurants, accommodations, and pubs which feature traditional music. Towards the seashore is Clifden's only major antiquity, **Clifden Castle**, built by the town's founder who designed the town center in 1815.

Further north, drive through the dramatic **Inagh Valley** to the **Kylemore Valley** in the shadow of the quartzite cones of the Twelve Pins. Take the turn to **Kylemore Abbey** and be ready for one of Ireland's best known scenes – the granite and limestone abbey viewed across a reed-filled lake backed by forest the latter of which is especially attractive in autumn.

Built in the mid-19th century by an English surgeon, the mansion had a royal ballroom and a luxurious interior. Gutted by fire in 1959, it was restored as a Benedictine abbey and a girls boarding school. The nuns run a crafts center and cafeteria and welcome visitors.

Mayo, Sligo & Donegal

"Years ago you'd never have seen any foreigners in Donegal in March," said the young nurse talking of her hometown, "but now there are Germans, French and even Chinese coming through". "Last week," she added, "a boat from Angola came into port and it was the most blacks the town had ever seen. It was wonderful to see them". She once worked in France, but now with tourism "making jobs", as she called it, lots of young people could now work in the northwest instead of leaving it, as was the norm in the past.

The beauty that once was, Glenveagh Castle grounds.

From Mayo's rugged splendor through Sligo's farms and woodlands, and the lakelands of Leitrim to the heathery hills and whitewashed cottages of Donegal, Ireland's largest Gaeltacht, the northwest region offers some of the nation's most remote and diverse attractions.

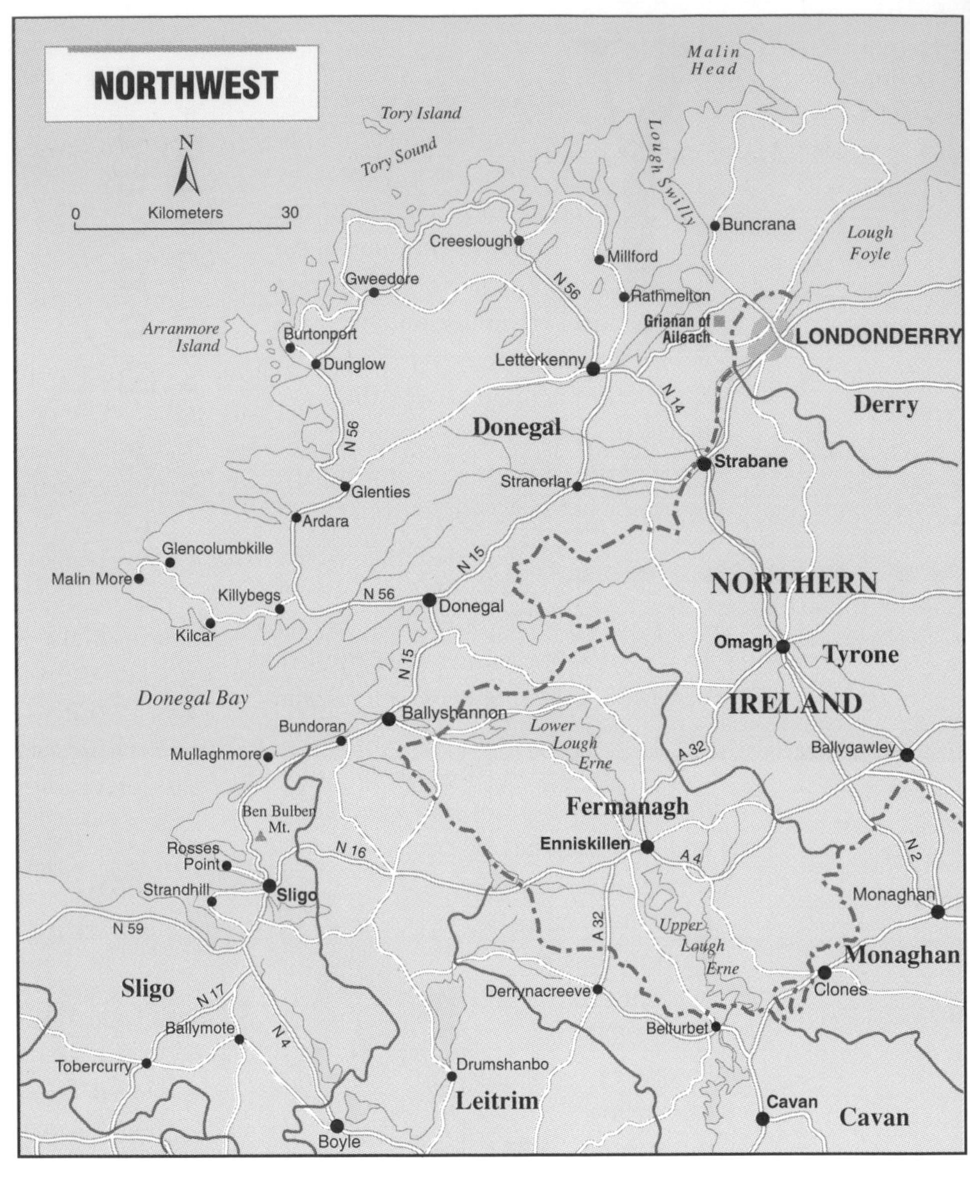

County Mayo

Westport, Mayo's attractive hub on a branch of Clew Bay, was planned by the same 18th-century architect who designed **Westport House**, a stately Georgian manor with antique-filled rooms open to the public. The Octagon in the center of town hosts an old-style **farmers' market** every Thursday, and the tree-lined **Mall** which runs alongside the river makes a pleasant stroll.

Head west from Westport around

the southern shores of **Clew Bay** past Croagh Patrick, the holy mountain which is thronged with pilgrims making their penitential summit-climb every July (see box story 'A Mountain Pilgrimage' p.112). Hikers start the three-hour climb from the small village of **Murrisk** and on clear days the views from the top of the 762-m (2,500-ft) high peak are spectacular, although the summit is often shrouded in cloud.

From **Roonah Point**, past Louisburgh, boats ply to **Clare Island**, which boasts a megalithic tomb, a 13th-century abbey, and the **Castle of Grace O'Malley**, the famous 16th-century pirate. Ireland's largest isle, **Achill Island**, further north, is approached by heading north from Westport around Newport Bay, and is linked to the mainland by a bridge. Bicycle or hike around Achill (pronounced "ack-ill") to another of Grace O'Malley's residences, the15th-century **Kildownet Castle**, and the **megalithic tombs** near Dugort where ferries also leave for visits to the local seal caves. **Currymore House** at Dooagh was once the home of Captain Boycott, the land agent who Achill's 19th-century farmers refused to pay rent to, and the originator of the term for such acts of defiance. Achill's coast is walled with magnificent cliffs including the quartzite, 244-m (800-ft) high **Minaun Cliffs** near Keel where weathered formations include the aptly-titled "**Cathedral Rocks**".

Boglands cover much of northern Mayo and the countryside is wild and deserted, particularly around the **Erris Peninsula** in the northwest. Due north from Westport is **Ballina**, the county's biggest town and a mecca for fishermen being a center for salmon fishing in nearby **Lough Conn** and the Moy River. East from Westport, via Castlebar, is **Knock**, the scene of miraculous visions in 1879, and now a place of pilgrimage for hundreds of thousands of believers who flock here every year.

Poetic Inspiration

Often dubbed "Yeats' Country" because of the poet's romantic attachment to this part of Ireland where he spent most of his boyhood summers, Sligo, is only just awakening to tourism, although it is hard to imagine why it took so long, as the county has a host of attractions. **Sligo**, the largest town in the northwest, with a population of 17,000 inhabitants, has long been a prosperous, commercial hub, which is perhaps one reason why tourism was so long in happening. Named after its "shelly river", the

Le Canvey Church, where the pilgrimage up Croagh Patrick begins.

River Garavogue, Sligo is at its liveliest during summer when the **Yeats Summer School** is in full swing. The school is held at the **Yeats Memorial Building** next to Hyde Bridge, and other memorabilia of the poet and his talented family, including his brother Jack, and father John, who were both well-known painters, can be found at the **Sligo County Library** and **Museum** on Stephen Street. Other historical sites in Sligo town include a ruined 13th-century **Dominican Abbey** on Abbey Street, a flamboyant **Victoriana Courthouse** on Teeling Street, and a swathe of churches, mainly Protestant, Sligo being well-known for its "Protestant stock" according to the writer Sean O'Faolain, who numbered Yeats' mother's family, the Pollexfens, among them.

Drive west from Sligo to **Strandhill**, an old-fashioned summer resort. Notice the prominent hillock of **Knocknarea**, a 305-m (1,000-ft) high mound with a massive stone cairn atop it which legend has it is the 1st-century burial place of Queen Maeve, the mythological Connaught ruler who was immortalized in the heroic saga *The Tain*. **Carrowmore**, nearby, is Ireland's largest collection of megalithic tombs, many of which date from 6,000 years ago.

Lough Gill, southeast of Sligo town, is so enchanting that it is easy to understand why Yeats was forever under its spell, and why its Irish name means "the beautiful lake". **Innisfree**, the island which Yeats immortalized in his poem *The Lake Isle of Innisfree*, is accessible by boat, but the solitude he writes of is probably only a reality during the off-season months.

Some of the interesting old buildings around the lake include **Parke's Castle**, a fortified Elizabethan house built from the stones of a historic O'Rourke fortress, and **The Old Hall**, built in the same era, also from the ruins of another O'Rourke castle, which was once the home of the pretty and notorious Dervorguilla. Dervorguilla deserted her O'Rourke husband for Dermot MacMurrough, the villian who invited Strongbow and the Normans into Ireland, the historic event that signalled Ireland's long travail with England. On the southern shore of Lough Gill is **Dooney Rock**, yet another Sligo site immortalized by Yeats in his poem *The Fiddler of Dooney*.

Farmers are plentiful in these remote parts.

A Poet's Resting Place

This region is not called "Yeats Country" for nothing, and for a look at the last resting place of the great poet, stop off at **Drumcliffe Church**, north of Sligo, where his limestone tomb beside St Columba's standing cross, records the immortal words from his poem *Under Ben Bulben*, as he prescribed:

A wayside country dwelling.

Cast a cold Eye
On Life, on Death.
Horseman, pass by!

Although the mountain is several kilometers away, the grey bulk of the poem's namesake, **Ben Bulben**, dominates the background of the church yard, a more fitting burial site could hardly be imagined, chosen by Yeats himself.

West of Drumcliffe is **Lissadell House**, the famed residence of the Gore-Booth sisters, Eva and Constance, who

were friends of Yeats, and the subjects of one of his poems. Eva became a poet, and Constance became the first woman elected to the *Dail*. Open to the public, the Georgian country home has interesting memorabilia and the surrounding forests are a wildlife reserve housing Ireland's largest colony of barnacle geese.

Other Sligo sites include the beautiful countryside around **Manorhamilton**, northeast of Sligo town, and the picturesque waterfalls of **Glencar Lough** nearby. At Ballymote in the south, is the medieval **De Burgo Castle**, ringed with six towers, and a friary. The castle is the place where the ancient text which deciphered the Ogham stones was written.

The Road to Donegal

Heading north from Sligo to Donegal, take a short detour to **Creevykeel**, a megalithic site dating from 2500 BC, then continue up the coast to **Bundoran**, a popular seaside resort, particularly with visitors from nearby Northern Ireland. Further along the coast the Atlantic swells roll into **Tullan Strand**, and other Donegal beaches making this stretch of coast one of Ireland's best for surfing. Just up the coast is **Ballyshannon** beside the River Erne, which is famed for its delicate chinawares. Stop off at the factory just outside of town where visitors can see these delightful ceramics being produced. Anglers are also well rewarded here for nearby **Lough Erne**, is a fisherman's paradise.

Keep north on the main road to Donegal, then turn east at Laghy, and then towards the border town of Pettigoe, to see the remote vastness of **Lough Derg**, where on a rocky outcrop named **Station Island**, pilgrims undergo a three-day penitence. Eating only scraps

Life is still traditional and going to mass requires one's best attire.

of toast and drinking tea, pilgrims abstain from sleep, and spend their pilgrimage walking barefoot around the isle. There are no lack of participants in Ireland's most rigorous penitential which has been famed since St Patrick's time. Pilgrimages are made from June to mid-August and during this time casual visitors are not permitted to visit the island.

Donegal Town

Donegal town, the gateway to the heathery hills, secluded glens and dramatic coastline of its namesake county, is attractively sited on a small harbor at the head of Donegal Bay. In Irish, Donegal means "fort of the foreigners", and was named after the Vikings who encamped here during the 9th century. After them the great Gaelic clan, the O'Donnells, including Red Hugh who warred against the Tudors, made Donegal the capital of Tyrconnel which was part of the old Kingdom of Ulster. Red Hugh was one of the many aristocratic Gaels who left Ireland during the Flight of the Earls in 1607 after his army had been crushed by the British might. Confiscated Donegal land was then resettled by Protestant farmers and the town was rebuilt during the Plantation Era.

Remnants of history still survive at **Donegal Castle**, built by the O'Donnells in 1470, and home to the last chief, Red Hugh. Repossessed by the English, the castle was rebuilt into its present shape as a turreted Jacobean castle. Located in Donegal's center, the Diamond, the castle boasts stone spiral staircase and carved crests over the fireplaces. Also in the Diamond is a monument to the Four Masters, four monks who prophetically realized that the English were set to destroy Irish culture and set down the history and mythology of Ireland in their 17th-century manuscript, *Annals of the Four Masters*, which now resides in the National Library. The remains of the old **Franciscan Friary** by the river is probably where the monks wrote their monumental history. On Main Street, **St Patrick's Church of the Four Masters,** also immortalizes the patriotic foursome.

Also on Main Street and around the

Diamond there are a number of shops selling the tweeds which Donegal is rightly famed for. At the **Magee Tweed Shop** (their jackets are world-renowned), handweaving demonstrations are offered, the factory where the handwoven tweeds are produced is just a short distance from the shop beside the River Eske. Its waters, softened by the upriver peat bogs, are said to be the reason that Donegal tweeds are so superior as the wool is still washed here.

Western Donegal

Killybegs, Donegal's major fishing port, 27 km (17 miles) west of town, is the start of the Gaelic-speaking region. Keep on the coast road beyond Killybegs passing the seaside village of **Kilcar**, also known for its tweeds, to **Carrick**, a center for traditional music. The town is also renowned for its towering 305-m (1,000-ft) high cliffs which plummet down to the Atlantic, backed by the lofty Slieve League mountains. The best cliff views can only be seen by hiking around the coast, not advisable for vertigo sufferers, but breathtaking, nonetheless.

At Donegal's western extremity is **Glencolumbkille**, named after the 6th-century missionary St Columba (an O'Neill from Ulster) who founded a monastery in this attractive valley. Every old stone cross and dolmen here has associations with the saint, and 15 of them are said to mark Columba's penitential route, followed by barefoot pilgrims every year on 9th June. A Stone-Age ring fort used by the pagan Celts is known as the **House of St Columba** and as the copious legends relate, a stone bed and chair inside were once used by the master of austerity – the saint himself. Glencolumbkille survives with its summer **Irish-language school**, a **Folk Village**, and a craft co-operative founded by a visionary priest in the 19th century.

Take the scenic road through the Glengesh Pass to **Ardara**, a pretty village of limewashed cottages renowned for centuries for its thriving wool trade. Every year at the start of July, a **Weavers' Fair** is held here and the village is an excellent place to purchase hand-knitted sweaters at a reasonable price.

Northern Donegal

To explore the spectacular scenery of Northern Donegal, start from the county's largest town, **Letterkenny**, which has little to offer apart from its location. **Ramelton**, an attractive town 13 km (8 miles) north, is the gateway to the great fiord-like inlet of Lough Swilly, and the old harbor of **Rathmullan**, scene of the historic Flight of the Earls, where the defeated chiefs of Ulster, the last great Gaelic Catholics to try and halt English rule, boarded a French ship in 1607 and went into exile. Their story is told at the town's **Heritage Center**.

From Rathmullan, a scenic route loops around the arid, rock-strewn **Fanad Peninsula** to the resort town of

Glenveagh Castle, the focal point of Glenveagh National Park.

Kerrykeel on Mulray Bay. Further south at Milford, head up the other side of the bay for the picturesque village of **Carrigart**, gateway to the scenic beaches of the **Rosguill Peninsula**. Continue southwest to 15th-century **Doe Castle** overlooking **Sheep Haven Bay**, home of the McSweeney clan who occupied the castle until late last century. To the west of the bay is **Ards Forest Park**, where trails wind around an old **Capuchin friary** and further north is **Horn Head**, a dramatic headland overlooking the Atlantic which is home to

various colonies of seabirds.

To the northwest is barren, remote **Tory Island**, accessible in good weather from Meenlaragh. Home to an independent population of fishermen and artists who speak their own unique Irish dialect, Tory Island is scattered with stone relics from prehistoric times, including the powerful **"wishing stones"** that once apparently sank a boatful of English tax-collectors. Continuing around the coast from Meenlaragh, there is **Bloody Foreland Head** named after the color of its rocks at sunset, and **Burtonport**, the famed salmon-fishing hub where boats depart for **Aranmore**, another remote Donegal island with Celtic stone ruins and magnificent scenery.

Heading back towards Letterkenny, stop off at the **Glenveagh National Park**, a 9,600-hectare (24,000-acre) expanse of heathlands, glens, and rocky mountains. Trails lead into the remote interior where herds of red deer still roam. Inside the park is the 19th-century **Glenveagh Castle** surrounded by delightful gardens and rhododendron walks.

Ireland in Miniature

Northwest of Letterkenny is the remote **Inishowen Peninsula**, the nation's most northerly extremity, sometimes called "Ireland in miniature". Highlights include: the hilltop Celtic **Fort of Grianan of Aileach**, the "stone palace of the sun", which dates from 1700 BC and affords marvellous vistas of the surrounding countryside; the beach resort of **Buncrana** with its castle of the same name; the famous carved Donagh or **St Patrick's Cross** at Carn-donagh; and **Malin Head**, Ireland's most northern extremity, and a fitting place to end a tour of not only Donegal, but of the republic itself.

Sports & Recreation

Valued for battle and sport, the most sacred animal in the Celt's divine menagerie was the horse. Today, 2,000 years later, at racetracks around Ireland, their descendents still seem to worship the horse with just as much fervor. Compared to the size of the population, the island republic boasts more race-courses than any other nation, a legacy from the pagan days when the warrior knights galloped their steeds across the grassy plains on festive race days. For centuries, horse-meets have been held on the majestic limestone plains of **The Curragh**, in the hub of Kildare's horse-breeding country, southwest of Dublin. At the important meets, a throaty roar issues from the great grandstands as the silk-clad jockeys urge their mounts to the finishing line, an emotion-packed, and thrilling spectacle for anyone who appreciates fine horseflesh

Angling, one of Ireland's most popular sports.

Racing the Irish Derby at The Curragh.

and the art of racing on the flat, not to mention a good wager. **The Derby**, the **1,000 and 2,000 Guineas, the Oaks**, and the **St Leger**, Ireland's classic races, are all held at The Curragh during the summer season. Other less sophisticated race-venues which manage to keep alive the festive spirit of the ancient horse-fairs include, the unique **Laytown Strand Races** which are held every summer on a beach 48 km (30 miles) north of Dublin; the summer meet in **Killarney**, and the renowned **Galway Races**. "It's there you'll see the gamblers, the thimbles and the garters. And the sporting Wheel of Fortune with the four and twenty quarters", wrote an anonymous 19th-century poet.

Steeplechasing

"Over the sticks", the local phrase for steeplechasing, has just as many, if not more Irish followers as flat racing, probably due to the sport having originated in County Cork in 1752. It all started when a couple of country gentlemen by the name of Blake and O'Callaghan, raced their horses 7 km ($4^1/_2$ miles) across country, jumping whatever was in the way, from one village church to the other. Known thereafter as "steeple-chasing", the new sport quickly became a countrywide favorite, and today Ireland is still where the world's best steeplechasers are bred and trained. The **Irish Grand National** at **Fairyhouse**, held on Easter Monday, is the biggest event of the steeplechasing year. The second-biggest, which draws around 20,000 Irish spectators around St Patrick's Day, is the Cheltenham Gold Cup, which is held on the other side of the Irish Sea in England. It has been said that so much Irish money is bet here that the nation's economy is threatened. It is all part of the art of winning and losing heroically, that the Irish put into whatever they do, but most particularly into horses.

The pick of the nation's top thoroughbreds strut their stuff every August at the **Dublin Horse Show**, in the elegant suburb of **Ballsbridge**, when the week-long horse show draws affecionados from all over Europe, the US, and the Middle East. However for an event which still preserves the spirit of the old days nothing beats the **Great October Horse Fair** at **Ballinasloe** in the east of County Galway. Legend has it that Napoleon's famous mount Marengo, now stuffed and on display in a Paris museum, was even bought here. Old ways, probably dating from pagan times, still prevail at Ballinasloe, like a seller's habit of spitting in his hand before passing "luck money" to the buyer.

Greyhound-racing is another sport favored by the Irish, but on a far less popular scale than horse-racing. It is however another opportunity to indulge in camaraderie and a good round of betting. The breeding industry is also steadily climbing in reputation and in profits made.

Gaelic Sports

Hurling, the world's fastest and most skillful ball-and-stick game, is unique to Ireland, and has a pedigree as old as horse-racing, as the epics of mythologi-

When the sun comes out who can resist a dip.

cal times relate. Teams of 15 players a side, wielding hockey-like sticks known as hurleys, score points by hiting a hard, orange-sized ball through goal posts, which are 6-m (20-ft) high by the same distance wide. Goals placed under the 3-m (10-ft) high crossbar score three points, while those over the bar only rank a single point. The team which scores the highest points after a 60-minute game is the winner, and in true die-hard fashion the game only halts at half-time and not for minor injuries. Hurling is played all over Ireland, but the southern teams of Cork and Kilkenny are considered the masters of the game and are home to all the greatest players, among them the legendary Christy Ring.

Gaelic football, Ireland's greatest crowd-puller, is played in a similar fashion to hurling, minus the sticks and with a football-sized ball. It is an offshoot of the medieval mêlée which involved entire parishes in day-long matches across kilometers of countryside. The sport is characterized by its free-for-all spirit which to the uninitiated looks very much like anything goes. The game is only played in Ireland and by Irish expatriates in the United States and the United Kingdom, although Australian Rules is similar and was obviously introduced by Irish emigrants.

Both hurling and Gaelic football are amateur sports and were revived during the 1880s' land agitations when the Gaelic Athletic Association (GAA) was founded to protect traditional Irish

Gaelic football is truly for everyone and the rules are free-for-all.

games. Fiercely nationalistic from its very beginnings, the GAA banned its members from playing non-Gaelic games, which effectively removed the threat of British soldiers from participating as they played cricket in the summer. The GAA's fiery founder Michael Cusack, an ardent nationalist was immortalized by James Joyce in *Ulysses*, where he is known as "The Citizen".

This promotion of Gaelic sports encouraged the Irish language and was instrumental in building up the Irish morale, and by the 1890s the GAA boasted a massive membership, which not only organized traditional sports but played a major role in encouraging militant nationalism.

In September, both hurling and Gaelic football hold their All-Ireland finals in Dublin's **Croke Park**, the headquarters of the GAA, and Ireland's largest sports stadium with a seating capacity of 72,000. Needless to say tickets are hard to come by and the teams play to a packed house every year, when Kerry, the undisputed champions are always the team to beat. As Brendan Kennelly, says in the *Irish Independent,* "Somehow or other, when the Dubs topple the Kingdomn (Kerry team), there is more to the triumph than a mere All-Ireland medal. There's a satisfaction beyond words, a victory that defies expression. Beating Kerry is like triumphing over history itself." If you are not lucky enough to be around for the finals, the

With Ireland's strong horses and beautiful countryside, horse trekking is an excellent choice of sport.

season for both Gaelic games runs from mid-February to November, and often there is just as much action and excitement in the provincial games as there is in the All-Ireland, and you can easily buy a ticket at the turnstiles. Jack Lynch from Cork, is Ireland's most famous hurler and football player, though in soccer Pat Jennings was an internationally-famous goalkeeper.

Soccer and rugby also have a large following in Ireland, and home games for the Irish rugby team are played from October through to March at Dublin's **Lansdowne Road Stadium**. The **International Rugby Championship** is staged here in January and February when Ireland plays against the world's best teams.

Another popular ball-game in some districts of Cork, Waterford, and Limerick is road bowling. No special course is needed as any public road can suffice for this game between two participants. The object is to see who can bowl an iron ball down a specified distance with the least amount of throws. Known as a "bullet", the bowling ball can weigh from 453-798 g (16-28 oz), and players are penalized if it lands off the road, in the rough, although they are allowed to sling it cross-country where the road bends. The betting, as in most popular Irish games, is fast and furious. Road bowling is actually illegal, because of the way it blocks traffic, but the *gardai* (police) seldom interfere, it would not be considered sporting.

Horse racing, hurling, Gaelic football, and other ballgames are all more or less spectator sports for travelers to Ireland, but there are many enjoyable pursuits like fishing, golf, cycling, hiking, and watersports that are freely available to all visitors.

Angling

Fishing falls into three categories: sea angling which includes shore fishing (from beaches, piers or rocks.), and deep-sea fishing; game angling for salmon, sea trout and brown trout; and coarse angling for all freshwater fish. No permits are needed for sea angling and anyone can wander off to the seashore and fish to his or her heart's content. Deep-sea fishing trips, with the likelihood of snagging a shark or a decent-sized tuna, can be organized from ports like Youghal, Kinsale, and Schull in County Cork, and Achill Island and Ballina in Mayo. A licence is needed for salmon fishing and is easily bought from most tackle shops, and in addition fishermen usually have to pay a fee for fishing rights, but these are not unreasonably priced.

The angling season runs from the start of January through to the end of September with river-openings dependent on the time of year. Donegal's **River Bundrowse** opens on New Year's Day, and Munster's **Blackwater River** opens a month later. **Burtonport**, or as the road signs say, *Ailt an Chorrain* (Irish), in Donegal, is said to land more salmon than any other Irish port. Auspiciously, fishermen arrive at **Mount Falcon Castle**, near Ballina, in County Mayo, on St Patrick's Day, when the salmon begin their run on the nearby River Moy.

Coarse angling, which includes fishing for freshwater fish like pike, bream, roach, dace and others, is open all year round with no permit required. The fishing grounds are extensive and cover all the Midlands drained by the **River Shannon** and its prolific loughs, the **Grand Canal**, the **Rivers Barrow** and **Blackwater**, and the extensive lakelands of **Westmeath** and **Cavan**. In **Drumsna**, near Carrick-on-Shannon, an **Angling Information Center** supplies tackle, bait, and all kinds of advice. If you really like to fish without the crowds head off to one of **Cavan's** 365 lakes, where the odds on pulling in supper are even greater than coming across another angler.

Golf

Golf is another Irish passion, and probably because of the ease with which grass grows on the shamrock isle, and the fact that it stays green all year round, there is no shortage of golfcourses across the country (see box story "Ireland's Best Golf Courses" p.304). There are links that are set in such enchanting scenery, like in **Killarney's lake district**, or overlooking the coast and the castle at **Howth**, that even non-golfers

Ireland's Golfing Greats

Ireland boasts a host of world-class and amateur courses.

Greens that stay green the year round are one reason why the "emerald isle" is a top golf destination for enthusiasts the world over, but almost as big a lure is that this wealth of different courses are blessed with such a variety of settings, from dramatic sand-dune seascapes, and clifftop locations, to forested glades and scenic lakesides. With over 250 clubs to choose from, Ireland boasts more quality courses per square mile than any place in the world, and visitors are warmly welcomed to the clubs and encouraged to make themselves at home, another reason why golfing holidays are becoming so popular.

Dublin Links

Beginning in Dublin, start with the **Royal Dublin Golf Club**, at North Bull Island, Dollymount, a traditional links which has hosted many major events and presents a fine test of golf. Lee Trevino once remarked that "the finish here, from the 13th tee onwards, is as tough as you will find in golf."

Portmarnock Golf Club, outside of Dublin at Portmarnock, is Ireland's premier tournament venue and consistently ranks as one of the world's top-20 courses. When Ben Crenshaw won the Irish Open in 1976 he remarked that "the 15th has to be the best par 3 hole on earth."

St Margaret's Golf Club, off Ashbourne Road, is Dublin's newest international-standard course featuring speedy, sand-based greens, and seven man-made lakes for a challenging round. Other excellent courses close to Dublin include the **County Louth Golf Club** near Drogheda, designed by Tom Simpson; **The Kildare Hotel and Country Club** course designed by Arnold Palmer in the upper reaches of the River Liffey; and the exposed **Dundalk Golf Club** at Blackrock near Dundalk, which is a tough course when the wind howls in off the Irish Sea.

Scenic Splendors

Many of Ireland's most famous and scenic courses are found in the rugged southwest in County Kerry, and are frequented by most of the world's top golfers. **Ballybunion Golf Club** is a superb test of golf as the course meanders, "menacingly", as one golf-guide describes it, through sand dunes overlooking the Atlantic. The legendary Tom Watson considered it "a true test of golf" and thought the course "the best in the world".

Waterville Golf Club, superbly sited on the Ring of Kerry nestled between the mountains and the sea, provides a truly unforgettable experience. Sam Snead once called Waterville "the beautiful monster" and he could have been talking about the par-five 11th which runs for 445 m (1,460 ft) along a rugged valley.

One of Ireland's most popular and picturesque courses is the **Killarney Golf Club** sited beside the scenic loughs and overlooked by the towering hills of Killarney National Park. Killarney has hosted all the major domestic events and the European Tour's Irish Open in 1991.

Also in County Kerry, is the rugged seaside course of **Tralee Golf Club**, which golf-guides say was "built by Arnold Palmer and created by Nature". Its feature hole is the 17th par four which is played from an elevated tee to a high green overlooking the Atlantic Ocean.

Often referred to as "the St Andrew's of Ireland", **Lahinch Golf Club** in County Clare, is possibly the country's most legendary course and has hosted every important Irish amateur event and the Home Internationals. The wild, and unhurried West Coast also boasts many excellent courses like **County Sligo Golf Club** at Rosses Point, where golfers get a chance to play as Henry Cotton describes, "the most satisfying shot in golf, the downhill drive", on the third, the fifth, the tenth, and the 14th.

At the parkland course of **Westport Golf Club** at Carrowholly in County Mayo, golfers can admire the views of nearby Clew Bay and the holy mountain of Croagh Patrick. Another top west-coast course is **Connemara Golf Club** at Ballyconneely, Clifden, in County Galway. The finish here is described as "robust golf at its best", and the scenery which encompasses a dramatic stretch of the Atlantic coast, is hard to beat.

Other great westcoast courses include **Donegal Golf Club** at Murvagh, County Donegal, which offers an international-class course in an incredibly peaceful location far from the madding crowds. Described as a "crafty course", **Bundoran Golf Club**, also in Donegal, has links which run along high cliffs above Bundoran beach.

Other top courses include **Cork Golf Club** which winds around a quarry overlooking the River Lee and was designed by Dr.Alister MacKenzie. **Mount Juliet Golf and Country Club** at Thomastown in County Kilkenny, is Ireland's first and only Jack Nicklaus-designed course.

With such prestigious courses and spectacular scenery, Ireland must be the place to truly enjoy your golf. For a tour of stunning views and golf, follow the chain of coastal links around the coast from Sligo to Clare and Kerry and finally to Dublin.

could be persuaded to take up clubs in Ireland. It is a casual game here. Golfers often wander up to the local course with a couple of golf clubs in their hands for a round after work. Most golfers shoulder their own bags, or pull a trolley, and golf-carts are just about unheard of. Course fees are extremely reasonable throughout Ireland and visitors are welcome to play at around 180 golf courses.

Cycling

Cycling is not only a great way to exercise, but in some parts of Ireland it is by far the best way to see the countryside, particularly if you are not partial to organized tours. Top of the list would have to be the ride around **The Ring of Kerry**, (see "Ring of Kerry" chapter p.235), a 175 km (109 miles) journey which winds around the rugged Iveragh Peninsula. There is spectacular mountain and coastal scenery, some gruelling passes, and marvellous glides down the other side. Off-season is the best time for traffic-free roads, although before Easter many B&Bs and restaurants are still closed for the season.

Bikes can be rented from a number of bike shops in Killarney and come complete with patch-kits, pumps, and bike-bags large enough to stow essentials and gear for a week. The "Ring" can be done in three days. Kerry's **Dingle Peninsula** is also popular with cyclists, as is **the Burren**, the limestone hills of Clare, and the nearby coastline from

Biking, both a great way to exercise and to see the magnificent countryside.

Doolin to the **Cliffs of Moher.** Most sizeable towns have a bike-rental shop, and there is even a bike-rental service available through the Irish Tourist Board which arranges for a bike to be ready for you on arrival at Shannon Airport. Prices for rental are reasonable.

Hiking

Hiking is a great way to really see the countryside in depth, and books and maps are readily available at tourist offices and bookshops throughout the

republic. The 113-km (70-mile) long **Wicklow Way**, a government-sponsored, long-distance walk, starts just outside of Dublin and follows the Wicklow Mountains to **Clonegal** in Country Carlow. There are marvellous views and hostels are spaced conveniently within hiking distance from the trail. Another excellent high-country walk is the **Kerry Way,** which starts from Killarney and follows the Ring of Kerry, at a high altitude, through spectacular countryside. Enquire for maps in the Killarney tourist office.

The 62-km (43-mile) **Munster Way,** runs from Tipperary's Cahir through the Galty Mountains. Other good hikes, or climbs, include the old pilgrimage route up Kerry's **Mt Brandon**, or up Mayo's **Croagh Patrick**, or Donegal's **Muckish Mountain**.

Watersports

Watersports are rapidly gaining in popularity around Ireland and there are a number of annual regattas. In August, there is an annual regatta at **Dingle**; at Galway's **Spiddal** you can watch the ancient sport of *curragh* (leather boat) racing, and at **Mountshannon Sport Weekend** on Lough Derg, there are a variety of watersports staged.

At **Caherdaniel** on the Ring of Kerry, **Sweeney's Diving Center** organizes scuba-diving trips, and at **Killorgan**, at the start of the Ring of Kerry. The **Cappanalea Outdoor Education Center** offers canoeing and boardsailing, as well as hiking and rockclimbing. At **Devil's Glen** in the Wicklow Mountains, the **Tiglin Adventure Center** runs courses on canoeing and kayaking, as well as rock-climbing and mountaineering. The **Irish Surfing Association** is based at the famed beach of **Rossnowlagh** in County Donegal.

ORIGINAL
PENCIL DRAWINGS
AND
PAINTINGS
By: KATHLEEN Kiely

Shopping

Aran sweaters, Donegal tweeds, Irish linen, Waterford crystal, four of Ireland's most well-known products which are "must-buys" for visitors. However, in addition to these notable souvenirs there is also a huge range of superb arts and crafts available as well as reasonably-priced antiques, famed potables and edibles, books on Ireland and by Irish writers, tapes and CD's of Irish music, chinawares and jewelry. Naturally, the traveler who has time to shop around and go to where the products originate will usually score the best bargains and have the added advantage of knowing that they are buying from source. But for those visitors who are pressed for time, Dublin has a marvellous variety of shops and galleries which specialize in Irish-made products from all over the country. To a

Portraits of Ireland's great figures make interesting souvenirs.

Not surprisingly Ireland's woollen wear is of the very best quality.

lesser extent, the other major tourist centers like Killarney, Galway and Cork, also offer an extensive collection.

Aran Sweaters & Woollen Wear

Top of every shopper's list has to be a real, hand-knitted Aran sweater preferably purchased on the **Aran Islands** from the knitter herself. These days, Aran sweaters, characterized by their interwoven cable designs, are a winter-fashion necessity, but they were originally produced as an indispensable, warm and hard-wearing, piece of clothing for the rugged fisherman of the Aran Islands. Designs are patterned on religious and other symbols and a rather macabre story tells that when an islander drowned often the sweater designs were the only way of identifying the wearer.

The very best, and often the most expensive sweaters, are made by Aran women who spin, card and dye their own fleeces before hand-knitting the garments which will last for a lifetime. There are a wealth of different patterns to choose from so make sure that you have a good look before making your final choice. The most traditional sweaters are cream-colored, but these days they come in a variety of colors. On the Aran Island of **Inishmore**, Siobhan McGuinness knits authentic sweaters from her own fleeces, and in Galway

Irish crystal is of the highest quality and coveted throughout the world.

Irish tartan on sale at woollen mills.

and throughout Connemara, there are a host of craft shops which specialize in not only traditional Aran sweaters, but also colorful ones knitted from cotton, which are marvellous for Ireland's summer evenings.

Donegal is also an excellent place to buy Aran sweaters which are still worn by most of the fishermen there. If you do not have time to journey to the west, Dublin's **Blarney Woollen Mills** at College Park House in Nassau Street, have a good range as do the **Kilkenny Design Centers** which can be found throughout the country, notably at Kilkenny.

Cheaper Aran sweaters which still look good but are not as long wearing, are referred to as hand-loomed and these can be picked up throughout Ireland, especially in village woollen shops around the **Ring of Kerry** in the southwest. Other good hand-knits include navy-blue fishermen's pullovers, soft mohair sweaters and cardigans in either pastel or jewel-like emeralds and ruby tones, and marvellous "picture" jumpers which are colorful hand-knitted sweaters with floral or animal designs.

Other woollen items which are popular and make excellent buys include blankets and shawls woven in Irish tartan designs or mohair weaves, and rugs made of goat and sheep skins. Another interesting handicraft from the Aran Islands are hand-painted belts known as *crioses*.

More fashionable products can be purchased along Grafton Street, Dublin.

Tweed & Linen

Donegal in the far northwest is famed for its hand-loomed tweeds, and although a tailored suit can be a costly, albeit a fabulous buy, machine-loomed tweed cloth is also available, sold by the meter (as are the expensive tweeds). Real tweed can also be made into less-expensive items like caps, or even placemats. Obviously the top region for purchasing tweed has to be **Donegal**, particularly Donegal Town and **Ardara**, as country weavers who often live in remote hamlets still bring their hand-loomed tweeds into these centers for sale. The soft waters of the River Eske and the humid Donegal air is said to be why the tweeds from this region are of such a superior hard-wearing quality, yet soft to the touch. Donegal Town's most famed tweed vendor is **Magee's**, on the Diamond, which is still run by the founding family who started the business in 1866. Despite their international reputation, Magee's tweed jackets are reasonably priced, and the riverside factory is definitely worth a tour even if you are just browsing.

The picturesque village of Ardara, northwest of Donegal Town, was once the scene of monthly cloth fairs, and although these have now died out there are still many weavers who work in the surrounding countryside and supply the village stores. The village's market tradition still lives on at the annual **Weav**

The relaxing ambiance of Powerscourt Shopping Center, Dublin

ers' Fair and Vintage Weekend which is held on the 1st July.

In Dublin, muted-colored tweeds are readily available in either ready-to-wear fashions or sold by the meter at the **Dublin Woollen Company**, opposite the Halfpenny Bridge on the north bank of the River Liffey, and at the **Blarney Woollen Mills**, **The Kilkenny Shop**, and **Kevin & Howlin**, all on Nassau Street (opposite Trinity College).

Irish linen is another excellent fashion buy and the above shops also have a good range of blouses and women's suits in this long-wearing and versatile fabric. Most garments are in classic styles which can be worn without fear of fashion changes dating them. Less expensive souvenirs in this famed fabric include handkerchiefs, place-mats, and damask tablecloths.

Waterford Crystal

Waterford crystal is the best-known, and most expensive of Ireland's lead-crystal, however, pieces hold their price and are a safe investment. The superb cutting, and the weight of this crystal is proof, indeed, of its superior craftsmanship. Naturally, the best place to buy Waterford crystal is at the factory in **Waterford**, which is one of the town's biggest tourist attractions and is a great place to visit even if you are just interested in the crystal-making process. As Waterford crystal is so well-known it is readily available anywhere in Ireland.

It would be a rare town that did not have at least one store dealing in this renowned product. Although they are dwarfed by the fame of Waterford, there are other centers that also produce fine quality crystal wares. These centers include Tipperary, Dublin, Cork and Galway, while uncut glass can be bought from Stoneyford and Jerpoint.

Arts & Crafts

Arts and crafts are enjoying a revival in Ireland and the quality and quantity available these days is fantastic compared to a decade or so ago when creative "Made in Ireland" products were harder to find. Top of the board must be the **Kilkenny Design Center**, in **Kilkenny** opposite the castle, and also in Dublin (though not quite as good). In the stables behind the showroom gold and silver-smiths, ceramicists, and photographers, work in the government-sponsored **Crescent Workshops**, turning out inspired pottery and jewelry. Good buys include hand-turned ceramic mugs; marvellous Irish-green woollen capes which are fastened at the shoulder by a Tara brooch (a silver pin which is still made in the same design as the Celtic originals); candles and dried flowers. Silversmiths are also plentiful in **Dublin** and **Cork**, and in **Connemara** silver is combined with the region's polished marble to create a unique style of jewelry. **Galway** is the home of the Claddagh Friendship Ring, an ancient design which features hands clasped about a heart; the design originated in the riverine region of the same name on Galway's west bank. Irish folk wear the ring as a wedding ring and it is a popular souvenir with visitors, crafted in either gold or silver.

Antique jewelry is available mainly in the antique shops of the capital and is very pricey, but for those who like the ancient designs but not at exorbitant prices, there are many excellent reproductions made by Irish silver and goldsmiths. Another innovative gift.

Antiques & Books

Antiques are best bought in Dublin where all the best stores are situated on **Grafton Street** and prices for 18th and 19th-century furniture and *object d'art* are quite reasonable compared to shops on the Continent. There are also some interesting shops specializing in old wares on the north bank of the Liffey in downtown Dublin. On the south bank near the Halfpenny Bridge is a photography shop which stocks historical photos, framed and unframed of Ireland in the old days, a souvenir with a difference.

Bookshops have to be one of Dublin's greatest diversions, especially when the weather turns inclement which is not infrequent. There are all kinds of book stores ranging from the huge display at **Eason's** in O'Connell Street to the quirky **Winding Stair**, on Lower

Ormond Quay, where you can browse the extensive second-hand book array, and then relax with a coffee and a wholefood snack overlooking the River Liffey.

With such a pedigree of famous writers, Dublin certainly lives up to its literary reputation and the book shops are legion. **Fred Hanna's** on Nassau Street is good for travel and Irish titles; **Waterstone's** on Dawson Street has a wide selection of titles on and by Irish authors; **Greene's** on Clare Street is good for second-hand books, while **Hodges Figgis** on Dawson Street is renowned for its sheer quantity of volumes. Good buys for gifts include works by James Joyce, Yeats, and all the other famed Irish writers, JM Synge's titles on the Aran Islands, and coffee-table books which do ample justice to Ireland's great houses, castles, gardens, pubs, or just general scenery.

Musical Buys

After your stay in Ireland, having experienced a country where music is such an essential and vibrant part of life, you will probably want to take something back with you. While Sinhead O'Connor, Chris De Burgh and U2 can be bought anywhere in the world, traditional Irish music can not, so you must buy recordings during your trip. Irish music is readily available both on CD's and cassettes and ranges from recordings of contemporary rock groups like U2, to traditional music. A good selection of the latter can be found in **Claddagn Records**, 2 Cecilia Street, and Gael Linn on 26 Merrion Square. Recordings by popular groups and soloists can be found at any of the big music shops in Dublin including **HMV** on Henry and Grafton Streets.

Value Added Tax

There is a bonus for shoppers from the United States and Canada as they can have the Value Added Tax (VAT) refunded to them at either Dublin or Shannon airport when they depart the country. The VAT is at the time of writing 21% of the retail price and applies to most luxury products that overseas visitors are likely to buy. Known as "Cashback", the refund system is used by many crafts shops and department stores, so if you are in doubt, ask, as the savings on larger priced items are quite substantial. If goods are to be shipped, however, the VAT is taken off the purchase price.

Food & Drink

Irish whiskey and Irish liqueurs, like Irish Mist (made with whiskey and honey), and Bailey's Irish Cream (mixed with cream), are excellent gifts which seldom fail to please. Edible gifts include smoked salmon, smoked trout, and gourmet cheeses like Milleens and Gubbeen.

BUSHMILLS
IRISH WHISKEY
BLACK BUSH

Cuisine

Irish stew, potatoes baked in their jackets, crunchy soda bread, this is traditional Irish cuisine; fortifying, filling, and tasty, the kind of food that every traveler to Ireland expects. But what comes as a surprise is that in addition to these well-known foods, there is a wealth of tantalizing seafood from Galway oysters and Wexford mussels, to smoked salmon and other freshly caught fish. Healthy salad bars that specialize in vegetarian quiches and other delicacies are extremely popular and there is a pizzeria in every town. Gone are the days when Irish food was considered bland and unimaginative, for these days the nation is not fully dependent on what is grown locally, as admittance into the European Community has opened the market to a vast array of exotic fruits and vegetables. In Dublin's **Moore Street market** there are bananas from Ecuador, oranges from

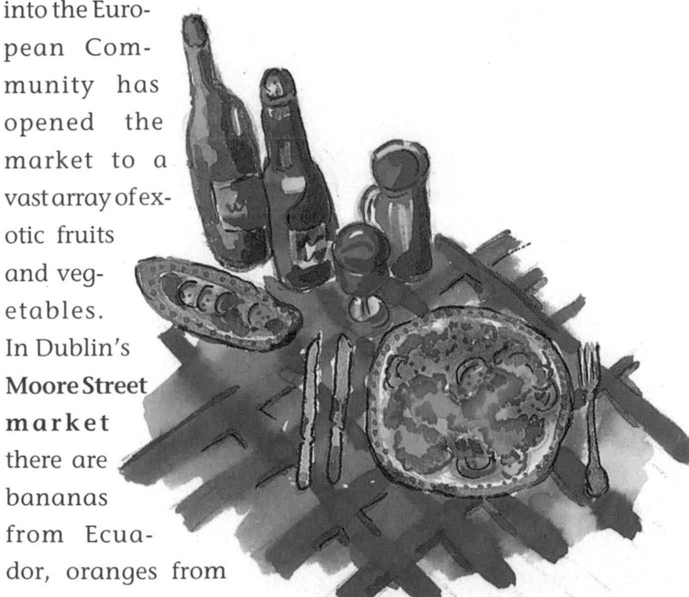

Presenting the cream of Ireland's tipples.

Neat and cheerful pantry-restaurants line the streets of many Irish towns.

Morocco, and even potatoes, believe it or not, from Cyprus!

Dublin Delights

It goes without saying that the larger the town, or city, the better the variety of food that is offered. **Dublin**, at the top of the scale, offers the diner gastronomic delights at astronomical prices, and for the less fastidious there is a wonderful selection of restaurants, cafés, and diners to suit all pockets. Among the cel-

ebrated are the renowned **Bewley's** on Westmoreland Street, famed as much for its brewed coffee, home-style breads and cakes, and salad bar, as it is for its atmosphere and conversation. For a genuine meal in real "working-class" Dublin, wander up to **Philomena's Café** at the north end of O'Connell Street, where for IR£3.75p you can fill up on a "fixed" three-course menu consisting of mutton soup, roast beef with three huge potatoes, carrots, cabbage and bread; custard and jelly, and a pot of tea. Frank Pearse, who started the café in 1953, has penned a rather cryptic ditty on the cafe wall, "A good meal is good value whatever the price".

Irish Staples

Despite the proliferation of pizzerias, and fast-food joints, Irish traditional food is still readily available especially in the countryside. Most bed-and-breakfasts (B & Bs) offer "Full Irish Breakfast" which consists of bacon, eggs, tea and toast, but many still include a couple of slices of Irish soda bread, together with the far less nutritous white-sliced toast.

Crunchy on the outside and soft on the inside, soda bread made of wholemeal flour, is an Irish staple, and is still baked every day, for it turns stale quickly. Even in the old days if a housewife offered a visitor two-day-old bread it would have been considered an insult. Named after the bicarbonate of soda which causes the bread to rise, Irish cooks of the early 18th century originally used yeast or sour dough as their leavening, and breads were made from a variety of grains including oat, barley, and maize, as well as wheat flours. Try fresh soda bread with a generous pat of butter alongside a plate of Galway oysters and a pint of Guinness, to appreciate its true flavor.

Ireland's Finest Cuisine

Good food is easy to find in Ireland, as every city, town and village has its cafés, and restaurants. Fine food is however a little harder to come across, and many establishments that offer Ireland's most exceptional food are found out of town in Georgian country houses which also offer excellent accommodations. The following list is of some of Ireland's top restaurants, many of which are found in superb, historical manor-homes, surrounded by beautiful gardens, and all of which offer award-winning cuisines and legendary Irish hospitality:

King Sitric, The Fish Restaurant is located in a former harbor-master's house on the East Pier overlooking Balscadden Bay, at **Howth**, a renowned fishing village just north of Dublin. Chef, Aidan MacManus even has his own lobster fishermen who provide the kitchen with these delicacies fresh from the sea. Specialities other than lobster include Howth crabs, Black Sole, oysters, Turbot, and John Dory. Licensed with private dining in the Harbor Room. Open Monday to Saturday, 1830-2300 hours. Dinner costs around IR£22.

The Old Rectory, as its name suggests is housed in a former Victorian rectory on the Dublin side of **Wicklow town**. Reservations are essential as the tiny dining room only seats 10 guests. Hosts Paul and Linda Saunders specialize in pure wholefoods, fresh local seafood, and organically-grown vegetables. Linda's exceptional "Garden of Ireland" salads even utilize edible flowers and fresh herbs, and vegetarians are made especially welcome. Open for food and accommodations from April to October. Dinner costs around IR£25 and is served at 2000 hours.

Longueville House and President's Restaurant a historic Georgian "great house" is set in a spacious estate beside the Blackwater River near **Mallow**, in County Cork. This river is famed for its salmon and trout fishing and along with these specialities the kitchen serves food which is produced from their own gardens. Loungueville boasts Ireland's only vineyard and their dry, fruity-flavored wine is also on the menu. Accommodations are also excellent and the house and restaurant opens from the 12th March to 19th December. Lunch costs IR£15, while dinner ranges from IR£24-£30 per person.

Blairs Cove Restaurant housed in a superbly-restored Georgian manor house has spectacular views of **Dunmanus Bay**, County Cork, and is located outside the village of Durrus on the Goleen/Barley Cove Road. Their *hors d'oeuvre* have been described by *Taste Magazine* as the best Ireland has to offer, and the main-dish specialities of fresh, local fish and fine Irish lamb and beef, are cooked on a wood-burning grill inside the restaurant. Desserts are displayed on the grand piano, and the ambiance and fine food is well worth the drive. Open 1st March to 1st November. Dinner costs around IR£23.

Aherne's Seafood Bar at 163 North Main Street, **Youghal**, in County Cork, is housed in a former pub run by the Fitzgibbon family. The historic port is famed for its seafood and this family restaurant specializes in fresh, locally-caught lobster, prawns, salmon, turbot and sole. Accommodations are also available all year round. Lunch costs around IR£12, dinner from IR£20.

Mustard Seed Restaurant housed in a traditional house, described as an "oversized dolls' house", is located in **Adare**, one of Ireland's prettiest villages 16 km (10 miles) south of Limerick city on the main road to Killarney. A walled cottage garden and open fires add to the marvellous ambiance of this restaurant which according to a 1991 *Vogue* food-critic "is turning out modern Irish cooking of the highest order". Open Tuesday to Saturday, closed during February. Dinner from 1900-2200 hours, costs around IR£22.

Mac Closkey's Restaurant is housed in **Bunratty House**, beside Bunratty Castle and Folk Park on the outskirts of Limerick city. The kitchen, staff quarters and cellars have all been restored to their original glory, and the restaurant offers choice salmon from Killybegs, lamb from Galway Bay, beef from the lush meadows of Meath, and herbs, vegetables, and shellfish from Munster. Closed from 23 December to 23 January. Open for dinner from Tuesday to Saturdays. Dinner costs around IR£26 per person.

Doyles Seafood Bar and Townhouse painted a post-box red, is hard to miss on

Dingle's John Street. Dingle is famed for its seafood and Stella and John Doyle specialize in serving it up as fresh as possible, they even keep their lobsters live in tanks. The menu changes daily according to the catch and Doyle's cuisine has won many awards for excellence. Accommodations are also available. Open from mid-March to mid-November. Dinner costs around IR£16 and is served around 1830 hours.

Drimcong House Restaurant, housed in a beautiful, white-washed house dating from the 17th-century, is run by Gerry and Marie Galvin, two of Ireland's most acclaimed restauranteurs. Set beside a lake just outside of **Moycullen**, 15 minutes from Galway city, this exceptional restaurant boasts turf fires in the winter, and a menu which is constantly influenced by what is fresh from the garden, the lake, and nearby Galway Bay. Held here every November/December are the popular four-day demonstration courses known as "The Drimcong Food and Wine Experience". Closed January and February. Open for dinner Tuesday to Saturday. A five course meal costs around IR£18, the vegetarian menu is around IR£18 per person.

Newport House, is a historic manor house once owned by the Earls of Tyrconnell, located in the famed angling center of **Newport**, in County Mayo. Kieran and Thelma Thompson use fresh produce from their own fishery, garden and farm, and house specialities include home-smoked salmon and local seafood. Accommodations are also offered in this superb residence filled with antiques and fine paintings. Open from 19th March to 6th October. Dinner costs around IR£27 and is served from 1930 to 2130 hours.

Crookedwood House, housed in a 200-year-old rectory overlooks the rolling fields around Crookedwood Village, outside of **Mullingar** in County Westmeath. Noel and Julie Kenny specialize in imaginative and creative cuisine using local produce including game, venison, homegrown vegetables and fresh herbs. Open all year except for two weeks in November. Dinner is served Tuesday to Saturday, only lunch is served on Sundays. Average cost per diner is IR£17. The Directory (p.346), lists more restaurants.

The Irish love of potatoes is as well-known as the Russians' love affair with vodka, but famous as it is, it was a relative late-comer on the Irish food scene, being introduced only in the Elizabethan era by Sir Walter Raleigh, in his Youghal kitchen garden. The town celebrates these historic links every year with the **Walter Raleigh Spud Festival**, a must for any "spud" (Potato) lover. Potatoes probably became popular because they were less trouble than other food for they could simply be dug out of the ground, dusted off, and put in the pot to boil. Potato eating was also a barometer of social standing; in general, the less potatoes that were eaten, the higher up the economic scale a family were, and vice versa.

The Great Potato Famine of the mid-19th century, when hundreds of people starved to death as their staple crop was stricken by blight, shows just how great the Irish dependence on the lowly potato was. Travelers through Ireland during the 18th century, while remarking on the relative prosperity of the Anglo-Irish towns, also noticed the poverty of the countryfolk and their monotonous diet. "As for their food it is notorious they seldom taste bread or meat..." wrote Edmund Burke, "their diet in summer is potatoes and sour milk; in winter...they are still worse, living on the same root made palatable only by a little salt, and accompanied with water." Compare this scene with Giraldis's comments on the Irish countryside when the Normans first invaded

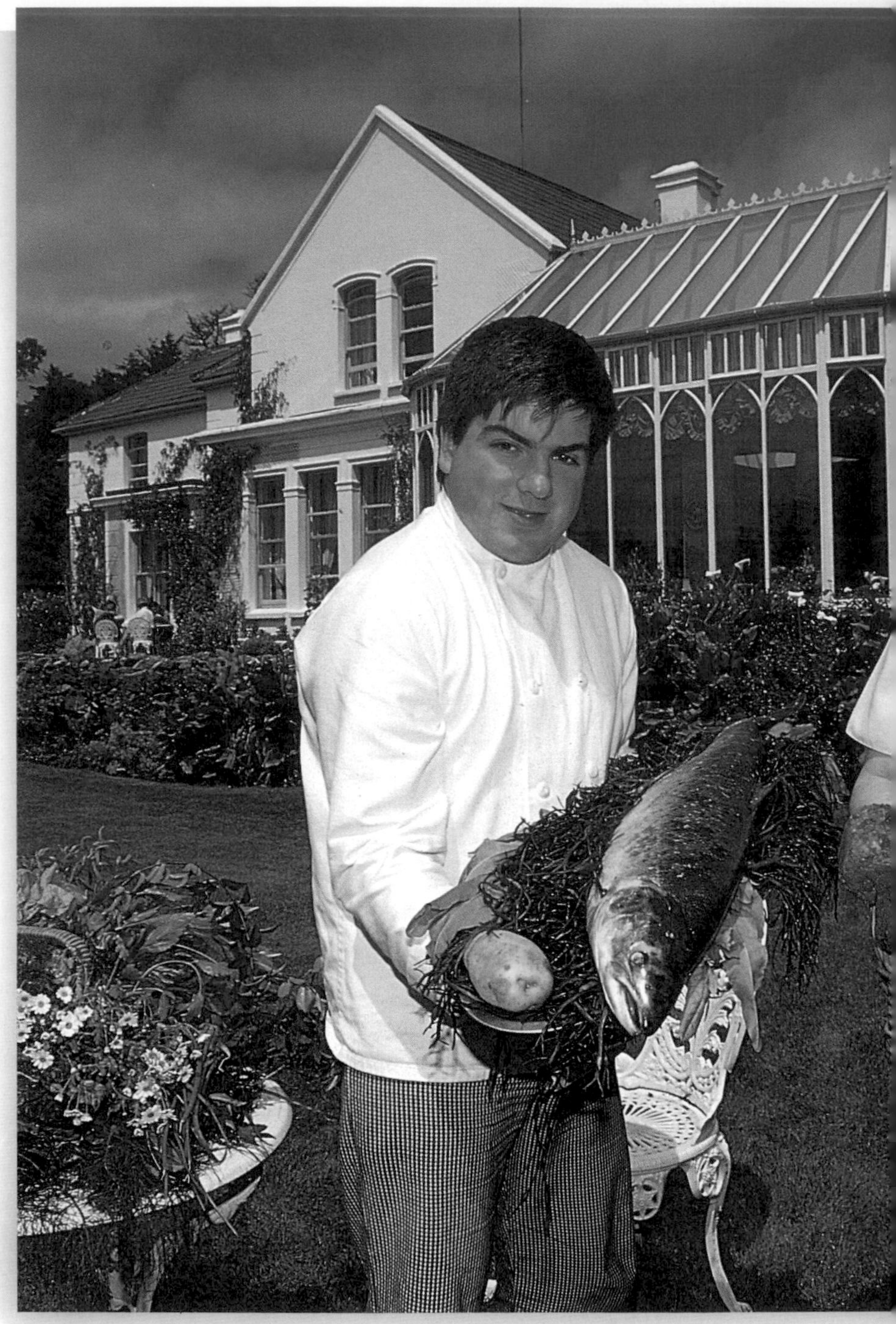

Seafood and kitchen bakes, hearty Irish offerings.

in the 12th century before colonialism had entrenched the Irish peasant into a unending cycle of poverty. "The land is fruitful and rich in its fertile soil and plentiful harvests. Crops abound in the fields, flocks on the mountains, wild animals in the woods. It is rich in honey and milk."

A Home-from-Home

But even if a peasant was poor, traditional Irish hospitality, which is still an enduring attribute, was warm and welcoming, whatever the family's circumstances. Asenath Nicholson, a mid-19th-century traveler, tells of a brief visit to the home of relatives of his Irish servant-girl in New York and the warm reception that was accorded to him, which was apparently the same as he had received wherever he went in Ireland, whether he had connections with the family or not. "After the usual warm greeting", he relates, "the girl was bidden to go out and dig some potatoes; the pot was hung over the fire, the potatoes boiled, the table was removed into the adjoining room, and a touch from the finger of the matron was the signal for me to follow her into supper. On a naked deal table stood a plate of potatoes and a mug of milk. The potatoes must be eaten from the hand, without knife, fork, or plate; and the milk taken in sups from the mug. I applied my nails to divesting the potato of its coat, and my hostess urged the frequent use of the

Break your shopping with a bite of Irish delights.

milk, saying, 'It was provided on purpose for you, and you must take it.' It must be remembered that a sup of sweet milk among the poor in Ireland, is as much a rarity and a luxury as a slice of plum-pudding in a farmhouse in America."

Seafood Specials

During the Great Potato Famine of the 1840s when the lowly potato became a rarity, famine victims were forced to survive by eating nettles and old cabbage leaves. The folk of the seashores were not however quite as bad off as they were never fully dependent on their rocky fields for a living and could at least catch fish, and gather shellfish and edible seaweed to supplement their diet, just as they always had. A century ago fish was much more popular than it is today, although it is currently having a revival with health-conscious people because of its fat-free, mineral-rich qualities.

In the old days fish, mainly herrings, but also cod and ling, were salted or smoked, and these were eaten all over the country during Lent and on Fridays when Catholics abstain from eating meat. Coastal dwellers also gathered shellfish like "the cockles and mussels, alive, alive, oh", hawked through Dub lin's streets by sweet Molly Malone in the popular ditty. Galway is rightly famous for its oysters, which are downed along with copious pints of Guinness every year at the rollicking **Oyster Festival** held every September. At other times of the year, those in the know, head for **Moran's Oyster Cottage**, near Kilcolgan, to pay their respects to a sumptous feast of crabs, mussels, oysters and smoked salmon. The latter can be seen during the spawning season, waiting in the river shallows of the **Salmon Weir Bridge**, right in the center of Galway town.

Seaweed, which during the 19th century was gathered for a variety of purposes including making iodine, soap and bleach, and for animal fodder and fertilizer, was also eaten. Saygrass was dried and chewed raw, sea-lettuce was boiled and eaten with meat, and *cairigin*, also known as Irish Moss, was sun-bleached, and then boiled with milk to make jelly. Tales are told that before the Great Famine the seaweed gatherers used to work naked, but that when the priests began blessing the operation the harvesters started working in their clothes, in order to preserve their morals in front of the churchmen. It was apparently a lot more comfortable and practical working nude as the gatherers' clothes ended up sodden and wet.

Meat From the Farm

Meat was always an important ingredient in Irish food as is evidenced by the massive quantities of bones which have been unearthed at ancient and medieval archaeological digs. Farmers would

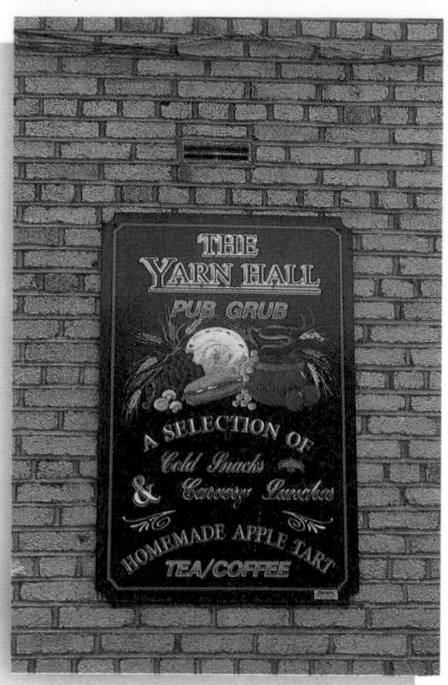

Hearty "pub grub" is a good choice in Ireland's hospitable pubs.

kill and butcher their own cattle, at least once a year, as well as sheep and pigs, which they would share around the neighborhood, a practice that was reciprocated whenever another household was butchering. Veal and kids were roasted, blood and entrails were made into blood puddings, and liver, kidneys, and hearts were eaten fresh. Nothing went to waste. Leftover meat was salted, hams were cured and smoked, and heads were made into brawn.

The famed Irish stew, sometimes hard to find in its native land, was originally made with goat or kid, as these were more expendable than lamb. Today's variety is usually lamb or mutton chunks softened to perfection by simmering for a long time in a stock of onions, potatoes, and herbs. Spring lamb is another delicacy usually served at Easter, for its religious association with the sacrificial paschal lamb.

Raising fowls was women's work and every farmer's wife kept hens, geese, ducks, and turkeys, which provided eggs and meat for the table. After harvesting the crops a goose was fed on the stubble, and the Michaelmas goose, as it was called, was meant to ensure the family's good fortune for the coming year. Fowl was also eaten at Christmas, as it still is, although turkey was formerly eaten only by the aristocrats, or by farmers who raised the birds.

Tales of Yore

In times gone by the landowners, or the ruling class, celebrated festivities like Christmas, with even more over-indulgence than that which occurs today. In Sir Jonah Barrington's *Personal Sketches* of Georgian times, he tells of a Christmas when he, and eight of his father's friends, who composed the "permanent bacchanalians", locked themselves in a hunting lodge for what they called their "shut-up pilgrimage" with a cook, his father and brother's pipers, "and Boyle, a blind but a famous fiddler", to eat a "fat cow" till it became a skeleton, and to drink a hogshead of superior claret until it was "on its stoop". The only other food allowed was chickens, bacon and bread.

"I shall never forget the attraction

this novelty had for my youthful mind", writes Sir Jonah, and he goes on with the skill of a writer on gourmet cooking to describe the banquet. "The luscious smoked bacon, bedded in its cabbage mattress, and partly obscured by its own savoury steam, might have tempted the most fastidious of epicures: while the round trussed chickens, ranked by the half dozen on hot pewter dishes, turned up their white plump merry-thoughts, exciting equally the eye and appetite" the list continues "... fat collops of the hanging cow, sliced indiscriminately from her tenderest points, grilled over the embers upon a shining gridiron, half-drowned in their own luscious juices, and garnished with little pyramids of congenial shallots, smoked at the bottom of the well-furnished board... Cherry-bounce (brandy) preceded the entertainment, which was enlivened by hob-nobs and joyous toasts."

The Cream of Dairy

Milk, cheese, cream and butter, are still just as popular as in the old days, although strangely enough cheese went out of popularity around the mid-19th century and was only revived in the 1950s. A jug of freshly-whipped cream is still standard fare in many cafés, and coffee shops, and diners help themselves to a spoonful for their coffee, or to lavish over their apple pie. Not for the faint-hearted who worry about cholesterol problems, but on a chilly day, after a long walk, nothing tastes quite as delicious as melting cream on a slice of warm pie.Corn beef and cabbage is often requested by tourists, but apparently the Irish never eat these two together, so if you find it on a menu, it is obviously there to serve a need, but whether it's traditional or not, it's still a satisfying and tasty treat. Cabbage forms the basis for the traditional Halloween dish of Colcannon. A mixture of mashed potato and boiled, chopped cabbage, flavored with minced onions, butter, milk, and nutmeg, this vegetable speciality often concealed hidden charms for the diners to find, including a ring which signified an impending marriage.

International Influx

These days a traveler could travel the length and breadth of Ireland and never taste traditional Irish food, except of course for the ubiquitous "Irish breakfast". With locals now taking their holidays in Spain, Italy, and Northern Africa, food tastes are changing as people become more adventurous and less restricted by tradition in their choice of food. What was exotic a few years ago, like pizzas, are now everyday fare. Baked potatoes are now eaten with chilli con carne, and Irish Stew is only served at tourist traps. But despite this, there is nothing quite like the taste of real Irish cooking, and like all good things, the rarer it is the better it seems to taste. The search is well worth the effort.

Nightlife

Without a doubt, Ireland's after-dark entertainment is mainly centered around the local pub, where not only does the liquor flow but so does the talk and the music. They are a home-away-from-home, a place to take it easy, to meet old friends and enjoy the *craic* (camaraderie) and are accorded a hallowed place in Irish society. In many rural districts, the pub usually provides the only entertainment available, but sometimes this may be a world-class fiddler who gives an impromptu performance, or the local traditional music group who never fail to get the discerning crowd foot-tapping.

Traditional music offering at Bunratty Castle.

By comparison, Dublin's night life offers a splendid line-up of not only great pubs, music venues, comedy clubs, cabarets, and cinema, but a smorgasbord of theatrical productions, often featuring past

Pubs such as O'Neill's, Dublin, are great places to join the Irish in their revels.

Temple Bar is Dublin's in place for rock music.

and present works of Ireland's renowned playwrights like Samuel Beckett, Sean O'Casey, Oscar Wilde, Brian Friel and John B Keane. The best guide to Dublin's after-dark amusements is *In Dublin*, available everywhere for IR£1.50p, which lists theater reviews, times, prices, and musical write-ups with band listings, details of who's on where, and cover charges.

Dublin Theater & Comedy

On Abbey Street, the famed **Abbey Theater**, Ireland's national theater, founded by WB Yeats and Lady Gregory, during the Literary Renaissance of the turn of the century, was the scene of riots when JM Synge's controversial *Playboy of the Western World*, and Sean O'Casey's *The Plough and the Stars* were first staged. Rebuilt in contemporary style after it was gutted by fire in 1951, the theater often stages classic Irish plays. The **Peacock Theater** in the Abbey basement puts on more experimental theater productions and often stages lunch time shows as well as poetry readings and concerts.

Orson Welles made his stage debut at the **Gate Theater** in Parnell Square, and the theater has a reputation for excellent dramatic works, including Irish classics. On South King Street is the superbly-restored **Gaiety Theater**, a Victorian-era theater which is also the home of the Dublin Grand Opera Society.

Dublin's Pubs

Drink and entertainment is not lacking at the myriad pubs in Dublin.

"The crack", or as it's spelt in Irish, the *craic*, is what Dubliners call their favorite recreation, gathering at the local pub for a chat, catching up on gossip, listening to some Irish music, and downing pints of the famed amber-colored fluid, Guinness. There is nothing like a Dublin pub for a quick introduction to typical Irish life, for the pub is not only a place to have a few drinks but it is a home-away-from-home, loved and revered by its fiercely-loyal customers.

Some pubs are famed for their traditional music sessions, some for the way the barman "pulls a good pint", and others for their atmosphere or their literary connections. Dublin even hosts a "Literary Pub Crawl" where literature buffs can do the rounds of the pubs immortalized by the city's famed writers like James Joyce, and Brendan Behan, amongst others. The "crawl" starts at 1930 hours from **The Bailey**, 2 Duke Street, and is a fascinating introduction to Dublin's watering holes and the gossip and tales which surround them. Joyce once said that a "good puzzle would be (to) cross Dublin without passing a pub", and indeed it would be a tortuous route indeed, for the city's public houses are not only renowned but incredibly numerous. The following listing does not even make a dent in Dublin's pub numbers, and many of the best "locals" are found by merely walking the streets and ducking in and out of establishments that appeal on the spur of the moment. However, the pubs that follow will be enough to give you a taste for further exploration.

A Choice Pub-Crawl

The **Brazen Head**, Dublin's oldest pub, is a fitting place to begin your tour. Located at 20 Lower Bridge Street, just off Merchant's Quay, this ancient drinking house was established in 1198. Soak up eight centuries of atmosphere

Pantomimes, ballet, opera, and serious dramas are staged here.

Another Victorian theater, the **Olympia Theater**, on 72 Dame Street, hosts musicals, and the occasional Gaelic play. Nearby, at 39 Essex Street, the **Project Arts Center**, hosts a spectrum of entertainment events from comedy and dance to avant-garde theater. Other smaller theaters include the **Andrews Lane Theater**, in the lane of the same name off Dame Street, which stages unusual modern plays and ***An Beal Bocht***, at 58 Charlemont Street, where traditional Irish theater is performed.

Dublin clubs which feature Irish

and join the locals for foot-tapping sessions of traditional Irish music. Walk downriver to Gratton Bridge and cross it to Capel Street where at No.29, **Slattery's Pub** offers Dublin's best traditional Irish music, set-dancing, and rock and blues, every night of the week. Further downriver overlooking O'Connell Bridge is the old-style **Clifton Court Hotel** which also hosts traditional music bands on Sunday and Wednesdays, and jazz on Thursdays. Wander up the south bank of the Liffey, past Aston Quay to Temple Bar, Dublin's "left-bank", and the site of the lively, refurbished **Temple Bar**, and the crowded, noisy, **Norseman**, popular with musicians and theater folk. Cross Dame Street and walk down South Great George's Street for one of Dublin's most picturesque bars, **The Long Hall**, with its carved wooden counter and antique mirrors. Head down nearby Wicklow Street for the **International Bar** which also boasts an antique wooden bar, and an eccentric clientele, some of whom could also be described as "antiques".

Pubs of James Joyce Fame

Make a side step into Grafton Street and into adjacent **Duke Street** the location of some of Dublin's best-known "watering holes". At No 2 is **The Bailey**, a superb Georgian-style pub with arched windows which houses the door of No 7 Eccles Street, the front door of James Joyce's fictional hero Leopold Bloom, whose wanderings around Dublin are immortalized in his epic novel *Ulysses*. At No 9 is **The Duke**, a hangout for real Dublin characters, who could have easily stepped out of a Joyce tale. Another must for his fans is **Davy Bryne's** at No 21, where Leopold Bloom stopped for a glass of burgundy and a gorgonzola sandwich on his epic-making *Ulysses* stroll. A block further south is South Anne Street where **Kehoe's** at No 9 still provides "snugs", wooden closed-in cubbyholes, for those who want to drink in private; snugs were made famous in Sean O'Casey's plays. Continue east to Merrion Row, where **O'Donoghue's** at No 15, hosts some of Dublin's best Irish folk music. This pub was where the famous traditional music group, *The Dubliners* first started out and the tradition has been continued ever since.

Head south to Lower Baggot Street, where at No 143 the **Baggot Inn** plays host to some of the city's best rock musicians. **Doheny and Nesbitt's** at No 5 also boasts "snugs" and plenty of good Dublin characters who have been propping up the bar here most of their lives. The famed poet WB Yeats once stopped by for a sherry at No 139, **Toners**, and then insisted on going home. As one Dublin guide says, "you might find yourself wanting to stay". The bard was not the pub-going type, unlike most of the city's famed literati.

Other well-known pubs include: **McDaid's** on Harry Street, where Brendan Behan worked on his legendary prowess as a writer and drinker; **Mulligan's**, at 8 Poolbeg Street, where the pints are said to be especially good; **Kenny's** on Lincoln Place where traditional music can happen at any time; and **Whelan's**, good for drinks, food, and comedy in a superbly restored setting.

comedians include **The Comedy Cellar**, upstairs in the International Bar, 23 Wicklow Street; the **Project Arts Center** (see above); **The Pulpit Comedy Club** at The Four Seasons, 199 North King Street; **The Underground** on Dame Street, and **The Purty Loft** out of town on the Dunleary Road, in Dun Laoghaire.

Popular Dublin Gigs

Dublin is where most of Ireland's best musicians congregate, and the nightly music scene is one of the main reasons

Live-entertainment is a feature of most Irish pubs and clubs.

many travelers are lax to get on the road. At scores of pubs where visiting musicians just get up and jam, the music is free but when a well-known band gets on stage there is often a small cover charge. In Dublin, you never know who might jump up from the audience and join in on a session. One guitar-playing traveler recalls the time he was playing a Van Morrison "golden oldie" for free Guinness, when the "Black Boy from Belfast" himself walked in the door and joined in. And with Bob Dylan and the Rolling Stones's guitarist Ron Wood re-

Take your buddy along for a beer.

cently buying homes in nearby County Kildare, the chances are that they too could make the occasional appearance at Dublin's nightspots. Top venues for rock music include the **Baggot Inn**, on 143 Baggot Street, where U2 used to play in the 1980s; gigs featuring up-and-coming Irish rock groups are held both upstairs and downstairs. Around **Temple Bar**, Dublin's latest "happening" scene, there are a number of rock-music venues like **Rock Garden** at 38 Crown Alley.

Traditional & Alternative Music

Traditional Irish music is extremely popular in Dublin's pubs and is not just staged for tourists, although in the height of the season it may seem that way. Well-known pubs with nightly sessions of traditional music include Dublin's oldest bar, the **Brazen Head**, at 20 Lower Bridge Street, the immortal **Slattery's** at 29 Capel Street, which was the former haunt of the *Dubliners*, and **O'Donoghue's** at 15 Merrion Row.

These well-known pubs have long been discovered by tourists and when they are "wall-to-wall", a Dublin guest-house proprietress hints, head for **Flynn's** in Upper Dorset Street, where the locals always outnumber the visitors. There you can be assured of an authentic night out with music, Guinness and *craic*. For an excellent night out

Some pubs are not only places of entertainment but are also architectural treasures.

with dinner and renowned traditional music, take the DART train just north of Dublin to **Ye Olde Abbey Tavern** in Howth.

Back in Dublin, **Bad Bob's Backstage Bar**, 35 Essex Street, hosts country and western music. Jazz is best at the **Night Train** (downstairs from O'Dwyers pub), **Rudyard's Wine Bar** in Crown Alley, and at **Bewley's**, Westmoreland Street, on Sunday sessions. Classical music concerts are staged at the **National Concert Hall**, situated in Earlsfort Terrace.

Dublin Dance & Nightclubs

Dublin's late-night scene is centered around a stretch of Georgian terrace-houses on **Lower Leeson Street**, south of St Stephen's Green, where basement dance-clubs rock until the wee hours. They usually do not really start jumping until after the pubs close, and although some stage live bands, DJs are more usual. Names of clubs change constantly. What is hip one week is passé the next. Many have no cover charge but drinks are expensive. Some of the current crop are as follows: **Suessy Street**, **Strings**, **Leggs**, **Buck Whaleys**, and **Bang Bangs.**

Other popular nightclubs in the city include **The Waterfront** at Sir John Rogerson Quay; **Lily Langtrys** at the Judge Roy Beans Restaurant, 45 Nassau Street; **Annabels** at the Burlington Hotel in Upper Leeson Street; **Clares** at Mont Clare Hotel, 13 Clare Street; and **Dungeon's** at Fitzpatrick Castle Hotel in Dublin's Southern Suburb of Killiney.

Wexford, Kilkenny & Cork

Leaving Dublin behind, head south to **Wexford**, the mecca for opera buffs every autumn when the town hosts its renowned **Festival of Opera** at the humble **Theater Royal**, also the venue for year-round theatrical events. The **Wexford Arts Center**, in the Cornmarket, also stages dance, music, and drama performances. **The Goal Bar Lounge** on Main Street hosts bands nightly during the summer. Further south at Waterford, the **Garter Lane Arts Center**, on the lane of the same name off O'Connell Street, stages drama, music and dance events.

Kilkenny town is well-known for its swinging pub scene. **The Pump House**

Bar, 26 Parliament Street, pumps out rock music, while **Cleere's Pub** (nearby) is the venue for traditional Irish music and the occasional poetry reading.

Cork has a lively pub scene especially for music lovers. **An Spailpin Famac**, 29 South Main Street, hosts traditional music on Tuesday, Friday and Sunday nights, and **An Bodhran**, 42 Oliver Plunkett Street on Union Quay is another top spot for traditional sessions. Open till late, **Nancy Spain's**, 48 Barracks Street, has weekend blues and country sessions.

For more high-brow entertainment in Cork, the **Opera House** on Emmet Place occasionally stages opera, as well as variety shows, theater and jazz. The more informal **Everyman's Theater** on MacCertain Street offers drama, music and dance. Cork's accommodations are packed to the rafters for the one-week **International Film Festival**, and the acclaimed **Guinness Jazz Festival**, both held in the autumn.

Outside of Cork, the resort town of **Kinsale**, offers a good pub scene during the summer with the **Shanakee's** crowd rocking to live music sessions, and **The Spaniard** hosting traditional Irish sounds. At **Clonakilty**, further around the coast from Cork, **Shanley's Pub** in Connolly Street, and **De Barra**, 55 Pearse Street, both have nightly music jams. Northwest, at the quiet town of **Bantry**, the **Bantry Bay Hotel** hosts live bands in the summer, and traditional-music fans flock to **Jimmy Crowley's Pub** on New Street.

County Kerry & Clare

Kerry's entertainment revolves around the pubs and the traditional music scene, and it is a rare town in this county that does not host at least one traditional music session a night. **Killarney** is good for ballad and folk sessions, whereas **Dingle** is best for spontaneous jams. Traditional Irish music can be heard at the following Killarney pubs: **Danny Mann**, New Street; **Laurels**, Main Street; **Scotts Hotel**, College Street; **White Gates Hotel**, Muckross Road; **Kate Kearneys Cottage**, Gap of Dunloe; **Buckleys Bar**, College Street; **Crock-of-Gold**, High Street; **Gleneagle Hotel**, Muckross. In Dingle head for **Murphys Bar**, **Garveys Pub**, and **O'Flaherty's**. Around the Ring of Kerry pubs well-known for their traditional music sessions include the **Ross Inn**, Rossbeigh, Glenbeigh; **Caitin Baiters** at Kells Beach; the **Old Forge Inn** and **Nunkers Bar** in Killorglin; **Sneem Tavern** and **Murphys Bar** in Sneem; **Ring Line Bar** on Valencia Island; and the **Lobster Bar** at Waterville.

At **Tralee**, Kerry's largest town, the **Siamsa Taire Theater**, Ireland's National Folk Theater, hosts an excellent summer programme of traditional mime, music and dance. **Comhaltas Ceoltoiri Eireann House** stages traditional music evenings and Kirby's Brogue Inn sometimes has jazz sessions.

The undisputed capital of Ireland's traditional music scene is the little, one-street town of **Doolin** on the Clare Coast, which has three of the nation's top Irish-music pubs; **O'Connors**, **McGann's** and **McDermott's**. If your idea of a holiday is to relax in a small-town atmosphere during the day, within easy reach of spectacular scenery, and then pub-crawl to the tune of Ireland's best traditional music at night, then peerless Doolin is the destination for you.

Galway, Dublin of the West

Galway is to the west what Dublin is to the east, and the entertainment scene here boasts a plethora of lively pubs, and a healthy theater scene. **Taibhd-hearc na Gaillimhe**, on Middle Street, is a renowned Irish language theater, but for those folks who like their plays in English, the **Druid Theater Company** on Chapel Lane, off Quay Street, hosts good Irish plays, as does the **Punchbag Theater** on Quay Lane.

Irish music, west-coast style, is at its best at the famed "**Noctons**", short for Seaghan Ua Neachtain, on Quay Street. Noisy, and crowded, this bar is where Galway's art and music crowd meet. Other traditional music pubs include **An Pucan**, 11 Forster Street, near Eyre Square; **Kings Head**, 15 High Street; and **Monroe's** on Dominick Street. Galway's late-night scene is liveliest at the nearby resort town of **Salthill** where dancers take to the floor at popular **C J's**, 143 Upper Salthill, and top rock bands perform at the **Hilltop Hotel's Hanger**, and **Setanta** on Salt Hill Road.

Off the Beaten Track

Offshore on the **Aran Islands**, summer is the only time when anything is happening at Kilronan's pubs. **Ti Joe Mac's** hosts traditional music, and the local dance hall is the venue for weekend set-dancing. Heading north through Connemara, **Spiddal's Ceol na Mara**, the town's cultural center, offers traditional music, song, and dance performances. At **Clifden**, musicians jam at **The Central** on Main Street, and **Mannions** on Market Street.

Mayo County is well-known for its traditional music scene and **Westport's** pubs are great places to hear the local sounds. The flutist of the legendary *Chieftains* is the proprietor of **Matt Molloy's Pub** in Bridge Street, and **Pete McCarthy's** on the Octagon also hosts live sessions. Further northwest, **Sligo town** boasts a lively pub-music scene. Top of the bunch is **McLynn's** pub on Market Street, where the well-known singer/proprietor entertains the drinkers. **Cyril O'Connors** in The Mall and the out-of-town **Thatch Pub** also host traditional music. **The Bear** and **The Cat** on Bridge Street, are good for reggae and blues throughout the year, and **The Clarence**, in Wine Street, is the favorite band venue after the pubs close.

In **Donegal town's** pubs traditional musicians often jump up for spontaneous sessions. Popular pubs include **Schooner's** and **Nero's** on Main Street, and the **Abbey Hotel** on the Diamond.

TRAVEL TIPS

ARRIVAL

By Air

All trans-Atlantic flights land at Shannon Airport, 25 km (15 miles) from Limerick City, even if they then proceed to Dublin. Aer Lingus, the national carrier of Ireland, has flights from New York, Chicago and Boston. Delta fly from Atlanta, and Aeroflot have flights from Washington D.C.

European, and United Kingdom flights touch down at Dublin Airport, 9km (5 miles) north of the city. From the UK Aer Lingus have 12 flights daily from Heathrow, and frequent flights from Gatwick, Birmingham, Bristol, East Midlands, Liverpool, Manchester, Leeds, Newcastle, Edinburgh, and Glasgow airports. English flights also land at Cork, Knock, Shannon and Waterford.

There are no direct flights to Ireland from Asia, so travelers usually get the airline of their choice to Heathrow and then connect with an Aer Lingus flight from there. British Airways and Quantas have a deal with Aer Lingus such that Aer Lingus will provide a free shuttle service from Heathrow to Dublin for all passengers taking a direct flight from Australia. Flights also connect with Dublin and/or Shannon from Toronto in Canada, Mexico City, Havana (Cuba) and Managua in Nicaragua. European flights ply regularly to Dublin from Amsterdam, Brussels, Moscow, Rome and Zurich airports, to name but a few.

By Sea

An alternative to flying to Ireland from England is to take the ferry across the Irish Sea. Express buses and trains connect with the ferry at Holyhead in North Wales which sails to Dun Laoghaire, just south of Dublin. B&I and Sealink both run ferries on this route. The alternative route is from Pembroke in South Wales to Rosslare near Waterford which is operated by B&I and is more convenient for travelers intending to journey around Cork and the southwest. Irish Ferries also have a service from Rosslare to Cherbourg and Le Havre in France.

BUSINESS HOURS

Banks

Banks are open Monday to Friday from 1000 to 1230 hours and 1330 until 1500 hours, with the exception of Thursdays, when they shut at 1700 hours.

Pubs

Pubs open Monday to Friday from 1030 to 2300 hours, but they close half an hour earlier during the winter months. On Sundays they open from 1230 to 1400 hours and from 1600 to 2300 hours. The only days that the pubs close are on Christmas Day and Good Friday.

Shops

Usually open from 0900 to 1730 or 1800 hours Monday to Saturday, but they often close at 1300 hours for one day in the week. Shopping malls keep later hours on Thursday or Friday evenings when they close at 2100 hours.

CLIMATE

Ireland's rain is legendary so visitors should be prepared for wet weather in any season. However, this is also one of the reasons why the climate is so mild compared with other European countries. Snow can occur in the winter but it is of short duration and the grass is usually green all year round. Taking the brunt of the Atlantic winds, the west coast is wetter than the east. The sunniest region is the southeast.

Winter temperatures average between 4-7°C(39-45°F) and the coldest months are January and February. Summer temperatures hover around 14-16°C(57-61°F) but can often get much warmer. The hottest and sunniest months are May and June. Although the summer is the most popular time for visitors, off-season, especially in the spring and autumn, is very pleasant as the climate is still exceptionally mild and you have the added bonus of less-crowded landscapes and lower prices.

CUSTOMS

There are two types of duty-free allowances for visitors to Ireland. The first is for purchases made outside of the European Community (EC), either on a ship, plane or in a duty-free store. Duty-free items in this category include 200 cigarettes, 50 cigars, 2 liters of wine, 1 liter of alcohol (over 22% proof) or 2 liters under 22% proof, three 50g bottles of perfume, and other goods to a value of IR£34 per traveler. The second category of duty-free allowance is for goods purchased in the EC which have already had duty and tax paid; under this category you are allowed; 800 cigarettes, 10 liters of spirits, 45 liters of wine, 55 liters of beer. Prohibited goods include: firearms, explosives, ammunition, narcotics and prohibited drugs; obscene publications; meat, poultry, plants, and products containing meat, poultry or plants; dogs and cats from countries other than the UK.

DOMESTIC TRAVEL

By Air

Air travel around Ireland is not all that popular with visitors as the distances are not great and most people prefer to see the marvellous scenery *en route* to their destination. But for visitors pressed for time there are ample domestic services operating between regional airports such as Kerry, Galway, Sligo, Knock and Waterford. Flights also ply from Connemara Airport to the Aran Islands.

By Bicycle

A marvellous option for those with plenty of time and energy is to hire a bicycle. Road, cross-country, and mountain bikes can all be rented in the major centers and in popular tourist hubs. Rent-A-Bike at 58 Lower Gardiner Street, Dublin, Tel: (01)–25931, even sells bicycles and buys them back at half the price. You can alternatively rent bicycles and leave them at other agencies around the country.

By Bus

Bus Eireann, the national bus company, is the quickest way to get between cities as the railway often takes a round-about route. Bus Eireann's comfortable, heated buses leave Dublin's Busaras, the central bus station, for all the major towns. There are regular daily services from Dublin to all of Ireland's major centers. Check at the tourist offices or at Busaras for a timetable. Most towns and all cities have good bus services which are a cheap way to get around town.

By Car

If you are traveling by road it is best to hire a car as many of the nation's prettiest sights are in the countryside and are difficult to get to by public transport. Many of the best country-house hotels are also only feasible if you have your own car. Road signs are written in both English and Irish, but in some parts of the Gaeltacht signs are only in the latter (Gaelic). Road distances are in kilometers, but sometimes the older signposts still have mileages. Vehicles travel on the left-hand side of the road, the opposite to the USA, and the speed limit on country roads is 88 kph, and 64kph in built-up areas. Safety belts must be worn by the drivers and the front seat passenger.

The cheapest car rentals are those which are incorporated into package fly/drive holidays. The next cheapest are pre-booked rentals. Every major center in Ireland has car-rental agencies including Hertz and Avis. Drivers only need a valid licence. Rates vary according to the make of car and the length of time you want to rent for, usually the longer, the cheaper. Unlimited mileage is generally the rule. See Directory for car-rental agencies.

By Rail

Ireland's rail system is a good way to travel between towns and for visitors intending to see the country mainly by rail there are some good deals like the EurailPass which gives unlimited, first-class travel throughout Europe including Ireland. Rambler Tickets are best if you only intend to travel in Ireland, these entitle the user to both bus and rail travel which is very convenient as many of the best spots are only accessible by bus. If however, you are not going to be traveling extensively and want to take your time it's often cheaper to merely buy tickets when you need them. Dubin's seaside suburbs are serviced by the fast, efficient DART train service.

MONEY

The Irish unit of currency is the *punt* (IR£) which is divided into 100 pence (100p). Notes are in denominations of 100, 50, 20, 10, and 5. Coins are minted as 1 pound, 50p, 20p 10p, 5p, 2p and 1p. Northern Ireland uses the English pound sterling (£). The Irish *punt* (IR£) and the English pound (£) are not inter-changeable.

American dollars and English pounds are only accepted in some hotels and tourist-orientated shops, but the exchange rate is usually exorbitant compared to what you can exchange for at the banks or the Bureau de Change. The best rates for travelers' cheques are found at banks as Bureau de Changes charge a slight commission. Bureau de Changes do however have the advantage of being open after hours, like the one at the General Post Office in Dublin which opens from 0800 to 2000 hours Monday to Saturday and 1030 to 1830 hours on Sunday.

In the countryside post offices often double as currency bureaus, but they charge a commission. Automated-teller machines (ATMs) are often affiliated with those in the US, the UK, and other countries, so check with your bank before traveling. Cash advances can also be made with ATMs. Major hotels, restaurants and shops also take international credit cards like Visa, Mastercard and American Express and these cards also offer cash advance services and other useful connections which should be looked into in advance.

PASSPORTS & VISAS

A valid passport is required for all visitors to Ireland except for British citizens. No visa is required for tourists staying up to 90 days, although tourists may be asked to show onward or return tickets. For visitors arriving from the United Kingdom by ferry there are no customs nor passport control. Most Commonwealth Countries need no visa to enter the United Kingdom, but it is best to check with the British High Commission in your own country before departure, if you are in doubt.

POSTAL SERVICES

Ireland's mail services are excellent. Dublin's General Post Office (GPO) is conveniently situated opposite the Tourist Office in O'Connell Street and is open from 0800 to 2000 hours, Monday to Saturday. Even-numbered postal codes are all south of the River Liffey and odd numbers are north of the river. Dublin is the only city big enough to require postal codes!

PUBLIC HOLIDAYS

The following days are public holidays: 1st January; 17th March (St Patrick's Day); Easter Monday; first Monday in June; first Monday in August; last Monday in October; 25 & 26th December (Christmas). Northern Ireland's public holidays are different but St Patrick's Day is the same.

TELEPHONE SERVICES

Local telephone calls cost 20p for three minutes, and long-distance (domestic) around 60p for the same time. There are public pay phones everywhere around Ireland, including pubs and shops. As is the case in most other countries, direct dialling is the cheapest way to phone as operator-connected calls are more costly. All Ireland is covered by STD. Avoid phoning from hotel rooms as the charges added are exorbitant.

International calls can be made from most post-office phone booths, and direct dialling services connect with more than 75 countries. Ireland's International Direct Dialling (IDD) code is 16, and all other country codes are listed in the phone book. Reduced rates for international calls take effect from 2200 hours and on weekends. Dial 10 for operator assistance including international calls, except for Dublin where the number is 114. For directory enquires in Ireland dial 1190.

TIPPING

If the hotel or restaurant charges a service fee which can be between 12 to 15% depending on how expensive the establishment is, tipping is not usually the done thing unless the service has been exemplary. The regular 10% is a good gauge at hotels and restaurants which have no service charge. The same percentage can be applied to taxi drivers. Porters expect about 50p and drink waiters around 20p.

VOLTAGE

220v is standard, AC current. Hotels usually have dual 220/110 voltage sockets for electric razors. Thirteen amp square pin plugs are most frequently in use. International adaptors are on sale in local shops.

WEIGHTS & MEASURES

Ireland is under the metric system. Road signs are in kilometers and food and other goods are purchased by the gram or kilogram.

DIRECTORY

AIRLINES

Aer Lingus
Aer Lingus Irish International Airlines, Dublin Airport.
Tel: (01)-705-2222

Aer Lingus Irish International Airlines, Shannon Airport.
Tel: (061)-415556

Aeroflot
Shannon Airport
Tel: (061)-472299

British Airways
Dublin Airport
Tel: (01)-844-5777

Delta Airlines
Dublin Airport
Tel: (01)-661-1880

Ryanair Ltd.
Dublin Airport
Tel: (01)-844-4400

AIRPORTS

Cork Airport
Tel: (021)-965974

Dublin Airport
Tel: (01)-379900

Horan International Airport
Tel: (094)-67222

Shannon Airport
Tel: (061)-61333

BUS TRANSPORT

Contact Dublin's central bus station:
Busaras Central Bus Station
Store Street, Dublin 2
Tel: (01)-366111

CAR RENTAL

The following list of car-rental firms is merely a guideline, for a full listing contact the Tourist Information Offices.

Avis Rent-a-Car
1 Hanover Street East, Dublin 2
Tel: (01)-776971

Flynn Bros
Ballygaz, Galway
Tel: (0903)-4668.

Hertz Rent-a-Car
19/20 Hogan Place, Lowet Grand Canal Street, Dublin 2
Tel: (01)-767476

Johnson & Perrott
Emmet Place, Cork
Tel: (021)-273295

EMBASSIES

Australia
Fitzwilton House, Wilton Terrace, Dublin 2
Tel: (01)-761-517

Belgium
2, Shrewsbury Road, Dublin 4
Tel: (01)-692082/691588

Britain
31-33 Merrion Road, Dublin 4
Tel: (01)-269-5211

Canada
65 St Stephen's Green South, Dublin 2
Tel: (01)-781-988

France
36 Ailesbury Road, Dublin 4
Tel: (01)-694-777

Germany
31 Trimleston Avenue, Dublin 2
Tel: (01)-269-3011

India
6, Leeson Park, Dublin 6
Tel: (01)-970843

Italy
63 Northumberland Road, Dublin 4
Tel: (01)-601-744

Netherlands
160 Merrion Road, Dublin 4
Tel: (01)-693444/693532

Spain
17A Merlyn Park, Dublin 4
Tel: (01)-691-640

Sweden
Sun Alliance House, Dawson Street, Dublin
Tel: (01)-715-822

USA
43 Elgin Road, Ballsbridge, Dublin 4
Tel: (01)-688-777

HOTELS & GUESTHOUSES

Prices are all in Irish pounds. Rates quoted are per person sharing.
B&B = bed-and-breakfast.
All prices inclusive of Value Added Tax (VAT) and service charges.

DUBLIN
Aberdeen Lodge
53/55 Park Avenue, Dublin 4
Tel: (01)-238155
B&B: IR£33-46.

Anglesea Town House
63 Anglesea Road, Ballsbridge, Dublin 4
Tel: (01)-683877
B&B: IR£43.

Ashling Hotel
Parkgate Street, Dublin 8
Tel: (01)-772324
B&B: IR£35.

Berkley Court Hotel
Landsdowne Road, Dublin 3
Tel: (01)-601711
B&B: IR£86.

Blooms Hotel
Anglesea Road, Temple Bar, Dublin 2
Tel: (01)-715622
B&B: IR£60.

Burlington Hotel
Upper Lesson Street, Dublin 4
Tel: (01)-605222
B&B: IR£62-68.

Clara House
23 Leinster Road, Rathmines, Dublin 6
Tel: (01)-975904
B&B: IR£20-24.

Conrad Hotel Dublin
Earlsfort Terrace, Dublin 2
Tel: (01)-765555
B&B: IR£69-98.

Georgian House
20/21 Lower Baggot Street, Dublin 2
Tel: (01)-618832
B&B: IR£26-40.

Gresham Hotel
O'Connell Street, Dublin 1
Tel: (01)-746881
B&B: IR£45-67.

Jury's Hotel & Towers
Road, Ballsbridge, Dublin 4
Tel: (01)-605000
B&B: IR£76.

Kelly's Hotel
36 Great Georges Street, Dublin 2
Tel: (01)-779277
B&B: IR£18-26.

Kingswood Country House & Restaurant
27/Pembroke Road, Ballsbridge, Dublin 4
Tel: (01)-682522
B&B: IR£30-38.

Marian Guesthouse
21 Upper Gardiner Street, Dublin 1
Tel: (01)-744129
B&B: IR£13-14.

Mount Clare Hotel
Merrion Square, Dublin 2
Tel: (01)-616799
B&B: IR£62-84.

Powers Hotel
Kildare Street, Dublin 2
Tel: (01)-6794388
B&B: IR£30-45.

Royal Dublin Hotel
Upper O'Connell Street, Dublin 1
Tel: (01)-733666
B&B: IR£44-54.

Sachs Hotel
Donnybrook, Dublin 4
Tel: (01)-680995
B&B: IR£32-49.

Shelbourne Hotel
27 St Stephen's Green, Dublin 2
Tel: (01)-766471
B&B: IR£95-121.

Stephen's Hall Hotel
114/117 Lower Lesson Street, Dublin 2
Tel: (01)-610585.

Tara Tower Hotel
Merrion Road, Dublin 4
Tel: (01)-2694666
B&B: IR£49-52.

The Fitzwilliam
41 Fitzwilliam Street Upper, Dublin 2
Tel: (01)-600448
B&B: IR£24-35.

Westbury Hotel
Grafton Street, Dublin 2
Tel: (01)-6791122
B&B: IR£86.

DUBLIN ENVIRONS
County Dublin
Court Hotel
Killiney Bay, Co. Dublin
Tel: (01)-28516122
B&B: IR£20-48.

Deer Park Hotel & Golf Course
Howth, Co. Dublin
Tel: (01)-321010
B&B: IR£30-35.

Finnstown Country House Hotel
Newcastle Road, Lucan, Co. Dublin
Tel: (01)-6280644
B&B: IR£35-49.

Fitzpatrick Castle Hotel
Killiney, Co. Dublin
Tel: (01)-2840700
B&B: IR£57-73.

Hotel Pierre
3 Victoria Terrace, Dun Laoghaire, Co. Dublin
Tel: (01)-2800291
B&B: IR£25-35.

Portmarnock Country Club Hotel
Strand Road, Portmarnock, Co. Dublin
Tel: (01)-8460611
B&B: IR£38-62.

Royal Marine Hotel
Marine Road, Dun Laoghaire, Co. Dublin.
Tel: (01)-2801911
B&B: IR£45-65.

County Wicklow
Bel-Air Hotel
Ashford, Co. Wicklow
Tel: (0404)-40109
B&B: IR£20-22.

Enniscree Lodge Hotel & Restaurant
Glencree Drive, Enniskerry, Co. Wicklow
Tel: (01)-2863542
B&B: IR£32-37.

Hunters Hotel
Newrath, Rathnew, Co. Wicklow
Tel: (0404)-40106
B&B: IR£35-37.

Rathsallagh House
Dunlavin, Co. Wicklow
Tel: (045)-53112
B&B: IR£44-55.

Rectory Co. House & Restaurant
Wicklow, Co. Wicklow
Tel: (0404)-67048
B&B: IR£42.

Wooden Bridge Inn
Woodenbridge, Vale of Avoca, Co. Wicklow
Tel: (0402)-35146
B&B: IR£23-25.

SOUTHEASTERN IRELAND

County Kilkenny
Butler House
16, Patrick Street, Kilkenny
Tel: (056)-65707
B&B: IR£29-32.

Club House Hotel
Patrick Street, Kilkenny
Tel: (056)-21994
B&B: IR£30-37.

Mount Juliet
Thomastown, Co. Kilkenny
Tel: (056)-24455
B&B: IR£72-117.

County Tipperary
Bailey's of Cashel
Main Street, Cashel, Tipperary
Tel: (062)-61937
B&B: IR£12-17.

Cashel Palace Hotel
Main Street, Cashel, Co. Tipperary
Tel: (062)-61411
B&B: IR£68-134.

Castle Court Hotel
Church Street, Cahir, Co. Tipperary
Tel: (052)-41210
B&B: IR£25.

Cedarfield House
Waterford Road, Carrick-on-Suir, Co. Tipperary
Tel: (051)-40164
B&B: IR£25-35.
Clonmel Arms Hotel
Sarsfield Street, Clonmel, Co. Tipperary
Tel: (052)-21233
B&B: IR£30-40.

Hotel Minella
Clonmel, Co. Tipperary
Tel: (052)-22388
B&B: IR£25-60.

Kilcoran Lodge Hotel
Cahir, Co. Tipperary
Tel: (052)-41288
B&B: IR£30-38.

County Waterford
Bridge Hotel
1, The Quay, Waterford
Tel: (051)-77222
B&B: IR£33-35.

Dooley's Hotel
The Quay, Waterford
Tel: (051)-73531
B&B: IR£25-32.

Grand Hotel
Tramore, Co. Waterford
Tel: (051)-81414
B&B: IR£33-36.

Granville Hotel
The Quay, Waterford
Tel: (051)-55111
B&B: IR£36-46.

Jury's Hotel
Ferrybank, Waterford
Tel: (051)-32111
B&B: IR£50.

Kelly's Strand Hotel
Rosslare, Co. Waterford
Tel: (053)-32114
B&B: IR£38-41.

O'Shea's Hotel
Strand Street, Tramore, Co. Waterford
Tel: (051)-81246
B&B: IR£20-30.

Waterford Castle
The Island, Ballinakill, Waterford
Tel: (051)-78203
B&B: IR£51-100.

County Wexford
Bayview Hotel
Courtown Harbor, Co. Wexford
Tel: (055)-25307
B&B: IR£32-35.

Cahore Castle Hotel
Cahore, Ballygarrett, Gorey, Co. Wexford
Tel: (055)-27338
B&B: IR£25-35.

Marlfield House
Gorey, Co. Wexford
Tel: (055)-21124
B&B: IR£62-73.

Rosslare Great Southern Hotel
Rosslare Harbor, Co. Wexford
Tel: (053)-33233
B&B: IR£36.

Slaney Manor
Ferrycarrig, Wexford
Tel: (053)-45751
B&B: IR£19-25.

Waterford Lodge Hotel
The Bridge, Wexford
Tel: (053)-23611
B&B: IR£28-30.

SOUTHWESTERN IRELAND
County Cork
Arbutus Lodge Hotel
Montenotte, Cork
Tel: (021)-501237
B&B: IR£36-55.

Ballylickey Manor House
Ballylickey, Bantry Bay, Co. Cork
Tel: (027)-50071
B&B: IR£46.

Blarney Castle Hotel
Blarney, Co. Cork
Tel: (021)-385116
B&B: IR£18-24.

Blue Haven Hotel
3 Pearse Street, Kinsale, Co. Cork
Tel: (021)-772209
B&B: IR£25-44.

Christy's Hotel & Restaurant
Blarney, Co. Cork
Tel: (021)-385011
B&B: IR£35-40.

Dunmahon Country House
Kilcrohane, Bantry, Co. Cork
Tel: (027)-67092
B&B: IR£14.

Fitzpatrick Silver Springs
Tivoli, Cork
Tel: (021)-507533
B&B: IR£45-53.

Garnish House
Western Road, Cork
Tel: (021)-275111
B&B: IR£17-20.

Glenvera House
Wellington Road, Cork
Tel: (021)-502030
B&B: IR£20-24.

Gougane Barra Hotel
Gougane Barra, Ballingeary, Co. Cork
Tel: (026)-47069
B&B: IR£25-30.

Imperial Hotel
South Mall, Cork
Tel: (021)-274040
B&B: IR£55-60.

Inchydoney Hotel
Inchdoney, Clonakilty, Co. Cork
Tel: (023)-33143
B&B: IR£17-20.

John Barleycorn Hotel
Riverstown Glanmire
Tel: (021)-821499
B&B: IR£22-24.

Jury's Hotel
Western Road, Cork
Tel: (021)-276622
B&B: IR£64.

Kieran's "Folk House" Inn
Guardwell, Kinsale, Co. Cork
Tel: (021)-772382
B&B: IR£20-30.

Longueville House & President's Restaurant
Mallow, Co. Cork
Tel: (022)-47156
B&B: IR£50-75.

Metropole Hotel
Mac Curtain Street, Cork
Tel: (021)-508122
B&B: IR£55-65.

Morrisons Island Hotel
Morrison Quay, Cork
Tel: (021)-275858
B&B: IR£54.

Victoia Lodge
Victoria Cross, Cork
Tel: (021)-542233
B&B: IR£15-22.

West Cork Hotel
Skibbereen, Co. Cork
Tel: (028)-21277
B&B: IR£25-27.

County Kerry
Arbutus Hotel
College Street, Killarney, Co. Kerry
Tel: (064)-31037
B&B: IR£22-30.

Ballyseede Castle Hotel
Tralee, Co. Kerry
Tel: (066)-25799
B&B: IR£35-45.

Barrow House
West Barrow, Ardfelt, Co. Kerry
Tel: (066)-36437
B&B: IR£29-35.

Blanconi
Annadale Road, Killorgin, Ring of Kerry, Co. Kerry
Tel: (066)-61146
B&B: IR£19-22.

Butler Arms Hotel
Waterville, County Kerry
Tel: (066)-74144
B&B: IR£37-47.

Cahernane Hotel
Mukross Hill, Co Kerry
Tel: (064)-31895
B&B: IR£43-56.

Dingle Skellig Hotel
Dingle, Co. Kerry
Tel: (066)-51144
B&B: IR£37-58.

Doyle's Seafood Bar & Townhouse
John Street, Dingle, Co. Kerry
Tel: (066)-51174
B&B: IR£29.

Dromuinna Manor Hotel
Blackwaterbridge Post Office, Killarney, Co. Kerry
Tel: (064)-41657
B&B: IR£20-60.

Glenbeigh Hotel
Glenbeigh, Co. Kerry
Tel: (066)-68333
B&B: IR£20-25.

Granville Hotel
Ballyferriter, Dingle Peninsula, Co. Kerry
Tel: (066)-56116
B&B: IR£15-26.

Great Southern Hotel
Killarney, Co. Kerry
Tel: (064)-31262
B&B: IR£50-56.

Great Southern Hotel Parnasille
Sneem, Co. Kerry
Tel: (064)-45222
B&B: IR£57-67.

Hotel Ard-Na-Sidhe
Caragh Lake, Killorgin, Co. Kerry
Tel: (066)-69105
B&B: IR£45-55.

International Best Western Hotel
Kenmare Place, Killarney, Co. Kerry
Tel: (064)-31816
B&B: IR£30-37.

Killarney Park Hotel
Kenmare Place, Killarney, Co. Kerry
Tel: (644)-35555
B&B: IR£40-70.

Lake Hotel
Lake Shore, Mukross Road, Killarney, Co. Kerry
Tel: (064)-31035
B&B: IR£28-39.

Park Hotel
Kenmare, Co. Kerry
Tel: (064)-41200
B&B: IR£88-126.

Scarriff Inn
Caherdaniel, Co. Kerry
Tel: (066)-75136
B&B: IR£27-33.

Smugglers Inn
Cliff Road, Waterville, Co. Kerry
Tel: (066)-74330
B&B: IR£16-28.

WESTERN IRELAND

County Clare

Aberdeen Arms Hotel
Lahinch, Co. Clare
Tel: (065)-81100
B&B: IR£33-44.

American Hotel
Eyre Square, Galway, Co. Clare
Tel: (091)-61300
B&B: IR£25-28.

Aran View Guest House
Coast Road. Doolin, Co. Clare
Tel: (065)-74061
B&B: IR£20-25.

Ballinalacken Castle Hotel
Lisdoonxarna, Co. Clare
Tel: (065)-74025
B&B: IR£20-25.

Dromoland Castle
Newmarket-on-Fergus, Co. Clare
Tel: (061)-368144
B&B: IR£69-109.

Gregans Castle Hotel
Ballyvaughan, Co. Clare
Tel: (065)-77005
B&B: IR£49.

Hylands Hotel
Ballyvaughan, Co. Clare
Tel: (065)-77037
B&B: IR£22-26.

Mountshannon Hotel
Mountshannon, Co Clare
Tel: (061)-927162
B&B: IR£24-28.

Mungovan's Guesthouse
78 Parnell Street, Ennis, Co. Clare
Tel: (065)-24608
B&B: IR£16.

Queen's Hotel
Abbey Street, Ennis, Co. Clare
Tel: (065)-28963
B&B: IR£20-30.

Sheedy's Spa View Hotel & Orchid Restaurant
Lisdoonvarna, Co. Clare
Tel: (065)-74026
B&B: IR£25.

County Galway

Abbeyglen Castle Hotel
Sky Road, Clifden, Co. Galway
Tel: (095)-21201
B&B: IR£33-50.

Ardilaun House Hotel
Taylor's Hill, Galway
Tel: (091)-21433

B&B: IR£33-52.

Ballynahinch Castle Hotel
Recess, Connemara, Co. Galway
Tel: (095)-31006
B&B: IR£38-56.

Brennans Yard Hotel
Lower Merchant's Road, Galway
Tel: (091)-68166
B&B: IR£35-45.

Great Southern Galway
Eyre Square, Galway
Tel: (091)-64041
B&B: IR£57-63.

Hayden's Hotel
Dunlo Street, Ballinasloe, Co. Galway
Tel: (095)-42347
B&B: IR£25-28.

Lough Inagh Lodge
Recess, Connemara, Co. Galway
Tel: (095)-34706
B&B: IR£38-56.

Rosleague Manor Hotel
Letterfrack, Co. Galway
Tel: (095)-45804
B&B: IR£30-55.

Sweeney's Oughterard House
Oughterard, Connemara, Co. Galway
Tel: (091)-82207
B&B: IR£15-19.

Zetland House Hotel
Cashel, Connemara, Co. Galway
Tel: (095)-311111
B&B: IR£40-53.

County Limerick
Adare Manor
Adare, Co. Limerick
Tel: (061)-396566
B&B: IR£62-100.

Castletroy Park Hotel
Dublin Road, Limerick
Tel: (061)-335566
B&B: IR£62-72.

Dunraven Arms Hotel
Adare, Co. Limerick
Tel: (061)-396209
B&B: IR£34-56.

Jury's Hotel
Ennis Road, Limerick
Tel: (061)-327777
B&B: IR£32-40.

Limerick Ryan Hotel
Ennis Road, Limerick
Tel: (061)-453922
B&B: IR£35-49.

NORTHWESTERN IRELAND
County Donegal
Castle Grove Country House
Ramelton Road, Letterkenny, Co. Donegal
Tel: (074)-51118
B&B: IR£23-35.

Fox's Lair Hotel
Church Road, Bunboran, Co. Donegal
Tel: (072)-41339
B&B: IR£12-14.

Hyland Central Hotel
The Diamond, Donegal Town, Co. Donegal
Tel: (073)-22208
B&B: IR£33-41.

Jackson's Hotel
Ballybofey, Co. Donegal
Tel: (074)-31021
B&B: IR£24-27.

Lake of Shadows Hotel
Grianan Park, Buncrana, Co. Donegal
Tel: (077)-61902
B&B: IR£19-22.

St Ernan's House Hotel
Donegal Town, Co. Donegal
Tel: (073)-21065
B&B: IR£38-55.

Strand Hotel
Ballyliffen, Inishowen, Co. Donegal
Tel: (077)-76107
B&B: IR£19-22.

Woodhill House
Ardara, Co. Donegal
Tel: (075)-41112
B&B: IR£16-24.

County Mayo
Ashford Castle
Cong, Co. Mayo
Tel: (092)-46003
B&B: IR£69-109.

Breaffy House Hotel
Castlebar, Co. Mayo
Tel: (094)-22033
B&B: IR£33-36.

Downhill Hotel
Ballina, Co. Mayo
Tel: (096)-21033
B&B: IR£35-43.

Grand Central Hotel
The Octagon, Westport, Co. Mayo.
Tel: (098)-25027
B&B: IR£22-27.

Mount Falcon Castle
Ballina, Co. Mayo
Tel: (096)-21172
B&B: IR£44.

Newport House
Newport, Co. Mayo
Tel: (098)-41222
B&B: IR£53-58.

Olde Railway Hotel
The Mall, Westport, Co. Mayo
Tel: (098)-25166
B&B: IR£25-33.

RAIL TRANSPORT

Connolly Station
Amiens Street, Dublin
Tel: (01)-363333
Passenger enquiries
Tel: (01)-787777

RESTAURANTS

**** Over IR£20 each.
*** Between IR£15-20 each
** Between IR£10-15 each
* Under IR£10 each.

Dublin

****Caesars**
18 Dame Street
Tel: (01)-6797049
Closed Sunday. Reservations advised. Italian restaurant.

**** **Celtic Mews**
109A Lower Baggot Street
Tel: (01)-760796
Open for dinner only, reservations advised. Closed Sundays. Irish & French cuisine.

*****Chapter One**
18/19 Parnell Square
Tel: (01)-732266
Closed for lunch on Saturdays & Sundays. Irish cuisine. Weekend reservations advised.

****Eastern Tandoori**
34 William Street
Tel: (01)-710428
Reservations advised. Real Indian food.

****Elephant & Castle**
18, Temple Bar
Tel:(01)-6793121
American food.

***Gallagher's Boxty House**
20, Temple Bar
Tel: (01)-772762
Traditional Irish food; country atmosphere.

*****Les Freres Jacques**
74 Dame Street
Tel: (01)-7694555
Closed Sunday. Reservations advised. French cuisine.

******Number 10**
Fitzwilliam Lower Street
Tel: (01)-761060
Dinner & lunch. Reservations advised. Traditional Irish cuisine.

*****Oisins Irish Restaurant**
31 Upper Camden Street
Tel: (01)-753433.
Closed on Sunday & Monday. Reservations advised.

****Pigalle**
14, Temple Bar
Tel: (01)-719262
Lunch served on weekdays, dinner all week. Closed Sundays. French food.

******Restaurant Partrick Guilbaud**
46 James Place, Lower Baggot Street
Tel: (01)-764192
Closed Sundays & Mondays. Reservations advised. French & Irish cuisine.

*****The Grey Door**
23 Upper Pembroke Street
Tel: (01)-763286
Closed Sundays. Reservations advised. The "food of the Tsars".

DUBLIN ENVIRONS

County Dublin

*****King Sitric**
East Pier, Howth, Co. Dublin
Tel: (01)-325235.
Closed Sundays. Extremely fresh seafood.

County Kildare

****Doyle's Schoolhouse Country Inn**
Castledermot, Co. Kildare
Tel: (0503)-44282
Lunch on Sundays only. Wholesome country-style cuisine.

*****Moyglare Manor**
Moyglare, Maynooth, Co. Kildare
Tel: (01)-6286351
No Saturday lunch. Irish cuisine.

County Louth

****Boyne Valley Hotel**
Dublin Road, Drogheda, Co. Louth
Tel: (041)-37737.
Swiss cuisine & wines.

County Wicklow

*****Hunter's Hotel Country House & Restaurant**
Rathnew, Co. Wicklow
Tel: (0404)-40106
Homegrown vegetables, fish & roasts.

******Rathsallagh House**
Dunlavin, Co. Wicklow
Tel: (045)-53112
Famous for breakfasts.

******The Old Rectory**
Wicklow, Co. Wicklow
Tel: (0404)-67048
Renowned "Green Cuisine" & wholefoods.

*****The Tree of Idleness**
Bray, Co. Wicklow
Tel: (01)-2863498
Closed Monday. Greek-Cypriot cuisine.

******Tinakilly House Hotel**
Rathnew, Co. Wicklow
Tel: (0404)-68274
Acclaimed for fish, game, brown & fruit breads.

****Wicklow Heather Restaurant**
Laragh, Co. Wicklow.
Irish cuisine.

SOUTHEAST IRELAND
County Kilkenny
*****Lacken House Guesthouse & Restaurant**
Dublin Road, Kilkenny Town
Tel: (056)-61085
International cuisine, local ingredients.

County Tipperary
******Cashel Palace Four Seasons Restaurant**
Main Street, Cashel, Co. Tipperary
Tel: (062)-61411
Seasonal game & local meats.

******Chez Hans**
Rockside, Cashel, Co. Tipperary
Tel: (062)-61177
Reservations required.
Closed Sunday & Monday.
French & Irish cuisine.

County Wexford
******Marfield House**
Gorey, Co. Wexford
Tel: (055)-21124
Country-style cooking.

SOUTHWEST IRELAND
County Kerry
****Beginish**
Green Street, Dingle, Co. Kerry
Tel: (066)-51588
French cuisine.

******Caragh Lodge**
Caragh Lake, Co. Kerry
Tel: (066)-69115
Seafood & Kerry lamb.

*****Doyle's Seafood Bar**
John Dingle Street
Tel: (066)-51174
Fresh seafood.

******Park Hotel Kenmare**
Kenmare, Co. Kerry
Tel: (064)-41200
Nouvelle-cuisine & seafood.

County Cork
*****Aherne's Seafood Restaurant**
163 North Main Street, Youghal, Co. Cork
Tel: (024)-92424
Freshly caught seafood.

*****Arbutus Lodge**
Middle Glanmore Road, Montenotte, Cork
Tel: (021)-501237
Closed Sunday. Reservations advised. French-Irish cuisine.

******Assolas Country House**
Kanturk, Co. Cork
Tel: (029)-50015
Traditional Irish cuisine.

******Ballymaloe House**
Shangarry, Midlton, Co. Cork
Tel: (021)-652531
Home-grown cuisine & cookery school.

******Blair's Cove Restaurant**
Durrus (near Bantry), Co. Cork
Tel: (027)-61127
Award winning *hors d'oeuvre* & wood-grilled meats.

****Chez Youen**
Baltimore, Co. Cork
Tel: (028)-30136
Local seafood, French chef.

****Dunworley Cottage**
Dunworley, Butlerstown, Clonakility, Co. Cork
Tel: (023)-40314
Swedish chef, local food.

***Halpins**
14, Cook Street, Cork
Tel: (021)-271534
Self-service. Salads & pizzas.

******Longueville House & President's Restaurant**
Mallow, Co. Cork
Tel: (022)-47156
Home-cooked cuisine, wine from local vineyard.

****The Oyster Tavern**
Market Lane, Cork
Tel: (021)-272716
Traditional Irish cuisine.

WESTERN IRELAND
County Clare
******Gregans Castle Hotel**
Ballyvaughan, Co. Clare
Tel: (065)-77005
Fresh seafood.

******Mac Closkey's Restaurant**
Bunratty House Mews, Bunratty, Co. Clare
Tel: (061)-364082
Fresh fish & meats.

County Galway
***Beezie's**
O'Connell Street, Galway
Tel: (071)-45239
Snacks & cheap lunches.

******Cashel House Hotel**
Cashel, Co. Galway
Tel: (095)-31001
Internationally-acclaimed cuisine. Fresh seafood.

*****Currarevagh House**
Oughterard, Connemara, Co. Galway
Tel: (091)-82312
Classic Irish cuisine.

****Drimcong House Restauarnt**
Molycullen, Co. Galway
Tel: (091)-85115
Classic Irish cuisine,
17th century ambiance.

****Lydon's**
Shop Street, Galway
Tel: (091)-64051
Irish cuisine.

***Noctan's**
17, Cross Street, Galway
Tel: (091)-66172
Literati & musican's pub.
Creative snack lunches.

****Rosleague Manor
Letterfrack, Co. Galway
Tel: (095)-41101
Fresh seafood, home-grown vegetables.

County Limerick
***Mustard Seed
Adare, Co. Limerick
Tel: (061)-396451.
Contemporary Irish cuisine.

NORTHWESTERN IRELAND

County Donegal
**Magee's
The Diamond, Donegal Town
Tel: (073)-21100
Inexpensive snacks & afternoon tea.

****Rathmullan House
Rathmullan, Letterkenny, Co. Donegal
Tel: (074)-58188
Prize-winning breakfasts.

****St Ernan's House Hotel
Donegal Town, Co. Donegal
Tel: (073)-21065
Irish home-grown cuisine.

*The Village Restaurant
Kerrykeel, Co. Donegal
Tel: (074)-50062
Home-cooked Irish meals.

County Mayo
***Enniscue House
Castlehill, near Crossmolina, Ballina, Co. Mayo
Tel: (096)-31112
Irish cuisine, Georgian ambiance.

***Mount Falcon Castle
Ballina, Co. Mayo
Tel: (096)-21172
Country-style fresh cuisine.

****Newport House
Newport, Co. Mayo
Tel: (098)-41222
Fresh home-grown cuisine & seafood.

County Sligo
***Coopershill House
Riverstown, Co. Sligo
Tel: (072)-65108
Traditional cuisine, romantic ambiance.

TOURIST INFORMATION OFFICES

In Ireland Tourist Information Offices can be found at the following addresses:

Carlow
College Street
Tel: (0503)-31554

Cavan
Farnham Street
Tel: (049)-31942

Cork City
Tourist House, Grand Parade
Tel: (021)-273251
Fax: (021)-273504

Dublin Airport
Tel: (01)-8445387
Fax: (01)-425886

Dublin City
14 Upper O'Connell Street
Tel: (01)-747733
Fax: (01)-786275

Bord Failte (Irish Tourist Board)
Baggot Street Bridge, Dublin 2
Tel: (01)-765-871
Fax: (01)-764-764

Dun Laoghaire
St Michael's Wharf
Tel: (01)-2806984
Fax: (01)-806459

Galway
Victoria Place, Eyre Square
Tel: (091)-63081

Kilkenny
Rose Inn Street
Tel: (056)-51500
Fax: (056)-63955

Killarney
Town Hall
Tel: (064)-31633

Limerick City
Arthur's Quay
Tel: (061)-317522

Rosslare Terminal
Tel: (053)-33622

Shannon Airport
Tel: (061)-61664

Sligo
Temple Street
Tel: (071)-61201
Fax: (071)-60360

Waterford
41 The Quay
Tel: (051)-75788
Fax: (051)-77388

Wexford
Crescent Quay
Tel: (053)-23111

Wicklow
Fitzwilliam Street
Tel: (0404)-69117

PHOTO CREDITS

Glenn Baker : 50
Randa Bishop : 38/39, 61, 64, 138, 144/145, 148, 157, 173, 174, 214, 241, 258, 262/263, 272, 310, 311, 313, 338/339
Holzbachova : x, xi (top), xii, xiii (top), xiv (top & bottom), 4, 5, 10, 14, 21, 30, 32, 35, 40, 41, 42, 44, 46, 52, 56, 57, 59, 60, 62, 69, 79, 82, 84, 85, 89, 93, 94, 97, 100/101, 105, 106, 108, 109, 110, 112, 114, 115 (top & bottom), 118, 119, 120, 121, 123, 124/125, 127, 128, 130/131, 131, 132, 134, 139, 149, 150, 154, 162, 168, 170, 172, 183, 185, 186, 187, 190, 192, 193, 194, 195, 196, 198, 201, 203, 204, 205, 207, 208, 210, 212, 221, 222, 223, 224, 227, 229, 230, 231, 232, 233, 234, 238, 239, 240, 248, 250, 251, 252, 253, 254, 261, 264, 265, 266, 274 (bottom), 275, 276, 278, 280, 281, 282/283, 288, 290/291, 292, 298, 300, 301, 304, 306/307, 312, 314/315, 318, 320/321, 324/325, 332, 334, 342, Back End
Bob King : xiii (bottom), 16, 66, 70, 81, 90, 92, 142, 147, 151, 160, 165, 277, 284, 294/295, 296, 308, 336
Life File/Keith Curtis : 2/3, 217, 266
Life File/Caroline Field : 19, 111, 171
Life File/Arthur Jumper : xv, 58, 75, 166, 167, 242
Life File/Keith Robinson : 78
Life File/Wayne Shakell : 337
Life File/Flora Torrance : 55
Theodor Maas : 25
R, Mohd, Noh : xi (bottom), xvi, 7, 8, 12, 28/29, 36, 80, 83, 96, 116, 122, 146, 153, 161, 178, 181, 182, 184, 209, 211, 216, 218, 220, 236, 237, 247, 268, 274 (top), 326, 328, 333, Front End, Back cover (top, left/right & bottom)
Carl & Ann Purcell : 67, 72/73, 76, 137, 141, 197, 270, 289, 302, 330
Retna Pic : 244/245, 246, 256, 257
Morten Strange : 86 (top & bottom), 87

INDEX

J

K

L

M

N

O

P